INTERPERSONAL PROCESS IN PSYCHOTHERAPY

A guide for clinical training

INTERPERSONAL PROCESS IN PSYCHOTHERAPY

A guide for clinical training

EDWARD TEYBER, Ph.D.
CALIFORNIA STATE UNIVERSITY, SAN BERNARDINO

BROOKS/COLE PUBLISHING COMPANY
PACIFIC GROVE, CALIFORNIA

Also by Dr. Edward Teyber
HELPING YOUR CHILDREN WITH DIVORCE:
A Compassionate Guide for Parents
Pocket Books, 1985
ISBN: 0-671-50826-1

© WADSWORTH, INC., 1989
© THE DORSEY PRESS, 1988

Acquisitions editor: Paul E. O'Connell
Project editor: Mary Lou Murphy
Production manager: Charles J. Hess
Designer: Jame A. Riley
Artist: Alice B. Thede
Compositor: The Saybrook Press
Typeface: 10/12 Palatino
Printer: Arcata Graphics / Fairfield

ISBN: 0-534-10861-X
Former ISBN: 0-256-65635-5

Library of Congress Catalog Card No. 87-71557

Printed in the United States of America

10 9 8 7 6 5 4 3 2

*Dedicated to those
who are struggling
to change.*

Preface

Therapists-in-training often read that the therapeutic relationship is the key to client change. However, guidelines for understanding and utilizing the therapist-client relationship are often vague and leave trainees uncertain as to how to proceed with their clients. Thus the purpose of this text is, first, to provide a conceptual framework for understanding the relationship between the therapist and the client in terms of their interaction or process. The second purpose of this text is to offer intervention guidelines for how to utilize this understanding to help clients change.

This book provides a practical introduction to the theory and practice of counseling and psychotherapy. It is an applied text written for therapists-in-training and is suitable for adoption as a primary text in clinical courses. Although the book may be used in prepracticum courses as well as by more experienced professionals, it is designed for practicum courses in which graduate students are seeing clients and receiving supervision. The book has the depth and versatility to be used by a range of beginning and advanced practicum students. This range occurs because trainees at all levels will find it personally challenging to enact these interpersonal processes with their clients, even after they have grasped them intellectually.

The text has ten chapters organized into four parts: (1) introduction and basic premises of the interpersonal process approach, (2) responding to clients' concerns, (3) conceptualizing client dynamics, and (4) resolving problems. The book is also organized to parallel the course of treatment from initial client contact to termination. Therapeutic goals and intervention strategies are presented for each phase of treatment, along with a developmental model for conceptualizing the overall course of therapy. Continuity is further provided by focusing on process characteristics of the therapist-client relationship at each successive stage of treatment. This text will replace the nebulous ideas beginning therapists have about therapy with a well-developed framework for the process of change and the role of the therapist-client relationship in this process.

There are several distinctive features designed to make this text highly readable and engaging for student therapists. First, this book captures the subjective experience of becoming a therapist. Beginning therapists bring a great deal of enthusiasm to their clinical training and their initial work with clients is often among the most important experiences in their lives. This book reflects this intensity and articulates the questions, concerns, and aspirations of the beginning therapist.

Second, more than other books, this text focuses on the personhood of the therapist. It examines how the therapist's own personality, developmental history, and current life situation are brought into the therapeutic relationship and influence the course of treatment. To focus on the process dimension and how the therapist-client relationship can be used as a vehicle for change, we must understand the therapist's participation in the relationship as well as the client's. Although students may initially find this approach somewhat anxiety-arousing, in the long run they find it personally fulfilling and productive of client change.

Third, because this book clarifies the process and relationship dimension, it is a useful guide for therapists of various theoretical orientations. One unique feature of the interpersonal process approach presented here is that family systems concepts are related to the practice of individual therapy. As a result, childhood and familial experience is brought to bear on many clients' problems in a relevant here-and-now manner that has not previously been available in a text.

Finally, therapists-in-training need concrete examples of how broad therapeutic principles can be enacted with clients, and they need case studies that illustrate specifically how theory guides clinical practice. Meeting these needs is the principal strength of this text. Each chapter is richly illustrated with numerous sample therapist-client dialogues, clinical vignettes, and extended case studies.

In sum, this text will enable therapists-in-training to use themselves and the relationships they provide their clients to help clients change.

ACKNOWLEDGMENTS

I wish to thank four individuals who have contributed generously of themselves. First and foremost has been my wife, Dr. Kathy Pezdek of Claremont Graduate School. Her loving support and talented editing helped greatly with this book. The meaning in the concepts presented here was brought to life for me by three fine teachers: Drs. Robert Hilton (Newport Beach, California), William Mueller (Michigan State University), and Sam Plyler (Okemos, Michigan). By providing the kinds of relationships they teach about, they have shown many clinical trainees how they can use themselves to help clients change.

Edward Teyber

Contents

An Interpersonal Process Approach

1

Introduction and Overview

Paul is a first-year practicum student about to see his first client. He has long and eagerly awaited this event. Like many of his classmates, Paul decided to become a therapist while working on his undergraduate degree. Psychotherapy was always intrinsically interesting to him, which is why this career choice held so much promise. Being a therapist meant far more than just a "good job" for Paul; it was the fulfillment of a dream. How exciting, he thought, to make a living by talking to people about the most important concerns in their lives. The potential for such meaningful human involvement filled Paul with anticipation as he began his clinical training.

At this moment, though, Paul felt the real test was at hand: His first client would be arriving in a few minutes. Worries race through his mind: What will we do for fifty minutes? How should I start? What if she doesn't show up? What if she doesn't come back next time? Needless to say, it was extremely important to Paul that he find a way to help this client with her problems. He had learned something about therapy in his undergraduate psychology classes, and a good deal more from his volunteer experience with callers on the local crisis hotline. But even with these experiences and a supervisor to guide him, Paul was painfully aware of his novice status and of the fact that he didn't know very much about actually doing therapy.

Although some of Paul's classmates thought he was a little too idealistic, they did share his excitement about becoming therapists. Many of them were older than Paul and far more experienced in life. Some had raised children, others had already had careers as teachers, nurses, and businesspeople. For these more seasoned classmates as well, a counseling career held new hopes. With the successive steps of completing undergraduate requirements, being accepted into a graduate program, and now starting their first practicum, their goals were becoming reality. Like Paul, however, realizing their dreams of new and rewarding careers also depended on their ability to help others. And the test of that ability, or so it seemed, was about to be met with the arrival of their first clients.

THE NEED FOR A CONCEPTUAL FRAMEWORK

Beginning therapists' anxieties about their ability to help are not necessarily neurotic insecurity or obsessive worrying. It is realistic to be concerned about one's performance in a new, complex, and ambiguous arena. Paul and his classmates, however, like most students who enter graduate training in clinical work, already bring many strengths to their new profession. Most students who are selected for clinical training already possess sensitivity, intelligence, and a genuine concern for others. Such personal assets, as well as their own life experiences, will prove enormously helpful to their future clients.

Although personal experience, common sense, and intuition are useful, they alone do not prepare one to negotiate an affect-laden therapeutic relationship. In order for a therapist to be effective with a wide range of people and problems, these valuable human qualities must be wed to a conceptual framework. Therapists must understand very specifically what they are trying to do in therapy—where they are going and why—in order to be consistently helpful to clients. Every therapist needs a conceptual framework as a guide, and this is especially true for the beginning therapist. Without this framework, decisions about intervention strategies and case management are too arbitrary to be trustworthy, and the therapist's confidence in the therapeutic enterprise lessens as a result.

Many therapists become exceedingly anxious in their early counseling work because of their conceptual uncertainty. Ambiguity over how to conceptualize client problems and proceed in the therapy session heightens their insecurity and preoccupation with their counseling performance. These performance anxieties arise because their strong needs to be helpful clash with ambiguous guidelines for how to proceed. When this occurs, the inherent abilities of novice counselors to help are diminished by their anxieties, and their effectiveness with clients actually declines.

Finally, the lack of a conceptual framework hinders novice therapists as they try to find their own identities as professionals. An important part of seeing oneself as a competent therapist is having a theoretical framework that is applicable across clients yet congruent with one's own values and life experiences. The purpose of this book is to provide one such conceptual framework for understanding the therapist-client relationship and the developmental course of therapy. Students will be able to refine this framework to fit their own personalities and preferred therapeutic styles as they continue to develop professionally.

THE INTERPERSONAL PROCESS APPROACH

Theoretical and Historical Context

The therapeutic model presented here will be referred to as the *interpersonal process approach*. This is not a new theory of psychotherapy but a synthesis of ideas from interpersonally oriented psychotherapy and family systems theory. This book links these ideas together and applies them to the practice of individual psychotherapy.

Harry Stack Sullivan (1968) first brought the interpersonal focus to psychotherapy. Many of the ideas in this book can be traced back in some form to Sullivan and his students (Karen Horney, 1950; Erich Fromm, 1941; Frieda Fromm-Reichman, 1950), as well as to other theorists who have been influenced by his interpersonal orientation (Erik Erikson, 1964; Carl Rogers, 1951). Sullivan also provided the distant roots of the family therapy movement through his study of close relational systems (Satir, 1967; Minuchin, 1974; Haley, 1980). This book will draw upon the ideas of these and other interpersonally oriented theorists.

Basic Premises

What are people's problems about? Where do they come from and how can they be resolved? Every beginning therapist grapples with questions such as these and will continue to do so throughout his or her life. One of the enduring satisfactions of a counseling career is in continuing to evolve one's own ideas about the nature of people and their problems.

This section introduces some ideas and assumptions that are central to the interpersonal process approach: (1) Problems are interpersonal in nature. (2) Familial experience is the most important source of learning about ourselves and others. (3) The therapist-client relationship can be utilized to resolve problems. In other words, this overview examines how problems are expressed, how they have developed, and how they can be resolved.

The Nature of Problems: A Separateness-Relatedness Dialectic. Most client conflicts arise in close relationships, and clients often enter therapy when they are beginning or ending a primary relationship. One useful way to conceptualize many of these interpersonal problems is along a continuum of separateness and relatedness. This is examined below from a family systems perspective.

Most family systems theorists agree that the basic dimension of family life is a developmental continuum of separateness-relatedness. Families must nurture young children and provide them with a secure sense of acceptance and belonging (relatedness). As children grow older, the developmental task of the family shifts from nurturing children to training them for independence and preparing them for emancipation (separateness). The family must have flexibility and a range of interpersonal responses in order to meet offspring's needs for both closeness in early childhood and autonomy in later years.

If there are problems in forming an attachment bond in infancy or in meeting the strong dependency needs of young children, family members will be disconnected from one another. Children will develop neither a shared sense of family identity nor loyalty to each other. Most important, children will not be motivated to comply with parent's socialization demands unless an affectional bond exists. Young children fail to relinquish their own wishes and adopt more mature and responsible behavior if they are not concerned about maintaining parental approval. As a result, children from such disengaged families do not internalize social rules and self-controls adequately. They do not feel responsibility toward others or the culture at large and are likely to develop acting-out symptoms and to externalize blame. These offspring are more likely to come in contact with police and judges than with mental health professionals.

Problems also arise at the other end of the continuum. When there is too much closeness and family members are enmeshed, parents cannot tolerate the individuation or emancipation of their offspring. An example of this can be seen when enmeshed families stifle individuation by making anger an unacceptable feeling and by avoiding conflict rather than addressing and resolving it. Individuation is also blurred by ineffective communication patterns, such as when family members express what another is thinking or feeling or speak to each other through a third person rather than directly.

Enmeshed families also inhibit emancipation by discouraging developmentally appropriate steps toward independence and autonomy. For example, these families do not give offspring in late adolescence permission to leave home psychologically and succeed on their own. Such offspring often feel a binding guilt as they try to become independent adults and make commitments to love relationships and career choices (Teyber, 1983).

In contrast to offspring in disengaged and enmeshed families, offspring in families that function well integrate the relatedness and separateness dimensions. These offspring develop a sense of self that allows them to feel emotionally connected to others while still remaining separate or individuated from them (Stierlin, 1972; Mahler, Pine, and Bergman, 1975; Boszornemyi-Nagy and Spark, 1973).

The same dialectic of separateness and relatedness continues into adulthood. Here again, the challenge of successful relationships is one of balancing intimacy and autonomy. On the one hand, we need to have a sense of belonging and being cared about. It is important that others acknowledge our experience and respond to us in caring and confirming ways. At the same time, however, we must also be separate and independent. All of us have the right to our own feelings and perceptions, even if they differ from those of significant others. We need to be able to express our own preferences and beliefs and to pursue our own interests and goals. Healthy individuals can accommodate the polarities of separateness and relatedness at the same time.

The problems that most clients present reflect an inability to achieve an integrated sense of self as both an independent and competent person and an emotionally available and committed person. Thus, several unifying themes encompass many of the varied problems clients present. Client conflicts will often embody *separateness* issues of autonomy, initiative, and power on the one hand, or *relatedness* issues of intimacy, trust, and commitment on the other.

The Source of Problems: Affective Learning in the Family of Origin. Social learning in the family of origin is the most important source of long-standing personality strengths and conflicts. Family homeostasis requires that many patterns of interaction and communication become repetitive and rule-bound. These transactional patterns are strongly maintained in the family of origin and can be highly resistant to change in adulthood.

There are two reasons why familial experience has such a powerful, long-term impact on the individual. The first factor is the sheer repetition of family transactional patterns. The same types of affect-laden interchanges are reenacted thousands of times in daily family life. Suppose, for example, that a parent has difficulty responding positively to a child's successes. Every time the young child enthusiastically seeks the parent's approval for an accomplishment, the parent might ignore the child and change the topic, compare the child unfavorably with a sibling's greater accomplishment, turn away and look vaguely sad or hurt, or take the success away from the child by making it his or her own.

The same type of parental response occurs every time the child shows the parent a favorite drawing, makes a new friend, wins a race at school, or earns a star from his/her teacher. This transactional pattern becomes a powerful source of learning when it continues over a period of years and even decades. As an adult, the child is likely to feel conflicted about completing his/her educational degree or about taking pleasure in a promotion earned at work. Thus the most important problems in people's lives are the generic conflicts that develop from these characterological or habitual response patterns. Long-standing personality problems are shaped more by repetitive family transactional patterns than by isolated traumatic events or time-limited stressors (Wenar, 1982).

Second, the learning from these repetitive transactions is even more significant because of the intensity of the affect involved. Parents are the pillars of the child's universe, and children depend on them with a life-and-death intensity. Thus these repetitive transactional patterns are even more influential because they have been reenacted in highly charged affective relationships with the most important people in one's life. The child in the example above may well feel a desperate need somehow to win the parent's approval, yet simultaneously feel increasing anxiety about trying to succeed or about approaching the rejecting parent. Thus, our sense of self in relation to others is learned in the family of origin, and, in many ways, will carry over to adulthood.

In summary, family interaction patterns may be hurtful and frustrating for the individual, or they may be validating and encouraging. For better or worse, these repetitive patterns of family interaction, roles, and relationships are internalized and become the foundation of our sense of self and the social world. Of course, other factors are influential as well and familial experience will not be relevant to many situational problems that clients present. Familial experience, however, does provide our first and most long-lasting model for what goes on in close relationships. It will figure significantly in one's choice of marital partner and career, in how adult offspring will, in turn, parent their own children, and in many of the other most enduring problems and satisfactions found in adult life.

Although such important learning as this has taken place in the family of origin, ineffective and painful transactional patterns can be relearned. Change is indeed possible and, as we will see below, occurs in part through a relational process of affective relearning.

Resolving Problems: It Is the Relationship that Heals. The relationship between the therapist and the client is the foundation of the therapeutic enterprise. The nature of this relationship is the therapist's most important means of effecting client change, and it determines the success or failure of the therapy. In order to utilize the therapeutic relationship systematically as a vehicle for change, however, therapists must understand very specifically the meaning of their dynamic interactions with their clients. Thus the interpersonal process approach focuses on understanding what goes on between the therapist and client in terms of their interaction or *process*.

The therapist-client relationship is complex and multifaceted, as different levels of communication occur simultaneously. For example, one subtle but important distinction is between the overtly spoken *content* of what is discussed, and the *process* dimension of how the therapist and client interact. In order to work with the process dimension, the therapist must make a perceptual shift away from the overt content of what is discussed and begin to track the relational process of how two people are interacting as well. Although the process dimension in psychotherapy cannot be explained so briefly, the following vignette introduces the concept.

Suppose that during their first session the client tells the therapist that he resents his wife because she is always telling him what to do. He explains that he has always had trouble making decisions on his own, and as a result his wife has often interjected and simply told him what to do. Even though he felt that she was just trying to help him with his indecisiveness, he resented her "bossiness" and "know-it-all attitude." After describing the presenting problem in this way, the client asked what the therapist thought he should do.

Let us look at the process dimension of their interaction. Suppose the therapist complied with the client's request and said: "I think that the next time your wife tells you what to do you should . . ." If therapy continues in this didactic vein, the therapist and client will begin to reenact in their relationship the same conflict that led the client to seek treatment. That is, the therapist will be telling the client what to do, just as his wife has done. The client has certainly invited this response, and will probably welcome the therapist's suggestions at first. In the long run, however, he will probably come to resent the therapist's directives just as much as he resents his wife's, and will ultimately find the therapist's suggestions to be of just as little help as hers.

Alternatively, the therapist might respond to the other side of the client's conflict and say: "I don't think I would really be helping you if I just told you what to do. I believe that clients need to find their own solutions to their problems." Frustrated, the client responds: "But I told you I don't know what to do! It's hard for me to make decisions. Aren't you the expert who is supposed to know what to do about these things?"

This response throws the client back on the other side of his conflict and leaves him stuck in his own inability to make decisions. If this mode of interaction continues and comes to characterize their relationship, their process will recapitulate the other side of the problem that initially brought the client to therapy. That is, the client's inability to initiate, make his own decisions, and be responsible for his own actions will immobilize him in therapy, just as it has in other areas of his life.

The key point is that clients do not just talk with therapists about their problems in an abstract manner; rather they actually recreate and act out in their relationship with the therapist the same conflicts that have led them to seek treatment. *This recapitulation of the client's problem in the therapeutic relationship is a regular and predictable phenomenon that will occur in most therapeutic relationships.*

In order to resolve problems, clients must experience in their real-life relationship with the therapist a new and more satisfying solution to their problems. When clients terminate prematurely or therapy reaches an impasse, the therapist and client are usually reenacting in their relationship the same conflict that the client has been struggling with in other relationships. For example, clients may feel that they are being controlled by the therapist and have to do everything the therapist's way, or that they have to take care of the therapist and meet her needs, or that they must please the therapist and win her approval, or that they have to compete with the therapist . . . just as they are doing with others in their lives. When this occurs, the therapeutic process has metaphorically repeated the same type of conflicted interaction that the client has not been able to resolve in other relationships, and that he has often experienced in earlier formative relationships in the family of origin.

Thus, clients will begin to play out with the therapist the problem that brought them to therapy. The issue is whether they will elicit the same problematic response from the therapist that they have received from others, or whether the therapist can respond in a new and more effective way that enables clients to resolve the conflict within their relationship. It is easier to understand this conceptually, however, than it is to carry this out in affect-laden relationships with clients.

In successful therapy, clients experience a different kind of relationship, one in which their old conflicts are intensely aroused without the therapist responding in the same problematic way that others have. The primary working goal of the therapist is to provide this *corrective emotional experience* (Alexander and French, 1946). Only if the therapist and client are able to resolve the conflict in their own relationship can the client generalize from this real-life experience of change and successfully adopt more adaptive responses with others. Frieda Fromm-Reichman (1950) has captured this best by saying that the therapist must provide the client with an *experience* rather than an *explanation.*

In order to provide this corrective emotional experience the therapist must be able to work with the process dimension. In the previous illustration, when the client asked his therapist what he should do, one option would have been for the therapist to make a *process comment* that described their current interaction, making it an overt topic for discussion.

⁜ For example, the therapist might have said: "It seems to me that you are asking me to tell you what to do, which will bring up the same problem for us in therapy that you are having at home with your wife. Let's see if you and I can do something different in our relationship. Rather than having me tell you what to do, let's try and work together to understand what is going on for you when you are feeling indecisive. Where do you think is the best place to begin?"

In this instance, the therapist is being supportive by offering the client a new and different *collaborative* relationship in which they can work together on the client's problems. If this collaborative effort continues to develop over the course of treatment, their working relationship will provide the facilitative context necessary for change to occur. Of course, the therapist's initial attempt to offer the client a corrective response to his conflict will need to be repeated in many different ways for change to occur. If the therapist can establish this type of collaborative relationship, however, it will facilitate other types of therapeutic interventions as well. Educational inputs, behavioral alternatives, dynamic interpretations, and interpersonal feedback will all be more effective when they occur in this type of interpersonal context.

⁜ A guiding principle in the interpersonal process approach is to provide a therapeutic relationship in which the client experiences a more satisfying response to old conflicts. This requires a great deal of personal risk and involvement on behalf of the therapist and is, therefore, difficult to do. For this type of corrective emotional experience to occur, the therapist must be personally engaged and emotionally available to the client. The relationship must hold real personal meaning for both participants in order to have the emotional impact necessary to effect change. If the therapist is psychologically removed or safely distant from the client, the relationship will be too insignificant to be utilized as a vehicle for change. Again, the client needs an experience, not an explanation, for this type of emotional relearning to occur. In this simple human way, it is the relationship that heals.

The dialectic of separateness-relatedness similarly applies to the client/ therapist relationship. Just as the extent of change is limited if the therapist is distant and merely serves as an objective technician, so therapy will also falter if the therapist becomes inappropriately close. If therapists overidentify with the client or invest in the client's changing in order to shore up their own feelings of adequacy, therapy will not progress. This is when therapists are most likely to stop seeing the process they are enacting with the client and begin to respond in problematic ways that recapitulate the client's generic conflict.

In this regard, the most common problem beginning therapists have is experiencing the client's situation or concerns as identical to their own. The solution is a supervisory relationship that helps therapists see the ways in which their own experience differs from that of the client's. Once able to differentiate their own issues from those of the client, therapists will often be able to see how the therapeutic process has been reenacting the client's generic conflict. This understanding usually enables therapists to return to the therapeutic relationship and provide the client with the interpersonal experiences needed for change.

While learning to attend to this process dimension, beginning therapists should expect to make many mistakes with their clients. All therapists are going to become overinvolved or underinvolved with some clients, recapitulate the client's conflict in the therapeutic relationship at times, and make many other mistakes. Few clients are fragile, however, and therapeutic relationships are often remarkably resilient. Mistakes can be undone. As their performance anxiety declines, beginning therapists will find that they are better able to identify and work with the process dimension. In turn, this focus on process will be one effective way to undo mistakes and realign the therapeutic relationship when it has gone awry.

Limitations and Aims

Limitations. This text introduces beginning therapists to the practice of interpersonally oriented psychotherapy with individual adult clients. This therapeutic approach is best suited for clients with long-standing problems in close interpersonal relations. These problems include issues of dependency, trust, control, and commitment in interpersonal relations. This approach is also directed toward resolving developmental ego conflicts that may include identity and self-esteem problems, concerns over initiative and adequacy, and accompanying emotions of anxiety, depression, guilt, and shame.

Other types of therapeutic approaches are better suited for many clients. For example, many clients who function well need short-term supportive therapy. These clients need help coping with situational crises that do not reflect broader problems in living or with problems that do not tap into other enduring personality conflicts. Behavioral approaches are the treatment of choice for clients who have circumscribed problems such as an isolated phobia or who are seeking only symptomatic relief from their problems. Some clients will not be suited for the more intensive, interpersonal process approach because they are too impulsive or are psychotically disorganized. These clients will not be able to tolerate the anxiety aroused by this affectively uncovering approach. Finally, many clients require educational and skill-development approaches. Sex education, time management, assertion training, or parent training is the treatment of choice for many clients.

This text focuses on the process dimension in psychotherapy and on how the therapist-client relationship can be used as a vehicle for change. This applied focus prevents us from addressing other important aspects of clinical training. Basic information about ethics, confidentiality, report writing, record keeping, informed consent, legal reporting, and other practical concerns is beyond the scope of this text. Similarly, clinical interventions in many important situations are not addressed, such as responding to client emergencies, managing suicidal crises, or mandated reporting of abuse. Further, this text does not address other therapeutic modalities such as child, marital, or family therapy or treatment complications when clients are referred by a court. Although the information presented here may be relevant to some of these treatment concerns, the subjects themselves are beyond the scope of this presentation.

Aims. The interpersonal process approach presented here emphasizes three broad aims that are essential to helping clients change. First, therapists must try to establish a significant emotional relationship with their clients. In addition to the relationship issues discussed earlier, this means that therapists must maintain their own internal commitment to helping clients change. It is especially important, but challenging, for therapists to do this during periods of intense client resistance, ambivalence, and negative transference toward the therapist. Conceptions of therapeutic change often vary on a continuum from the application of discrete, problem-solving techniques on the one hand, to some vague allusion to "the relationship" on the other. Somehow, the relationship is supposed to produce change but it is not clear how or why change occurs. The interpersonal process approach presented here offers a middle ground between these two extremes. Change *is* predicated on the nature of the therapist-client relationship, but specific guidelines are provided to show how the therapeutic relationship can be utilized to effect change.

Second, in order to effect change, therapists must also be able to respond effectively to the client's emotions and inner life. Therapy is a private and intimate sharing in which therapists respond to clients' pain and help them understand their conflicted emotions. Making contact with clients in these very personal ways is a critical aspect of therapy, yet it is the dimension along which therapists are most likely to stumble. Most therapists, like other people reared in our culture, have been socialized to avoid rather than approach strong feelings, such as anger, despair, fear, and shame. In addition, it is often difficult for therapists to respond to their clients' emotions because they arouse the therapist's own conflicted feelings as well. The most effective way for therapists to facilitate change, however, is to help clients integrate emotional reactions that they have not been able to resolve on their own. Thus, specific guidelines will also be provided to help beginning therapists understand and respond to their clients' conflicted emotions.

The third component of effective therapy is to conceptualize the client's personality and problems and formulate what experiences the client needs to undergo in therapy in order to change. This conceptualization should enable the therapist to identify the client's central conflict, understand the resistance and defenses that have kept the client from changing, and provide direction for the ongoing course of treatment. Typically, the least developed skill for beginning therapists is their ability to formulate a useful conceptualization of the client's personality and problems. However, the most effective therapists are equally adept in the conceptual as well as the affective and relational domains. Thus, this text aims to facilitate the therapist's effectiveness in all three areas.

A final aim of this text is to provide an overview of the nature and course of a therapeutic relationship. Therapeutic relationships usually have a coherent life course and follow a predictable developmental pattern from beginning to end. Although variations and exceptions occur with every client, therapists can often identify an ordered sequence of successively unfolding stages. At each successive stage of therapy, the therapist must negotiate certain therapeutic tasks with the client. If the therapist achieves this, the next set of issues and concerns will often emerge from the client. This epigenetic unfolding provides an integrating structure for conceptualizing the temporal course of therapy and suggests intervention goals and strategies for each successive stage. The chapters that follow are organized to reflect this developmental schema and to parallel the course of therapy from beginning to end.

With these general considerations in mind, we can now examine more specifically how to begin a therapeutic relationship. We turn now to the first stage of therapy: establishing a collaborative relationship.

SUGGESTIONS FOR FURTHER READING

1. The reader is strongly encouraged to examine the book by William Mueller and Bill Kell entitled *Impact and Change: a Study of Counseling Relationships* (Englewood Cliffs, N.J.: Prentice-Hall, 1966). Chapters 1 through 4 provide a rich conceptualization of the therapist-client relationship and how it can be used to help clients change. This is a brilliant and illuminating book that deserves to be read and reread by beginning and experienced therapists alike.

2. The reader may also wish to examine Salvadore Minuchin's book, *Families and Family Therapy* (Cambridge, Mass.: Harvard University Press, 1974). Chapters

3 and 5 provide a succinct presentation of structural family relations and family developmental processes. This discussion will help individual therapists understand the genesis and familial context of their clients' problems.

3. The great novelists best bring to life the profound impact of childhood and familial experience on adult personality. John Steinbeck's *East of Eden* (New York: Viking, 1952) and Franz Kafka's *Letter to His Father* (New York: Shocken, 1966) put flesh and blood to the conceptual skeleton of familial influences on personality development.

Responding to Clients

2

Establishing a Collaborative Relationship

CONCEPTUAL OVERVIEW

Psychotherapy is a profession of trust. Clients enter therapy with a need—they are in pain, asking for help with something they have not been able to alleviate on their own. A trustworthy response is to honor the dependency in clients' requests for help and to respond compassionately to their pain. Yet to be most effective, the therapist must also respond in a way that helps clients gain a greater sense of their own capabilities. Thus the goal is not only to resolve specific situational problems, but to do so in a way that leaves clients with a greater sense of their own competence and mastery. In this way, the interpersonal process approach to psychotherapy fosters independence as it aims for broader personality growth and maturation.

Clients cannot resolve problems and achieve a greater sense of their own personal power in a hierarchical or one-up/one-down therapeutic relationship. This means that clients need a *collaborative relationship* in order to grow beyond their situational dependency. Clients must be active participants when working with the therapist, rather than being passively "cured" or told what to do. This chapter presents a model for a collaborative relationship that accepts the client's need for comfort, understanding, and guidance, yet does so in a way that equally encourages the client's independence.

CHAPTER ORGANIZATION

This chapter presents issues that are fundamental to a successful initial therapist-client interview. The first section elaborates the concept of a collaborative relationship in terms of a balance of directiveness/ nondirectiveness in the therapeutic relationship. Sample therapist-client dialogues will be used to illustrate how the therapist can establish a collaborative working alliance in the initial session.

The second section presents ways to foster the therapeutic relationship and further engage the client in treatment. Principally, these goals are achieved by listening carefully and understanding the subjective meaning in what the client is saying. The therapist can better understand the client's experience by (1) clarifying the repetitive themes that recur in the different stories and vignettes the client presents, (2) identifying the central conflicts that link the client's problems and concerns, and (3) approaching the client's central affect in a direct but caring way. Following the central theme of this book, both sections will focus on interpersonal process characteristics of the therapist-client relationship, and how they can be used to facilitate change.

A COLLABORATIVE RELATIONSHIP

At each successive stage of treatment the therapist has a different overarching goal to guide her interventions. At the beginning stage of therapy, the therapist's goal is *to establish a collaborative relationship or working alliance* with the client (Greenson, 1967). In the initial sessions the therapist must "join" with the client, set expectations for how they are going to work together, and behaviorally enact these spoken expectations by giving the client the *experience* of working together on her problems. If a collaborative relationship is established early in the course of treatment, it will facilitate change later in therapy and ultimately help clients to achieve a greater sense of their own mastery and competence.

A Directive/Nondirective Balance

At the outset, the therapist should explore the client's expectations for how they are going to work together and how change is going to occur. For example, does the client believe that the therapist is the authority or healer who is the agent for change—perhaps via advice, explanations, interpretations, information-giving, modeling, reinforcing, encouraging, confronting, challenging irrational thinking . . . ? That is, will the process of therapy be a hierarchical doctor-patient or teacher-student relationship where the powerful therapist leads and the dependent client follows? Many clients believe the process of therapy is primarily having the therapist tell them what to do. When this one-up/one-down relationship occurs, it fosters the client's continuing dependency on the therapist. Although few therapists overtly subscribe to this type of therapeutic process, it is commonly enacted without the therapist realizing it.

Many clients enter therapy expecting the therapist to be the "doctor" who is going to prescribe their route to mental health. This doctor-patient role will work well with many clients in the *short run*. The client's expectations will be fulfilled if the therapist takes the role of leader or healer, but little client change will occur in the long run from this teacher-student mode of interaction. Clients will not be able to gain a greater sense of their own personal power as long as they believe that the source of potency resides in the therapist rather than in themselves.

Whereas a directive stance may work in the short run, a purely nondirective approach will often sputter right from the start. Typically, clients feel frustrated if their requests for help or direction are continuously reflected back upon them. A negative cycle may ensue in which the client becomes increasingly angry and demands direction from the therapist, who further eschews this role and talks about inner direction and finding one's own answers. This, in turn, further frustrates the client who does not feel he has the answer to anything at that moment.

The client often sees the therapist's attempts to be strictly nondirective and avoid the leader role as manipulative and evasive. Clients do need advice and direction from an expert. They need suggestions and guidance for how to proceed and the therapist should provide it. However, the therapist must provide this structure and direction without falling back into the other extreme of a counterproductive authoritarian role.

How can such a structured but nonauthoritarian relationship be achieved? In the initial interview the therapist must make *an overt bid to establish a collaborative relationship in which the therapist and client work together to resolve the client's problems.* For example, this attitude may be conveyed in the following type of message:*

Therapist:
I would like for you and I to become partners. I cannot figure out what is wrong and tell you what to do on my own, and you have not been able to solve your problems by yourself, so let's work together on them. You are the world's foremost expert on you, and I have skills and knowledge about problems such as yours to contribute. By working together we have the best chance of succeeding. How does that sound to you?

---

*Throughout this book sample dialogues are provided to illustrate the concepts that are discussed. Beginning therapists should not use these words (or try to say what a supervisor might say in a similar situation), but should find their own ways to express these concepts. Beginning therapists will lose their creativity with their clients if they try to imitate someone else.

This type of message communicates that the therapist is going to be an active participant and respond to the client's need for help. However, the client is not going to be a passive recipient who is being cured by the therapist, but an active participant who is sharing the driver's seat with the therapist. Clients must be given the expectation that they share responsibility for the direction and outcome of therapy. The therapist is also taking herself off the pedestal and defining the client as an equal participant with valuable information, abilities, and resources to contribute. Whether the therapist and client can continue this process of mutual collaboration will largely determine the eventual outcome of therapy. Let us look now at some specific ways to establish a collaborative relationship in the initial therapy session.

Beginning the Initial Interview

Therapists must begin to establish a collaborative relationship in their initial contact with the client. The therapist structures the session by providing the client with guidelines and direction for what is going to occur in the interview. This can be done simply and briefly by offering clients an open-ended bid to talk about what brings them to therapy. For example:

Therapist:
I'd like to begin by learning more about the concerns that have brought you to therapy. What has been the difficulty?

This type of message communicates several important things to the client. At the simplest level, it ends the opening phase of social interaction that occurs as the therapist and client are introduced and walk to the interview room. More important, it tells clients that the therapist is someone who is willing to talk directly about their personal problems, and is ready to respond to their need for help by listening. However, it does this in a way that still gives clients the freedom to choose where they want to start and leaves them in charge of how much they want to disclose. From the outset, clients are sharing control of the interview by choosing what they want to talk about, yet the therapist is an active participant who has offered some direction for where they are heading. This type of constructive collaboration does not occur if the therapist gives the client a more specific cue such as:

When we talked on the telephone you said you were having trouble with your boss. What is the problem there?

Although the difference between these two openings may seem insignificant at first, it is important to communicate that clients should talk about what they want to talk about and not feel that they have to follow the therapist's agenda. Why? From the start, we want the client to take an *active role* in directing the course of therapy, while still feeling that the therapist is participating as a supportive ally. *Enacting this process dimension in the initial session is more important than the content of what is discussed.*

In most cases, clients will readily accept the therapist's open-ended bid and begin to share their concerns with the therapist. The therapist can then follow the client wherever she leads and begin to learn more about this person and her problems. Therapy is underway when this occurs. Before we go on to the next step, however, we must examine two exceptions in which the client does not accept the therapist's offer to begin.

Previous Screening Interview. If another therapist has previously conducted an intake interview, the client may not be so ready to begin. For example:

Client: [impatiently]
> I've already been through all of this in the intake with Dr. Smith. Do I have to go over it all again just for you?
>
> or
>
> *[hesitantly]* I don't know how much you already know about me. What has Dr. Smith told you about me?

Our initial goal is to develop a working alliance between the therapist and the client. In the two hypothetical responses above, the previous intake therapist is a third party who is psychologically still in the room with them. This is especially problematic for many clients who have come from families in which a third person was triangulated into every two-person relationship (Bowen, 1966). That is, whenever two people were close, or in conflict, a third family member would be drawn in and disrupt the dyad (Haley, 1967). To keep therapy from recapitulating this transactional pattern, the therapist and client must begin their own relationship as a stable dyad. It is important to maintain a dyadic therapeutic relationship that does not allow others to disrupt the therapeutic alliance, especially as so many clients have a strong propensity to bring a third person into every relationship. For example:

Therapist:
> I know that you have already spoken with Dr. Smith, and I have learned a little bit about you from his intake notes. But just you and I are going to work together from now on, and I'd like to hear about you in your own words. It may be a little repetitious for you, but this way we can begin together at the same point.

Most clients appreciate this offer for a dyadic relationship and will begin to share their concerns with the therapist.

Conflicts over Initiating. There is another common circumstance in which the client does not respond to the therapist's initial request to begin. The central conflict for some clients involves issues of leading, initiating, or accepting responsibility. This type of client cannot begin at the therapist's request. By asking the client to begin, the therapist has inadvertently presented the client with her central conflict. Asking these clients to initiate in the therapy session is precisely what they cannot do in their lives. It is difficult for this type of client to decide what to talk about or to assume any responsibility for the course of therapy. Thus an impossible demand is placed on this client when a therapist nondirectively sits and waits for the client to lead.

On the other hand, it merely reenacts the client's conflict when a directive therapist begins the session by telling the client what to talk about. Thus, therapy stalls right from the start if the client has problems with initiative and the therapist responds in either a directive or nondirective manner. What can the therapist do in this case? One way to find a more effective middle ground is to make a process comment, as discussed in Chapter 1. An effective intervention is simply to describe, ask about, or make overt what is occurring between the therapist and client at that moment. For example:

Therapist:
It seems to be hard for you to get started. Maybe we can begin right there. Is it often hard for you to begin, or is there something about this situation in particular that is difficult for you?

By first identifying this as a problem and then encouraging the client to explore it, the therapist has offered the client a focus and helped her to move forward. However, the therapist has provided this focus without taking over and telling the client what to do, which would only recapitulate the client's conflict with the therapist. The therapist's open-ended inquiry is supportive in that it responds to the client's immediate concern. Yet it allows the client to take this issue of initiating where she wants, and to share responsibility for the course of treatment. This type of response provides a new opportunity for clients to explore their problems in a supportive environment. Our first goal is met as the client *experiences* a collaborative interaction with the therapist, rather than merely having a conversation about "the need to work together." Such a collaborative experience sets important expectations for the future course of therapy.

UNDERSTANDING THE CLIENT

The therapist has begun the session by giving the client an open-ended bid to talk about whatever is most important to her. Now imagine that the client has now begun to share her concerns with the therapist and is clarifying the background and context of her problems. The therapist must find the subjective meaning that each successive story or vignette holds for the client. It is critical for the therapist to be able to see what is most significant to the client *from the client's point of view* (Kelly, 1955). The client will feel *understood* by the therapist when the therapist can find a common meaning that links together the client's concerns or distills the central feeling in her experience. When this occurs, clients become more interested in exploring their problems and more engaged with the therapist. They are encouraged to reveal even more about themselves and their problems.

The section that follows examines what it means to understand the client's experience. We will see why it is important to acknowledge the client's experience, explore what therapists can do to better understand what their clients are saying, and see how the beginning therapist's own performance anxieties make it difficult for her to listen effectively to the client. Finally, therapists will be encouraged to share their understanding with the client in a caring and compassionate way.

Clients Do Not Feel Understood

Most clients are concerned that others do not really listen to them, take them seriously, or understand what they are saying. Clients often describe themselves as feeling invisible, alone, strange, or unimportant. Many clients feel this way because their subjective experience was not validated or responded to in their family of origin. For example, while growing up, others often responded to the client by saying:

Why would a silly thing like that make you mad?
You can't possibly be hungry now.
I'm cold, put your sweater on.
How can you be tired, you've hardly done anything?
You shouldn't be upset at your mother, she loves you very much.
You don't really want to do that.

Most clients have repeatedly received messages like these that deny their feelings and invalidate their experience. Further, family members often changed the topic or simply did not respond when the client expressed a feeling, concern, or interest. One of the most effective ways therapists can help their clients change is to validate and confirm their subjective experience. R. D. Laing goes so far as to suggest that people stop feeling "crazy" when their subjective experience is validated (Laing and Esterson, 1970). Therapists can respond effectively by listening intently to the client, taking seriously whatever matters to the client, and communicating understanding and acceptance of what the client has said. Although this type of empathy and validation may sound like a simple and common human response, it is not. In many current and past relationships, clients have not had their feelings and perceptions acknowledged. Therapists must validate the client's experience by identifying and articulating the central meaning that this particular experience seems to hold for the client. For example, in the phrases below the therapist is trying to capture the central meaning or issue in what the client has just said:

It didn't seem fair to you.

You were frightened when he did that.

Here again, you have to take care of everyone else.

It's been too much for you, more than you can stand.

It felt great to be so effective and in charge.

It was disappointing; you wanted more than that.

It is profoundly reassuring to clients when therapists can consistently and accurately offer such validation.

Therapists Must Demonstrate Their Understanding

To engage a client in a working relationship, the therapist must listen to the client's experience, find the feeling and meaning the stories hold for the client, and accurately reflect back what is most significant in the client's experience. An accurately empathic reflection that *captures the meaning of the client's experience* is a complex and significant intervention. It is never just a rote parroting of what the client has said. An effective reflection is more akin to an interpretation that goes *beyond* what the client has said and communicates that the therapist understands what is most important in the client's experience (Rogers, 1951). Therapists become credible to their clients when they *demonstrate* their understanding in this tangible way.

It is easy to trivialize the response I am suggesting and allow it to become a cliché. The simplistic, inauthentic stereotype of the therapist is someone who readily says: "I hear you," "I know just what you mean," "I understand completely." This type of global, undifferentiated response is not effective and, paradoxically, often furthers the client's sense of never being seen, heard, or understood. It is not just a matter of saying, "I understand," but of demonstrating that understanding by articulating the central meaning or issue in what the client has said. Therapists show the client that they can be helpful when they capture and express the specific meaning in the client's experience, rather than offering well-intended but vague reassurances.

The therapist does not have to be an exceptionally insightful or perceptive person to understand the client's experience. Therapists can check out their perceptions with the client and invite the client to clarify them. For example, the therapist replies: "As I listen to you, it seems as if you feel so hopeless that you just want to give up. Is that how it is for you?" This dialogue takes the pressure of having to be right off the therapist and furthers the collaborative alliance. And, even though the therapist's perceptions will be inaccurate at times, clients often feel cared for by the therapist's sincere efforts to understand their experience.

Therapy offers clients an opportunity to be understood more fully than they have been in other relationships. When this understanding occurs in the initial session, clients begin to feel they have been seen and are no longer invisible, alone, strange, or unimportant. At that moment, the client begins to perceive the therapist as someone who is different from most other people, and possibly as someone who can help. In other words, hope is engendered when the therapist understands and articulates the personal meaning that each successive vignette holds for the client. With this in mind, let us look more specifically at how the therapist can find the central meaning in what the client presents.

Identify Recurrent Themes

At the beginning of this chapter it was suggested that therapists start the session by encouraging the client's initiative, following the client's lead, identifying the meaning in what the client relays, and sharing this understanding with the client. Although this may sound simple to do, it is not. To accomplish it, the therapist must give up a great deal of control over the direction of therapy and over the timing of when issues are brought up for discussion. The therapist is placed in the far more demanding position of responding to the diverse and unpredictable material that the client produces, rather than simply directing what the client will cover. This approach gives clients more control and responsibility in resolving their problems, but puts a greater demand on the therapist to understand the varied material that clients present. If the therapist can identify *recurrent themes* in the client's material, it will help the therapist make sense of the client's experience and better understand what is important to the client.

Suppose the client is telling the therapist about himself and the concerns that have brought him to therapy. As the therapist follows the different recollections and descriptions the client chooses to relate, the therapist needs to find an *integrating focus* for the wide diversity of material that the client is presenting. The therapist can do this by identifying a superordinate *theme, conflict,* or *affect* that recurs throughout the different material the client presents. For example, a client's various experiences are often linked together by a common *theme* (e.g., "No one is trustworthy"; "I have no power"; "It's my fault"; "It wasn't fair"). Although the disparate material that clients present often seems unrelated and disconnected, synthesizing themes are usually present and can be found if the therapist listens for them.

Similarly, the different vignettes the client presents often contain a repetitive *conflict*. For example, the problems and concerns clients discuss often embody a central underlying conflict (e.g., "I have to give up what I want in order to be close; if I follow my own interests and feelings, I have to be alone. Either way I lose."). Usually only two or three central conflicts recur throughout the varied problems that clients present.

Most important, there is often a repetitive *affect* that comes up again and again for the client (Mueller and Kell, 1966). As the therapist listens to the client, an overriding feeling such as sorrow, bitterness, or shame may pervade the client's mood or characterize the different experiences he relates. Thus, if the therapist can identify the repetitive theme, central conflict, or primary affect that links together the client's experience, the client will feel that the therapist understands. We will explore these ideas further in later chapters, but for now, let us examine some issues that make it difficult for beginning therapists to understand their clients.

Performance Anxieties Impede the Therapist's Understanding

Therapists, like other people, often do not really hear what their clients are telling them. They are not accurately empathic and often do not capture the feeling and meaning in the client's experience. This section examines performance anxieties that make therapists less empathic and cause therapists to push clients to change prematurely.

Therapists will not be as effective with clients when they are burdened by their own excessive performance demands. Commonly, beginning therapists are trying too hard (e.g., to be helpful, to win approval from a supervisor, to prove their own adequacy to themselves, to be liked by the client). When therapists are trying too hard in one of these ways, it is almost impossible to de-center and be emotionally available to the client.

Too often, novice therapists are thinking about where the interview should be going next, wondering how best to phrase what they are going to say next, or worrying about what their supervisors would expect them to do at this point in the interview. This self-critical monitoring can immobilize student therapists, block their own creativity, and prevent them from being as sensitive and empathic to the client as they could be. Beginning therapists should slow down their own inner process of planning what to do and focus more on finding the meaning that this particular experience seems to hold for this particular client.

Beginning therapists' anxiety about their helping abilities can also be translated into a need to *do* something to make the client change. Novice therapists often believe they are supposed to make the client think, feel, or act differently within the initial therapy session. Paradoxically, when these unrealistic expectations come into play for the therapist, clients are more likely to drop out of therapy because they feel that the therapist is not with them or does not understand.

Therapists with excessive performance anxieties are less effective because they are responding more to their own internal need (to be helpful, competent, or liked) than they are to the client's need to be understood. Beginning therapists may be alerted to their own excessive performance demands if clients express that they are not being heard or are being told what to do, or hurried up. When this occurs, the most effective way for therapists to manage their performance anxieties is to discuss them with a supportive supervisor or colleague. We will elaborate on this point later.

Change Occurs in the Context of Care and Understanding

The therapist does need to help the client change, of course, but change is most likely to occur if the client first experiences the therapist as someone who understands and cares. In the initial sessions, the therapist's primary goal is to establish an emotional connection with the client and to begin a working alliance. This is more important than obtaining any specific information about the client or effecting any change. In this regard, one of the best ways to evaluate the success of an initial session is for therapists to ask themselves: "Do I feel like I made contact with this person and have a genuine feeling for who he is?" Therapists are building an affective bridge to the client and creating the interpersonal context necessary for change when clients feel that the therapist is available, concerned, and sincerely trying to understand. If therapists provide this type of responsiveness throughout the initial session, they are already being helpful to the client.

Finally, we must address the most important component of what it means to understand the client. Therapists must *actively* extend themselves to the client and *directly* express their feeling and concern for the client. That is, therapists must articulate their understanding of the client's experience in a way that also communicates their compassion and care for the client. Therapists must find their own personal ways of communicating that they are moved by the client's pain and are concerned about the client's life and well-being. Clients' inability to care about themselves is central to many of their conflicts, and most clients cannot care about themselves until they feel someone's caring for them (Gilligan, 1982). Therapists provide this care when they recognize what is important to the client, express their genuine concern about the client's distress, and communicate that the client is someone of worth and will be treated with dignity in this relationship. These are the therapist's goals in the beginning stage of therapy.

CLOSING

The interpersonal process approach tries to resolve problems in a way that leaves clients with a greater sense of their own capacities and abilities. This independence-fostering approach to psychotherapy can only be achieved through a collaborative therapeutic alliance. The client must be an active participant throughout each phase of treatment—not a "good patient" waiting for the "doctor" to cure him or to tell the client "what to do." This process dimension of how the therapist and client work together is more important than the theoretical orientation of the therapist or the content of what they discuss. This chapter has also underscored the profound therapeutic impact of listening and understanding. Perhaps because they are so simple, these basic, human responses are too easily overlooked. They are the foundation of every helping relationship, however, and the basis for establishing a collaborative therapeutic alliance.

SUGGESTIONS FOR FURTHER READING

1. Illuminating ideas about the effects of multigenerational family relations on individual personality are found in these two articles on triangular coalitions: J. Haley, "Toward a Theory of Pathological Systems," in G. H. Zuk and I. Boszormenyi-Nagy (Eds.), *Family Therapy and Disturbed Families* (Palo Alto, Calif.: Science and Behavior Books, 1967), pp. 11–27; and especially, M. Bowen, "The Use of Family Theory in Clinical Practice," *Comprehensive Psychiatry* (1966), pp. 345–376. Both of these articles will help therapists apply family systems concepts to the practice of individual psychotherapy.

2. For some, client-centered therapy connotes passivity on the part of the therapist and the lack of an effective treatment focus. However, Carl Rogers's original discussion of the therapeutic reflection (chapter 4 of Carl Rogers, *Client-Centered Therapy* [Boston: Houghton Mifflin, 1951]) remains an enormous contribution to psychotherapy that therapists should examine.

3. Chapter 1 of Ralph Greenson's book *The Technique and Practice of Psychoanalysis, Volume 1* (New York: International Universities Press, 1967), lucidly describes a collaborative therapeutic relationship. The reader does not have to be interested in psychoanalysis in order to glean valuable insights about this basic therapeutic dimension.

3

Honoring the Client's Resistance

Joan was nervous about seeing her first client, but the initial session actually went very well. The client talked at length about his concerns and, to her relief, she found it was easy to work with him. The client expressed some difficult feelings and Joan felt that she understood what was important to him. She was sure they had begun a good working relationship when the client parted and said he looked forward to meeting again next week. One week later, however, Joan received a telephone message from the client saying that he was no longer interested in therapy. Confused and dismayed, Joan sat alone in her office wondering what had gone wrong.

CONCEPTUAL OVERVIEW

Just when the therapist feels that something important is getting started, some clients put their foot on the brakes. The client cancels his second appointment, shows up 25 minutes late, or asks to reschedule for Sunday at 7:00 A.M. This *resistance* is puzzling and frustrating for the novice therapist: "Why didn't he return; we had a great first session!" Although most clients will not be resistant in this particular way, other forms of resistance will occur regularly throughout the course of therapy. The purpose of this chapter is to help beginning therapists recognize, understand, and respond to client resistance.

All clients have both positive and negative feelings about entering therapy, although the positive feelings are usually more apparent initially. Clients are distressed and want relief from their suffering, and these painful feelings motivate them to seek therapy. We must look further into the complexity of the client's feelings, however. Clients also bring resistant feelings to therapy that must be acknowledged as well. Paradoxically, at the same time as clients are seeking help and trying to change, they are also fighting against it. Why? Layers of fear become entwined with the original core of hurt, which makes it even more threatening for clients to approach their problems. The reasons for these fears differ for each client, but common themes include:

If I let myself depend on the therapist he might leave me, or take advantage of me, or try to control me as others have done when I needed them.

I cannot ask for help or need anything from others because I must be perfect and in control all of the time.

I am afraid of what I will see or what a perceptive therapist will learn about me if I stop and look inside of myself.

Asking for help is admitting that there really is a problem, and if therapy does not help then I surely will be hopeless.

If I cannot handle this by myself it means that I really am weak or dependent, just like they told me I am.

It is easy to respond to the *approach side* of clients' feelings, the hurt and pain that motivates them to enter therapy. If you gently scratch the surface it is usually right there in front of you, and the client wants you to respond to it. In contrast, the other side of the client's feelings—the reactive emotions to having a problem and needing help—may not be so accessible. These concerns over what it means to enter therapy or ask for help act as a countervailing force to the client's motivation to enter therapy. If unaddressed, these ambivalent feelings may draw clients out of therapy prematurely, as occurred in the opening vignette.

CHAPTER ORGANIZATION

The first section of this chapter discusses why it is difficult for both therapists and clients to approach resistance and work with this important aspect of clients' experience. The second section provides a working definition of resistance, clarifies when resistance is occurring, and suggests how therapists can conceptualize each client's resistance. The third section presents intervention guidelines for responding to some of the different types of resistance that clients may present. Common expressions of client resistance are illustrated at three different points in time: during the initial telephone contact, at the end of the first session, and during subsequent sessions. Sample therapist-client dialogues illustrate effective and ineffective responses at each point.

BOTH THERAPISTS AND CLIENTS WANT TO AVOID RESISTANCE

Imagine your client has missed, come very late for, or twice re-scheduled her second appointment. Perhaps this has no significant meaning at all. Cars do break down, traffic jams occur, children get sick, and employees get called for work at the last minute. It is also possible, however, that this behavior reflects the client's ambivalence about some aspect of being in therapy. You may not know what this behavior means, but by trying to find out, you can increase the chances of the client's continued participation.

The Therapist's Reluctance to Address Resistance

To a greater or lesser degree, every client will be ambivalent, defensive, or resistant. This push-pull occurs at the beginning of therapy and will continue to wax and wane throughout treatment. Although therapists need to address signs of potential client resistance, this is difficult to do for many beginning (and experienced) therapists. Let us examine three reasons why therapists are often reluctant to approach their clients' resistance.

Many beginning therapists are not aware of the multiple meanings and conflicted issues that entering therapy arouses for new clients. In their initial therapy sessions, these therapists are surprised to find that their clients actually resist the help they are overtly seeking. For other therapists, the concept of resistance is more familiar but it has a pejorative connotation. These therapists have observed that resistance can be used to keep the therapist in a superior position, and to deny the validity of the client's own experience. This occurs, for example, when a therapist says to a working, single mother of three, "Hmm, I notice that you are four minutes late for our appointment today." Resistance does not have to be associated with this type of insensitive or hierarchical therapist-client relationship. Resistance can be used instead to strengthen the client's commitment to therapy and to enhance the therapeutic alliance.

There is another, more personal reason why therapists are often reluctant to approach their clients' resistance. Most novice therapists have strong needs for their clients to like them, find them helpful, and to keep coming to therapy. If the client does not show up or comes late, therapists often feel that they have failed. When this occurs, therapists become increasingly concerned about their ability to help others and overly invested in the next client's satisfaction with therapy.

In order to ward off unwanted criticism, therapists often do not inquire about signs of potential resistance. Most therapists, like their clients, are not eager to approach issues that arouse their own anxiety. Thus the beginning therapist may be hesitant to invite clients to express negative reactions they may have toward the therapist or being in therapy. Although it is difficult to invite critical feedback and approach conflicts, it is necessary to do. The paradox is that if therapists allow their own anxiety to keep them from approaching clients' resistance, their clients will be more likely to end therapy prematurely.

The Client's Reluctance to Address Resistance

Unfortunately, the client usually shares the therapist's reluctance to address resistance. Clients are confused by their own contradictory behavior when they see themselves resisting. For example, clients often exclaim with dismay:

Why do I go to all the trouble and expense of coming here to see you, when I can't think of anything to say as soon as I walk in the door?

Why would I forget our next appointment after we had such a great session last week? It doesn't make sense!

Why do I keep asking you for advice, and then say "Yes, but . . ." to whatever you suggest? What's wrong with me?

Clients also interpret their own resistance as being bad and project this critical attitude onto the therapist. When the therapist begins to inquire about resistance, most clients want to avoid the topic because they are afraid the therapist will blame them for not really trying, failing, or being unmotivated. The therapist must help clients reframe their critical attitude toward their own resistance, and appreciate the fact that they originally learned this defensive behavior for very good reasons. Both the therapist and client must *honor* the client's resistance, as it originally served a self-preservative and adaptive function. We will examine below what it means to honor the client's resistance, and will view it as *the best possible response to an unsolvable conflict that the client had available at that point in her development*.

Past experiences with family members and other significant relationships have given clients very good reasons for not wanting to ask for help, not sharing a painful feeling, or not risking a disclosing relationship. If the therapist and client explore how significant others have responded in the past, the client's resistance will become understandable. The feelings that underlie the client's resistance always make sense historically, although they are no longer necessary or adaptive in most current relationships.

For example, suppose that a client is having trouble entering therapy.

The therapist might ask:

> What might I do to hurt you or make things worse if you seek help from me?
>
> or
>
> How have others responded to you in the past when you have asked for help or needed someone?

These types of questions will help the therapist and the client identify the aversive consequences that occurred for the client when he asked for help. For example, clients may respond that they were ignored and felt powerless, were made fun of and felt ashamed, or were told that they were selfish and too demanding. They may have been told they didn't really need or want something, or felt there were strings or obligations attached to everything they received, and so on. In this way, the therapist and client can clarify both why and how the client originally learned to defend himself.

Thus the first thing the therapist must do is help clients *understand* why they originally needed to defend themselves and how they are continuing to do that now in therapy. Second, the therapist must confirm or *validate* the necessary protection this resistance once provided. That is, the maladaptive resistance in the therapeutic relationship was once an adaptive response. The original defensive behavior minimized the hurt and allowed the client to cope with the painful interpersonal response that repeatedly occurred. Third, the therapist must also *differentiate* his own response in the current relationship from the aversive ways that significant others have responded in the past. For example, the therapist might respond:

> In the past you learned that if you allowed your____to help you or take care of you, she wanted you to remain a child and continue to need her. I would like to respond to your need, but I am different from your____. I do not need for you to remain dependent on me. I would like to help you achieve your own independence so that you will not need me any longer, and will be able to go on with your own adult life.

Therapists must follow this three-step sequence: identify the original transactional pattern, validate the client's unmet need and defensive adaptation to it, and differentiate the therapist's current response from the past dynamic. This three-step sequence will need to be repeated many times with different manifestations of resistance throughout the course of treatment.

We have seen, then, that clients are far more likely to become stalled in therapy, or to drop out, if their resistance is not addressed. One of the most important ways to keep clients in treatment, and to identify conflict areas in clients' lives, is to invite clients' negative reactions toward therapy and the therapist. The guiding principle is that if clients *talk* about their feelings of not wanting to be in therapy, or express what they do not like about the therapist, clients will be less likely to *act* on their ambivalence and drop out. Before going on to illustrate specific ways to implement this general principle, we must first learn how to identify and conceptualize clients' resistance.

IDENTIFYING AND CONCEPTUALIZING RESISTANCE

Early in their training, many therapists will have several clients drop out of therapy within the first few sessions. The main reason clients prematurely terminate is because they are *acting on*, rather than *talking about*, their conflicted feelings about entering therapy. In order to help clients remain in treatment, the therapist must be prepared to identify when resistance is occurring, directly approach this issue with clients, and help clients resolve these concerns. To do this, the therapist must first be able to identify when resistance is occurring.

The Client's Difficulty Participating in Treatment

How does the therapist know when a client is resisting treatment? Resistance is usually operating whenever clients have difficulty participating in treatment. For example, clients are probably resisting when any of the following occur repeatedly or in tandem:

The client misses the appointment or comes late.

The client needs to reschedule the appointment.

The client has very limited hours available when she can be seen.

The client cannot make a firm commitment to attend the next session.

It is important to stress that the same behavior often means very different things to different clients. Therapists never know for certain what any particular behavior means, but whenever clients have trouble attending sessions it is likely that some form of resistance is occurring. In such cases, the therapist should *generate working hypotheses* about the possible meaning this resistance holds for the client.

The Therapist's Formulation of Working Hypotheses

Therapists must formulate *tentative hypotheses* about clients' conflicts, central feelings, primary expectations, and interpersonal style right from their initial contact. One systematic way to do this is for therapists to formulate answers to three successive questions for each client.

What Do Clients Elicit from Others? The first question therapists can assess is: What does the client's interpersonal style tend to elicit from others? Even in the initial telephone contact, clients' interpersonal style and what it tends to elicit from others is an important source of information about them. For example, if this client sounds helpless and confused on the telephone, does he regularly invite others to treat him as a victim and rescue him? Or, if the client presents himself in an angry and demanding way, do others often withdraw and leave him alone? If so, perhaps this client is testing whether the therapist can tolerate his angry challenges and still see his need and hurt. As therapy progresses and the therapist learns more about each client, many of these initial hypotheses will prove inaccurate and need to be discarded. Others will fit the client, however, and these formulations can be further developed and refined. It is important to formulate, evaluate, and revise hypotheses regarding each client's dynamics.

What Is the Threat? The second question therapists can ask themselves concerns the client's potential resistance: What might this particular client find threatening about being in therapy? Based on other information about the client's past relationships and interpersonal style, the therapist can begin speculating how this client could be averse to therapy. For example,

Is it incongruent with this client's perfectionistic demands to need help?

or

Is it difficult for this older Chicano male to seek help from a younger female therapist?

Therapists should formulate working hypotheses such as these about the feelings, issues, or concerns that are likely to be difficult for each client.

How Will the Client Express Resistance? Finally, therapists should formulate a third set of hypotheses that anticipate how the client will play out or enact these with the therapist. For example, suppose that the therapist has observed that her depressed client feels selfish and guilty whenever she does something for herself, or whenever someone does something for her. The therapist then hypothesizes that this client may withdraw from treatment as soon as she starts to feel better, or emotionally disengage from the therapist when she realizes that the therapist genuinely cares for her.

To illustrate further, let us look at working hypotheses for each of these three questions in the following example. Suppose that a male client whose problem is substance abuse telephones the therapist to schedule an initial appointment. During this initial telephone contact, the client tells the therapist that his alcohol and drug usage is more problematic than it has ever been and his mother believes that he "really needs to be in therapy." Based on this information and other impressions the therapist has gathered, the therapist hypothesizes that an important part of the client's interpersonal style is to let others know he is hurting, elicit help from them, but then avoid taking responsibility for his own needs and behavior.

Continuing with the second question, the therapist hypothesizes that this client may become resistant to treatment when she addresses the issue of how he meets his dependency needs, or when the client is given reality-based confrontations about how he eschews responsibility for his own decisions (e.g., to enter therapy, continue drinking, and so forth). Third, the therapist hypothesizes that this client is impulsive, and that he may act out his resistance by bolting out of therapy as soon as these anxiety-arousing issues are addressed.

Thus, the therapist must try to anticipate the concerns that might cause each client to drop out of treatment and the way each client is likely to express these concerns. This will enable the therapist to help clients anticipate their own resistance before they act on it, and it will help the therapist to respond more effectively once clients have already begun to act on their resistance.

As the therapist spends more time with the client, she will learn much more about this person and many of these general, initial hypotheses will need to be discarded. Some of them will probably be accurate, however, and these can be elaborated to help understand this particular client. In this way, the therapist identifies the enduring issues that arise for the client. The therapist will then be better prepared to *center treatment around these repeated themes*, which provides structure and focus for the ongoing course of treatment. As we will see in Chapter 7, this is part of the continuing process of formulating and refining one's conceptualization of client dynamics and treatment plans.

RESPONDING TO RESISTANCE

This section illustrates how therapists can respond to the types of client resistance that commonly occur at the beginning of therapy. Sample therapist-client dialogues illustrate effective and ineffective responses at three critical points. The first situation examines different ways of handling a telephone conversation in which the client has difficulty scheduling the initial appointment. Next, we will examine several ways of inquiring about resistance and ambivalence at the end of the initial session. Third, we will examine sample dialogues with clients who have difficulty attending subsequent appointments. As before, student therapists should find their own words to express the principles embodied in these dialogues.

The Client's Resistance During the Initial Telephone Contact

The first situation in which resistance may be encountered is in trying to schedule the initial appointment. The therapist wishes to obtain a firm commitment from the client that she will attend. The client, however, may be ambivalent about entering therapy and express this during the initial telephone contact. The therapist should be prepared to respond directly to this issue.

An Uncertain Commitment. In the first example below, the client is only somewhat ambiguous about attending the first session.

Therapist:
It's been good talking with you, and I'll see you on Tuesday at 4:00.

Client:
Okay, I guess I'll see you then.

Therapist:
You "guess so." Does that mean you are not certain you will be there?

Client:
Oh no, I will be there for sure.

Therapist:
Good, I am looking forward to meeting with you. See you next Tuesday at 4:00.

An effective response to the client's ambiguity ("I guess so") is modeled above. The therapist hears the indecision in the client's commitment and addresses it directly. An ineffective response would be for the therapist to let it pass by unnoticed. Indeed, chances are that the client will still arrive at the appointed hour anyway. However, the chances of the client not arriving are far greater if the therapist does not directly address the signs of uncertain commitment.

Further, the therapist should mentally note this indecision as a possible sign of resistance to treatment. This is an instance in which the therapist can begin to generate working hypotheses about the possible meaning of relevant client behavior. Of course, it is very possible that this client's ambiguous statement means little or nothing. On the other hand, it may reflect that the client has difficulty making commitments, entering into new relationships, doing things to meet her own needs, and so on.

A More Ambivalent Client.   Let us return to the topic of the client's resistance, but this time take it one step further with a more difficult client. Imagine that we have returned to the same telephone conversation:

Client:
Okay, I guess I'll see you then.

Therapist:
You "guess so." Does that mean you are not certain you will be there?

Client:
Don't worry, I'll be there unless something comes up.

Therapist:
I need a firm commitment from you to attend the first session before I will agree to meet with you. Maybe there is something about coming here that doesn't feel right to you. Can we talk about that for a minute?
or
Can we agree to meet only one time on Tuesday at 4:00? At that time we can discuss what therapy is and any concerns you may have about it.

An ineffective response would be to accept the client's uncertain commitment (e.g., "Okay, I guess I'll see you Tuesday at 4:00") and deny that an important issue is being played out. In this dialogue the therapist has continued to push for a firm commitment from the client, even if that is only to attend the first session. The therapist has taken what may seem like an unnecessarily hard line: She will not make an appointment based on a response of "maybe." The therapist wants to accept the client's ambivalent feelings, and make them overt as a topic for discussion. However, the therapist wants to discourage the client from acting on her ambivalence as much as possible. So, although the therapist invites the client to talk about her ambivalence, the therapist wants the client to make a decision whether to enter therapy.

It is important to emphasize that the therapist does not stop with the requirement of a firm commitment to attend the first session. The therapist also extends herself and addresses the client's difficulty in making a decision. In this example, the therapist offers to try and help the client ("Can we talk about that for a minute").

Why must the therapist take such a firm stance? Wouldn't it be more supportive to let clients leave the appointment a little bit tentative if that is what they need to do? Little or no therapeutic change will occur until clients take responsibility for the decision to enter therapy and work on their problems. Clients' commitments can be very short—for one session, or for just a few sessions to get a sense of whether therapy is for them. However, it is necessary for clients to take responsibility for this decision before therapy can progress. Without this, the therapist has little to work with. In fact, it is better for the client to remain out of therapy than to enter without commitment and have an unsuccessful therapeutic experience. The therapist must be concerned about preventing failed hope in the client. If clients have one or more unsuccessful therapy experiences, it may discourage them from trying to seek help with their problems again.

Clients Who Try to Make the Therapist Responsible. Let us continue the conversation above and examine a particular response that many clients will give the therapist. At this point in the telephone conversation, some clients will try to make the therapist take responsibility for their decisions. The therapist does not want to resolve the client's ambivalence by assuming responsibility for his decision, or by trying to provide the necessary motivation for therapy. Suppose the client says:

I'm not sure if I should start therapy or not, what do you think I should do?

Although well-intended, it is not helpful to automatically tell the client to go ahead and begin. For example, it might be easy for the therapist to say:

Oh, I'm sure I could be helpful to you.

or

Yes, you should definitely see me in therapy.

A more effective response is for the therapist to help clients take responsibility for their own decisions. The therapist does not want to cajole, coerce, or win the client into therapy. *The therapist must keep responsibility for the client's behavior squarely in the client's lap.* At the same time, however, the therapist does not want to leave clients stranded and alone. The therapist needs to reach out and work with clients on their ambivalence. If this is done skillfully, the therapist will help the client without taking the responsibility or providing an external solution for the client. Thus a more effective response is for the therapist to say:

It seems as if one part of you wants to be in therapy, but another part of you doesn't. Tell me about both sides of your feelings.

In this example the therapist is inviting the client to express all of his concerns about entering therapy. Thus the therapist is working with the client to reach a decision, but does this in a way that leaves the client responsible for his own decision. Here again, we are working with the process dimension in psychotherapy. Although this process distinction is subtle, it will make all the difference in the outcome of therapy.

The client in the dialogue above is providing the therapist with potentially important information about himself. Just as before, the therapist should begin generating working hypotheses about what this behavior may mean. For example, uncertain clients may not have been supported when they have tried to take responsibility for their own actions. These clients may now try to avoid the aversive consequences they have experienced in the past by getting others to take responsibility for them. If so, this could make it difficult for clients to initiate new activities (e.g., apply for college) or follow through on their own wishes and interests (e.g., select the major or career choice they are most interested in). Being held back in this way may leave clients feeling resentful and frustrated as well.

Therapists can generate hypotheses such as these and be alert for evidence of these themes in other arenas of the client's life. If these prove to be enduring and pervasive issues, the therapist is better prepared to focus on them later in therapy. The therapist must not become wed to these early hypotheses, however, but be ready to discard them if further supporting data is not forthcoming. As therapists become more experienced, their initial hypotheses will become more fruitful.

Even these initial tentative formulations can help therapists respond more effectively, however. As noted in Chapter 1, the therapist does not want to recapitulate the client's conflict in the therapeutic relationship. This can easily occur in an encapsulated way in the initial negotiations between therapist and client. This is another reason why the therapist should not take over and tell the client seeking advice what to do—for example:

> Based on what you've told me, I'm confident that therapy can help you and believe that you should begin now.

Assuming such a directive stance often reenacts a prototypic and problematic interaction for clients. Clients often feel that they cannot act on what they want, or that they need to be dependent and let others assume responsibility for their decisions. Although clients often feel they need to ask the therapist to tell them what to do, it also makes clients feel that their own autonomy is being suffocated at the same time. Paradoxically, clients resist the control they have just elicited by avoiding or rebelling against the therapist. As this scenario continues, clients come to feel badly about themselves—confused as to why they are rejecting the help they have just asked for and guilty for rejecting the therapist who was trying to help. The therapeutic responses suggested earlier prevent this reenactment from occurring, and may provide clients with a new and different response to an old conflict.

The Client's Resistance at the End of the First Session

At the end of the first session, the therapist should ask clients how the session felt to them. The therapist should also ask about any dissatisfaction with therapy or difficulty with the therapist that the client may have had. The therapist should ask about these concerns even if they were not evident in the session.

Approach Interpersonal Conflict. Even if the first session went very well, five minutes before the end of it the therapist should ask:

How was it to be here today?

Most clients will answer, "Fine." Thinking that you may need some reassurance, or to try and win your approval, many clients will go on to tell you how helpful you have been. If so, the therapist might respond:

Good, I'm glad you've found our first session helpful. You've told me a lot about yourself today, and I feel we have gotten off to a good start too. But was there anything about coming today, or anything that I did, that did not feel good to you? If so, it is important that we talk about that.

Client:

Oh no, I was eager to begin, and you have been very nice and understanding.

Therapist:

That's fine, but if in the future you ever have any uncomfortable feelings about me or therapy, I would like for you to talk with me about them. Would you be sure to do that?

In this vignette the therapist is trying to establish an important set of rules and expectations for what is going to occur in therapy. Unlike many relationships the client has experienced, the therapist is telling the client that she can tolerate the client's angry or dissatisfied feelings. The therapist is also saying that she is not afraid of conflict and wants to deal with problems between them straightforwardly. Although many clients will not be able to accept this bid initially, the therapist is laying the groundwork for an honest and direct relationship. These are important expectations to establish early in the course of treatment.

A More Assertive Client. Let us stay with the same situation, but imagine we have a more assertive client this time. What happens if the therapist raises the same type of query as before:

How has it been for you to talk with me today?

This time the client is critical of the therapist and says,

I thought you were trying to push me or hurry me up.

The therapist must learn to *approach* the conflict, rather than avoid it by moving on to another topic or ending it with a punitive response. The best way to approach the conflict is to encourage the client to express fully his critical reaction. For example, the therapist might respond:

> I'm sorry that happened. Let's look at that together and try to understand what happened for each of us. Tell me more about your feeling of being pushed or hurried up.

Of course, it is often difficult for beginning therapists to do this. The therapist's anxiety may be aroused by such confrontations, especially if the therapist has strong needs for the client's approval. In order to help therapists approach such anxiety-arousing confrontations, therapists must become aware of their own characteristic responses to interpersonal conflict. For example, many therapists will want to avoid or ignore the client's confrontation, or readily agree with it and apologize in order to abate the criticism. Other therapists will automatically begin to defend themselves and offer long justifications and explanations to the client. A few therapists will counter with their own hostility. Every therapist must become aware of how she typically reacts to difficult confrontations.

One of the best ways to do this is to recall how the therapist's own family of origin dealt with interpersonal conflict. Regardless of their age, therapists' initial reactions to conflict usually follow closely from how their parents dealt with conflict in their marriage, and how each parent dealt with conflict with the therapist when the therapist was a child. Rather than reflexively following their initial propensity, therapists must learn to *approach* conflicts with clients.

After inviting clients to express fully their concerns, the therapist must accept the validity of the client's perception. Perhaps the client is right and the therapist was pushing the client faster than he wanted to go. The therapist must honestly examine her own behavior and see if the client's perception is accurate. If so, therapists should not be afraid to admit to the client that they have made a mistake. For example:

Therapist:
> Yes, I think you're right. I was aware of the time going by and I wanted to touch on a few more issues before we had to stop. I probably was pushing you there, and I can see why that bothered you. I'm glad you made me aware of that; I'll try not to do it again.

It is liberating for beginning therapists to learn that they do not need to be afraid of making mistakes, although they may need to acknowledge them. In the example above, the therapist is responding to the client on the basis of reality and in an egalitarian way. The client's perception is validated by the therapist, which tells the client that the therapist is willing to have a genuine dialogue with him. It also tells the client that the therapist will respond to his concerns with respect and that the therapist-client relationship is going to be a two-way street. Too often, therapists and clients enact a relationship in which the client is the sick and needy one and the therapist is the healthy one who does not make mistakes or have problems. The response suggested above discourages this illusion. Overall, these messages can have a powerful effect on clients' expectations of therapy and accelerate the level of disclosure and exploration clients undertake in subsequent sessions.

In contrast, therapists can handle the confrontation in a way that hides their own humanity, keeps the relationship safely distant, and puts them in a superior position. For example, an ineffective response to this client's criticism would be to flip it back:

So you saw me as hurrying you up; how was that for you?

This response is an abuse of the client-centered reflection or psychoanalytic *blank screen*. With this type of *deflection* the client is told: It's always your problem, I will not look at my own contribution here, this will not be a genuine interpersonal encounter. This type of response limits the relationship to a superficial encounter and sets up a power battle between them. Little therapeutic gain will be realized as long as the relationship continues in this mode.

But what if the therapist does not agree with the client's complaint? The therapist should still accept the validity of the client's perception, but without agreeing to the comment. For example, the therapist can respond:

I'm sorry you saw me as being impatient with you; that wouldn't feel very good to me either. I wasn't aware of being in a hurry or trying to push you, but I'll be alerted to that in the future. If you ever feel that happens again, stop me right then and we'll look at it together.

The therapist should never agree to something she doesn't believe is true. In the example above the therapist is telling the client:

I will take your concerns seriously even if I do not see it the same way.

We can have differences between us and still work together.

It is important to me that you feel good about our relationship.

This type of response also tells the client that problems between them can be resolved, which lends hope that the therapist and client together will be able to resolve the client's problems.

Finally, it is very possible that the client is systematically misperceiving the therapist as hurrying him. For example, this client may readily experience the therapist and most other authority figures as demanding more than the client would like to produce, and then being dissatisfied with whatever the client does produce. If so, this client may have grown up with a parent who repeatedly demanded that the client do everything on the parent's timetable, and/or ignored the child's own wishes and accomplishments. Even if the therapist has gained further evidence to support such a hypothesis, this type of historical or transference interpretation should be held until later in therapy. Therapists stand to lose a lot if clients see them as sidestepping a reality confrontation. However, the therapist can use this information to generate working hypotheses that can be utilized later.

Clients Who Test the Therapist's Adequacy. Because it is usually difficult for beginning therapists to respond to client confrontations, we will examine another example of this. In the following situation the client challenges the therapist's competence. Although this taps into an anxiety-arousing area for the novice therapist, she still approaches the issue and invites the client to express his concern more fully.

Therapist:
You arrived late today. We should talk about that for a minute. I wonder if there is something about seeing me, or being in therapy, that doesn't feel right to you.

Client:
Well, aren't you just a student here? Isn't that what you said the first time we spoke?

Therapist:
Yes, I'm a second year graduate student in psychology, working on my master's degree.

Client:
Well, I don't really feel like a guinea pig or anything, but you really are just practicing on me, aren't you? Maybe you haven't had enough experience to help me?

Therapist:
Are you worried that if you go to all of the trouble of coming here, and talk about difficult problems with me, that I just won't know enough to be able to help you?

Client:
Yeah, after all, you really are just a beginner, and I must be fifteen years older than you. What do you think—are you certain that you can help me?

Therapist:
I certainly cannot offer you any guarantees, but I will do my best to try and help you. And as we continue to meet together a few times, you will be able to decide for yourself if I can help you or not. But for now, let's see if there are any questions I can answer for you about my training status, and then we should talk about how our age difference might get in the way.

In this vignette the therapist was able to approach the client's concern, even though this was difficult for her to do. The therapist did not act on her initial impulse, which was to try to assure the client that she would be able to help, and to try to convince the client of her competence. Instead of responding to her own need, the therapist was able to respond to the client by inviting him to express his reservations about her directly and fully. By tolerating her own discomfort and discussing the client's concerns with him, the therapist *demonstrated* her competence. This is always more effective than offering verbal reassurances that would only sound hollow to the client, and still leave the burden of proof upon the therapist.

The Client's Difficulty Entering Therapy. In the previous two examples, the therapist inquired about resistance and the client expressed concerns that personally challenged the therapist. In the following example, the therapist addresses the client's resistance and the client expresses her own concerns about entering therapy. This occurs more commonly than challenging the therapist and is usually far easier for the therapist to respond to. For example, a client may respond:

It's hard for me to ask for help.

I'm a little embarassed talking to a stranger. In our family, we kept our problems to ourselves.

I don't know if you can help me because you're (a woman, white, younger . . .).

First and foremost, it is crucially important to let clients know that you have heard their concerns, take them seriously, and want to do something about it. Again, the best way to communicate this respect and responsiveness is to invite clients to discuss their concerns more fully. For example, the therapist might say:

That does sound like an important concern for us. Let's talk more about it. What does it mean for you to need help?

or

How could my age (gender, color) keep us from working together productively?

In this example the therapist is able to follow the suggested guidelines and *approach* the client's conflict. As the therapist and client discuss it, some concerns will be taken away by educating the client more fully about the process of therapy. Other concerns will be resolved by correcting inaccurate assumptions about the therapist. However, some of the concerns that clients express cannot be assuaged so easily. The therapist can offer to be sensitive to these concerns and express a willingness to work with the client on them over the course of therapy. One way for the therapist to do this is by enlisting the client's help in better understanding the client's background and experience. For example, the therapist can invite clients to educate the therapist about their disparate life/cultural experiences when they feel the therapist is uninformed or doesn't understand. Giving clients an opportunity to express their concerns about treatment or the therapist, and sincerely trying to accommodate them as much as possible, will go a long way toward diminishing those concerns in therapy.

Approaching Resistance during Subsequent Sessions

The third and final section of this chapter examines therapeutic responses when a client cancels, does not show, or comes late to subsequent appointments. The therapist must consider the possible meaning that this holds for the client. In most cases, clients are not fully aware of their conflicted feelings about therapy. If the therapist inquires about resistance, clients often feel that they are being told they are bad or doing something wrong. Thus the client anticipates a punitive, critical, or disappointed response, so the therapist must be not only direct, but gentle, when approaching the topic of resistance.

Therapists should not try to pull away or expose a client's resistance as soon as they see it. A full frontal assault on perceived resistance will often be too much for a client. Resistance must be approached in a way that leaves clients with their dignity. One way to do this is to approach the client's resistance through a series of gradual steps that are progressively more direct. In the first example below, the therapist offers a *permission-giving and educative response* to encourage clients to express their conflicted feelings about therapy. That is, the therapist tells the client that resistance and ambivalence are understandable and expectable feelings. If this permission-giving does not work, the therapist can take a second step and encourage the client to explore the potential danger these feelings hold for her. This is focusing on the *defense* (e.g., "What could the threat be for you if . . ."). If clients continue to show signs of resistance but cannot talk about it, the therapist can draw on previous working hypotheses and try to interpret the *content* (e.g., "I wonder if it is difficult for you to become involved in therapy because. . ."). This progressive sequence will work well in many cases. For example:

Therapist:
Mrs. Smith, I would like to talk about how it feels for you to see me in therapy. I noticed that you were 20 minutes late today, and had to reschedule your appointment last week. I was wondering if there was something about coming here that didn't feel good to you. If so, it would be helpful for us to talk about that.

Client:
Oh no, I really do want to be here. And you've been very helpful already. It's just that my boss called.

Therapist:
Okay, but if in the future you ever find yourself having any difficulty about being in therapy, I want you to tell me about it. In therapy it is very important that we talk about any problems that come up between us. How would it be for you to tell me about something I did that you didn't like, or something about being in therapy that didn't feel good to you?

Client:
Well, that might be kind of hard for me to do.

Therapist:
What about that would be hard for you?

At this point the therapist and client are off and running together. The therapist can help clients work through the issues that would prevent them from expressing dissatisfaction or disagreement (e.g., clients concerned that the therapist or others will not like them unless they are always "nice"; clients are afraid of the intensity and destructiveness of their anger, etc.). Not only will this help keep clients in therapy, it has also provided the entreé into important conflict areas that need to be addressed in therapy.

In the example above, the therapist offered a permission-giving and educative response to try and free the client to talk about her ambivalent feelings toward therapy. If the client continued to show signs of resistance (e.g., missing, canceling, rescheduling, coming late), without being able to talk about it, the therapist should continue to focus on the resistance. In the example below, the therapist does this by addressing the *defense.*

Therapist:
It's important that you feel free to tell me about critical or troubled feelings you may have, because they are bound to occur. Would you be able to tell me if something about me or being in therapy bothered you?

Client:
I think so.

Therapist:
I'm not so sure you would. I think it would be difficult for you to tell me if I did something that you didn't like, or if there was something about being in therapy that was uncomfortable for you. Perhaps you believe "good clients" or "nice people" never have irritated, frustrated or disappointed feelings, or at least that they don't ever express them.

Client:
Well, yes, that's probably true.

Therapist:
> We need to look at that. You are having difficulty being in treatment, but you can't talk with me about that problem. What is the danger for you if you stop being "nice" and tell me what doesn't feel good about coming here? What do you think might happen?

In this example the therapist is trying to identify the threat that keeps the client from expressing her conflicted feelings about therapy. The therapist is not trying to find out why the client is not showing up for therapy, but why the client is having trouble talking about it. *It is more effective to address the defense itself than it is to probe for the conflict that is being defended against.* In most cases this will prove effective. If focusing on the defense does not work, however, the therapist can try to interpret the *content* of the client's resistance as a last resort. For example, if the therapist thinks the client's ambivalence is about to pull her out of treatment, and the client cannot talk about the conflict, the therapist can draw upon working hypotheses and interpret the resistance:

Therapist:
> It's been hard for you to get here; you've missed the last two sessions. I don't think that you just forgot. I think there is something about being in treatment that is difficult for you. Based on some other things we have talked about, I wonder if you are . . .?

Why does the therapist only take this more direct interpretive stance as a last resort? The interpretation (accurate or not) is the therapist's issue and puts the ball in her own lap. Whenever possible, it is better to try to follow the client's lead, or focus on the therapeutic process, rather than trying to pull the client along in the therapist's direction. That is, it is usually more effective to explore why the client is resisting, or make a process comment and address the current interaction, than it is to make interpretations or tell the client what to do. These responses are more effective because they leave more responsibility with the client.

CLOSING

Listening to the client with concern and respect is the most powerful intervention the therapist can make in the beginning of therapy. This is the basic tool the therapist uses to begin a working alliance with the client. Addressing ambivalence or resistance to therapy is the next step in maintaining the relationship that has just begun. Resistance will be more of an issue with some clients than others but it will occur to some extent for every client. This chapter has emphasized that if the client expresses these ambivalent or resistant feelings and the therapist responds to them, they will be far less likely to pull the client out of therapy. Resistance will remain a concern throughout the course of therapy and repeatedly emerge as clients address difficult personal issues. Responding effectively to the many different types of resistance that will occur for clients is an important way to keep clients engaged and progressing in treatment. If therapists formulate working hypotheses, it will help them anticipate client resistance and respond more effectively when it occurs.

Resistance, ambivalence, and defense provide a window to certain inner aspects of the self. Each provides an opportunity to observe the fascinating workings of internal conflict. People do not possess a unified self—humans are so complex and multifaceted that it often feels as if "a part of me is working against another part of me." By resolving an internal conflict a person becomes a little bit more integrated or whole. This process of integrating disparate parts of the self is the resolution of neurosis and the avenue to personal growth and change. When this occurs around the topic of resistance, the therapist and client stride forward in therapy. This early success experience can show clients that they possess the internal resources, and have the helping person necessary, to go on to resolve the bigger issues that lie ahead.

SUGGESTIONS FOR FURTHER READING

1. Beginning therapists are encouraged to read further about the concept of resistance. For example, one classic reference in this area is Ralph Greenson's book, *The Technique and Practice of Psychoanalysis*, Volume 1 (New York: International Universities Press, 1967), chapter 2. This chapter provides a lucid introduction to the topic of resistance and offers informative case studies to illustrate effective therapeutic responses. Again, the reader does not have to be psychoanalytically oriented to be informed by this discussion.

2. There are many different ways to work with resistance and beginning therapists will find it useful to examine other approaches. For example, therapeutic responses to resistance have been especially highlighted in the family therapy literature. Therapists who are interested only in individual psychotherapy may still find it useful to examine basic texts in this area, such as: C.M. Anderson and S. Steward, *Mastering Resistance: A Practical Guide to Family Therapy* (New York: Guilford Press, 1983). The "strategic" schools of brief therapy have also focused intensively on handling resistance. Some will find their paradoxical maneuvers too manipulative to adopt, but others will find them elegantly effective, especially with recalcitrant clients. See R. Fisch, J.H. Weakland, and L. Segal, *The Tactics of Change: Doing Therapy Briefly* (San Francisco: Jossey-Bass, 1982).

4

An Internal Focus for Change

CONCEPTUAL OVERVIEW

The first stage of therapy is complete when the therapist and client have established a collaborative relationship and begun to work together on the client's problems. This collaborative alliance is a necessary prerequisite to the beginning of the second stage of therapy—the client's journey inward. In order to change, clients must become less preoccupied with the problematic behavior of others and begin to explore their own internal and interpersonal responses. More specifically, this means that clients need to stop talking about historical events, past relationships, and the problematic behavior of others in their lives. Instead, clients must begin to clarify their own thoughts, feelings, and reactions to the troubling events they are experiencing. Why? Although clients will usually fail in their attempts to change or control others in their lives, they can often resolve problems by understanding and changing themselves.

The therapist's task is to help clients make the transition from seeing the source and resolution of problems in others to adopting an internal focus for change. This is a twofold process. First, the therapist must help clients to look within. That is, the therapist must focus clients away from complaining about or trying to change others and toward identifying and understanding their own reactions. Second, the therapist must help clients become active agents in their own change process. The therapist does this by fostering the client's own self-direction and initiative within the therapeutic relationship. In adopting an internal focus for change, clients can begin to adopt new and more effective responses to old problems and claim a greater sense of effectance in their lives. It will be difficult for many clients to begin looking at their own issues, however, and they cannot take this journey inward without the support provided by a secure and caring relationship with the therapist.

CHAPTER ORGANIZATION

The first section of this chapter introduces the need for clients to shift from an external to an internal focus for change. It describes how clients often externalize their problems onto others, maintaining their feelings of helplessness, "stuckness," and/or depression. It shows how therapists can help clients focus inward and begin to change themselves rather than continue to try to change others. And it illustrates how clients often resist the transition to an internal focus and how therapists can respond to this resistance.

The second section discusses how clients can become active agents in resolving their own problems. It discusses how therapists can use the therapeutic relationship to foster the client's own initiative and sense of effectance. It examines specific intervention strategies that therapists can use to place the locus of change within the client. Sample therapist-client dialogues will illustrate effective and ineffective ways to achieve this.

The third section shows how therapists can actively enlist clients in understanding and changing their own problems. A case study will illustrate how therapists can help clients remain responsible and contributing agents throughout each phase of treatment.

LOOKING WITHIN TO ADOPT AN INTERNAL FOCUS FOR CHANGE

Clients Externalize Their Problems

In the beginning stage of therapy, most clients see the source of their problems in others. Clients often want to spend more time describing the problematic behavior of others than their own experience of these problems. For example, many clients begin the first few therapy sessions by announcing that the problem is really with another person:

My wife is always on my back.

My husband won't pay any attention to me.

My children are impossible; they won't do anything I say.

My boss is a raging tyrant. If he doesn't back off, I'm going to have a heart attack.

My mother won't stop criticizing me; I can't do anything right according to her.

I'm twenty-seven years old, and my father treats me like a child.

My boyfriend has a drinking problem.

When therapy begins with these externalizing complaints about the behavior of others, the therapist must respond to the client's immediate experience and acknowledge these complaints as valid concerns that genuinely trouble the client. This is only the first step, however. After hearing and empathizing with the client, the therapist must begin to focus the client back on her own thoughts, feelings, and reactions to these problematic others. The following discussion examines why therapy is more productive when therapists focus clients inward and how this can be done.

In the examples above, the client is talking about the behavior of others that is troublesome for him/her. The client feels depressed, anxious, distrustful, enraged, or helpless because of the other person's behavior. In many cases, clients will try to get the therapist to join them in blaming, criticizing, or trying to change the other person. Therapy will not progress very far if the therapist joins the client in focusing on the other person's problematic behavior. Whereas the client's attempts to change the other person will usually fail, the client is much more likely to resolve the problem by changing her own way of responding (Wheelis, 1974). Thus, the therapist's task is to shift the client's focus away from the other person and back onto herself.

One of the most effective ways therapists can help clients change themselves is by increasing clients' awareness of their own thoughts, feelings, and reactions in problematic situations. Each of the questioning responses below can be used to focus clients back on themselves:

How do you feel when your wife is nagging you?

What do you find yourself thinking when your husband is ignoring you?

What do you do when your children do not mind you?

What is it like for you when your boss is being so demanding?

Tell me the thoughts you were having as your mother was criticizing you.

How do you react to your father when he diminishes you?

What is most troublesome for you about your boyfriend's drinking?

Simple inquiries of this type serve two important functions. First, it tells clients that the therapist is listening to their concerns and is taking them seriously. The therapist has not changed the topic or brought up something that was discussed ten minutes ago, but is responding directly to their concerns. Second, while inviting the client to say more about her concerns, the therapist is also shifting the client's focus away from others and encouraging the client to look more closely at herself. This bid to help clients become more aware of their own reactions is a critical step toward understanding and resolving their problems. As we will see throughout this chapter, the simple response of focusing clients on their own experience is a powerful intervention that will elicit strong feelings, memories, and associations.

In many cases, clients will welcome the therapist's offer to talk more about themselves. When clients begin to focus inward and learn more about *themselves*, they begin to change. The clients' active exploration of her own life and problems will lead to new feelings of mastery and effectance that often result in growth and change. However, not all clients will respond so positively to the therapist's bid to look more closely at themselves. Clients may avoid or actively reject an internal focus, continuing to talk about the problem "out there" in others. The therapist can expect this and can continue to inquire about the personal meaning that this particular situation holds for the client. For example:

Therapist:
Where would you like to begin this morning?

Client:
My wife is impossible to live with. She complains constantly; nothing ever pleases her.

Therapist:
It sounds like you've had a difficult week with her. What's been the hardest thing for you?

Client:
Do you know how hard it is to live with an angry, demanding wife who keeps trying to tell you what to do?

Therapist:
You are very angry at her. Tell me, what is it like for you to live with someone who keeps trying to boss you around?

Client:
She's just impossible, and her whole family is like that. They must think they're better than everybody else!

Therapist:
I'm struck by how strongly you react to their criticism. That makes me wonder if you may feel that they really are better than you in some way, or that you deserve to be criticized.

Client:
Well, sometimes I think I should be making more money or be further along in my career. Then they wouldn't be able to treat me like they do.

Therapist:
So their superior attitude does bring out your own feeling of not measuring up. That feeling may be a big part of the problem you have with them. We should work together and try to understand that feeling of yours better.

Client:
Well, I guess I do feel like I'm not really good enough sometimes, but it wouldn't be so bad if they would just stop criticizing me.

Therapist:
Let's talk about your feeling of not being good enough. If we could help you with that feeling, then it would be easier for you to learn new and better ways to respond to them than you have had in the past.

In this dialogue the therapist kept encouraging the client to look at his own reactions, while the client kept trying to focus on the problematic behavior of his wife and her family. The therapist's repeated bids to have the client look at himself served to mitigate the client's defensive, externalizing stance and, as a result, eventually moved the client closer to his own problematic feelings. By exploring and gaining a better understanding of his own feelings of inadequacy, the client will be better able to change himself and find more effective ways of responding to his wife and in-laws.

Focusing clients on themselves is a simple but powerful intervention that most clients have not experienced before. Many clients will resist this internal focus, however, because it demands that they come face-to-face with those difficult feelings that they have been unable to resolve alone. The paradox is that, as long as clients avoid their own conflicts by externalizing their problems onto others, they will feel powerless, dependent, and out of control. We must look further at why it is more effective for clients to focus inward and try to change themselves rather than others.

Many clients who are struggling with neurotic conflicts are inappropriately invested in changing others as a means of managing their own problems or insecurities. In attempting to shape or direct others, the client is seeking an external solution to an internal problem. Beyond clearly and directly expressing our preferences and personal limits (e.g., "I would like . . . "; "I will not . . . "), the reality is that we are limited in influencing the way others think, feel, and act. For example, clients usually fail in their attempts to make their spouse stop drinking, smoking, or overeating. Similarly, some clients try for decades to win the approval or recognition from others that they never received from a parent. Others try unsuccessfully for years to have their grown offspring choose a different mate, friend, or job. As a result of these failed attempts to change others, many clients enter therapy with feelings of frustration, helplessness, and depression.

A therapist can offer clients the more productive alternative of decreasing their attempts to change others and gaining more understanding and control over their own reactions. This internal focus is a necessary prerequisite before clients can adopt new, more effective responses to old problems. Only when clients begin to focus on understanding and changing themselves will they begin to feel in charge of their lives and capable of change. These feelings are experienced by the client as *empowerment*. Thus, as we saw above, a consistent therapeutic response should be to gently focus clients back onto themselves to learn about their own thoughts, feelings, and reactions. The following types of questions will help clients explore their own responses:

What is the main feeling you are left with when . . . ?

Tell me the thoughts you were having when . . .

What was the most difficult thing for you when . . . ?

How would you like to be able to respond when . . . ?

Therapists Must Focus Clients Inward

Focusing clients on their own behavior often reveals how they are contributing to or participating in their own conflicts. Often clients will not have realized their own role in these conflicts. As we will see below, clients who can focus on themselves and see their own participation in a conflict are usually motivated to change their own part in it. This, in turn, may allow the other person to respond differently as well. To illustrate, we return to the previous example of the husband who complained about his wife and in-laws.

Although the client began to explore his own feelings of inadequacy, he kept complaining to his therapist about his "obnoxious" wife and his "superior" in-laws. The therapist was genuinely empathic and supportive of his anger but, at the same time, she did not join the client in blaming or criticizing his wife. Instead, she continued to lead the client away from his preoccupation with his wife's behavior and repeatedly focused him on his own reactions to her. As this internal focus continued, it allowed the client to become more aware of his own reactions that contributed to their marital conflict.

For example, the client learned that he was quiet and unresponsive to his wife when he arrived home from work. The therapist helped him see that his silence escalated his wife's attempts to gain his attention, causing him to become even more unresponsive to her. Their problematic interaction escalated as the wife became more insistent and demanding of his attention, leading him to withdraw even further—by taking a nap, for example. Furthermore, by focusing on his own emotional reactions at that moment, the client realized that his wife's increasing requests for attention also made him feel overwhelmed by the prospect of trying to meet all of her needs. In this regard, he had held the unrealistic belief that, if he did not always respond to her, he was failing as a husband and again being inadequate.

If the therapist does not join with the client in complaining about his wife, but encourages the client to become more aware of his own internal and interpersonal responses to his wife, then the client is given an opportunity to change his part in the marital conflict. That is, this client stopped being a helpless and begrudging victim of his "obnoxious" wife only when he began to alter his part in their conflict. In this case, the husband began to express more directly to his wife when he would like to be close to her and when he would prefer to be alone. He also explained to his wife that he wanted thirty minutes alone to unwind when he returned home from work, after which they could then sit down and share their day together.

More important, as the husband gained a better understanding of his tendency to feel overwhelmed by the demands of others, he became less reactive to his wife's requests. He learned that he felt overwhelmed, in part, because he could neither say no to her nor express his wishes. If his wife wanted something from him, he thought that he was failing and felt bad if he didn't respond immediately. And because he couldn't set limits or ask for what he wanted without feeling selfish, he resented the "unfairness" in their relationship. The client also learned that he expressed this resentment to his wife indirectly—in critical and withholding ways. Over the next few months, his new awareness allowed him to respond to his wife's "demands" as if they were merely requests. He could choose to respond to them or not, without feeling controlled by them. As the client set these limits, he began to feel a new sense of control over himself in their relationship and was able to make some tentative steps toward greater closeness with his wife.

Thus, as soon as clients begin focusing on their own behavior, they will start to feel less "stuck," powerless, and depressed. Most clients will start to see more alternatives available to them and begin to feel more hopeful and in charge of their lives. Thus, the therapist's task is to discourage clients from passively complaining about others or from trying to manipulate and control others' behavior. Although clients usually fail in their attempts to change others, they can often succeed in resolving problems by gaining greater mastery over their own responses.

Both Therapists and Clients Avoid an Internal Focus

Therapists Join Clients in Externalizing. We have already seen that many clients externalize their problems onto others and that therapists can help clients change by focusing clients inward. Many therapists, however, will find it difficult to work with clients in this way. Focusing clients inward means that the therapist is *drawing out* the client's fears and concerns rather than diminishing or assuaging them. Some therapists have difficulty approaching client conflicts so directly, perhaps because they confuse being direct with being critical, blaming, or unsupportive. Other therapists are reluctant to approach the client's internal conflicts so directly because they believe that "good people do not make others hurt or feel bad." These therapists try to make clients feel better by reassuring them about their insecurities and by emphasizing their strengths and successes. Moving away from client conflicts in these ways are well-intended but ineffective responses that keep clients from fully expressing and exploring their problems. Still other therapists avoid an internal focus in order to maintain the client's approval. This occurs because some clients will become angry as the therapist encourages them to explore the threatening internal conflicts that they have been defending against.

For these and other reasons, therapists often join with the client in looking away from the client's internal conflict. Therapists collude with the client to externalize problems when they repeatedly respond in the following ways:

Give advice and tell the client what to do or how to respond to others.

Interpret or explain what the other person's motives or behavior really mean.

Reassure clients that their problems will go away or are not something to be concerned about.

Disclose what the therapist has done to cope with a similar person or problem.

Although each of these responses may be effective at times, they cannot come to characterize the ongoing course of treatment. If they do, they will keep clients from exploring their own experience and, ultimately, from being able to resolve their own conflicts. Thus, therapists must help clients expand and elaborate their awareness of their internal experiences and interpersonal responses. This must be done repeatedly throughout each therapy session. As we will see below, however, this is difficult to do because an intense focus on self and internal experiences may arouse clients' anxiety.

Clients Resist an Internal Focus. Why do clients often eschew an internal focus and how can therapists work with this resistance? A shift away from the client's focus on others can make some clients feel that the therapist does not really understand them or is not sympathetic to their concerns. Other clients fear that, if they give up their attempts to change others, they will either have to accept the blame for the problem or remain forever resigned to defeat. Still other clients may not yet be ready to approach the painful feelings or difficult choices that looking inside entails, or they feel that it is unsafe to share their personal concerns with the therapist. Thus, the therapist should *work with clients to explore their reasons for not wanting to look within* (this is called *addressing the resistance*). The therapist should not insist, however, when clients are not ready to look at their own issues.

We must look more carefully at how the therapist can best respond when clients have difficulty looking within. One thing the therapist can do is to follow clients along for awhile, giving repeated bids to reveal a little more about themselves. If the client's externalizing stance does not begin to change, the therapist can make a process comment that simply describes their interaction. For example:

Therapist:
I've noticed that you talk very easily about your husband and your daughter, but you don't say very much about yourself. Are you aware that that happens?
or
I think that we have been missing each other the last two sessions. I keep asking you what you were thinking about or trying to do in a particular situation, and you keep responding by telling me more about the other person. What do you see going on between us?

These process comments will help clients to become aware of their externalizing style with the therapist and to learn that they probably respond this way to other people as well. For example, if clients cannot share themselves in a personal way with others, many people will find them boring or aloof. The therapist and client may then have part of the client's presenting problem occurring in their relationship (e.g., client complaints of loneliness, isolation, or lack of meaningful contact with others).

Although it is often frustrating and discouraging for clients to realize that they are reenacting their conflict in the therapy session, this reenactment provides the client the opportunity to resolve the problem by changing the distancing pattern *within* the therapeutic relationship. That is, the therapist can help clients become aware of how they interact with others and how others experience them, and offer a new and more effective way of relating in the therapeutic relationship. For example, the therapist can describe their current interaction and offer to develop a more meaningful and sharing relationship with the client:

Therapist:
   I feel that I am being held away from you when you keep talking about others rather than yourself. That doesn't feel very good to me. I would like to learn more about *you!* Can we work together to try and change that?

A significant response often occurs when the therapist uses questions or process comments to focus clients inward. Clients will often *reveal a variety of new and important concerns* that they had not talked about before. For example:

But there really isn't very much about me to know.

I'm not used to telling people what I'm feeling.

It seems like something always goes wrong when I try to get close to someone.

You wouldn't like me very much if you knew what I was really like.

In this way, the therapist's process comment has brought out important new concerns that can now be addressed in therapy. The therapeutic relationship and the content to be explored have deepened. *This process of helping clients to focus inward and to explore their resistance to looking within will provide some of the most important material to be addressed in therapy.* It is important to note that these new client concerns are far less likely to be brought up for treatment when the therapist does not focus clients inward. Thus one of the most important reasons for adopting an internal focus is to *uncover* central conflicts that are operating in the client's life, and to do this in a way that makes them accessible for treatment. We will return to this uncovering aspect of the internal focus in the next section.

PLACING THE LOCUS OF CHANGE WITH THE CLIENT

The first component of the internal focus was to help clients *look* within and become more aware of their own reactions and responses. In addition to looking within, the client must also begin to *act* from within, by adopting an internal locus for change. This section examines how clients can gain a greater sense of *effectance* in their lives by becoming active agents in their own change process (White, 1959).

First, we will see how therapists can use the therapeutic relationship to foster the client's own initiative and self-direction. Second, we will examine specific types of therapeutic interventions that encourage the client's participation in and control over the change process. Throughout, the therapist's goal is to respond to the client's feelings, interests, and initiative and to thereby support the client's growing sense of effectance.

Using the Therapeutic Relationship to Foster Clients' Initiative

In the course of treatment, a therapist has the opportunity to convey to his clients the broader message that they are able to take charge and effectively manage their own lives. Effective therapists of every theoretical orientation nurture the client's own sense of personal power and dignity. Rather than just using words to encourage clients' initiative and autonomy, however, therapists must provide clients with the experience of *acting* more effectively during the therapy session. When clients experience a greater sense of mastery and control in their relationship with the therapist, this generalizes to other relationships (Bandura, 1977). We will see below how therapists can help clients assume an active, initiating role in therapy.

The first way to help clients feel responsible for and capable of change is to encourage them to bring up the issues that they feel are most important to discuss. Therapists should repeatedly encourage clients to talk about whatever their primary concerns are, to explore their own motivations and wishes, and to generate their own behavioral alternatives and options.

Why is it so important to encourage and respond to the client's own initiative? In one way or another, most clients are unable to act on their own wishes, preferences, and interests. In past relationships, these clients have not had significant others respond to their own true feelings or support their own interests. As a result, it will be very exciting—but threatening—for these clients to feel the therapist's support for their own feelings, perceptions, and self-direction. Whenever therapists can successfully engage clients in pursuing their own interests and examining their own conflicts, therapy will become an intense and productive experience.

When the therapist is able to help clients explore and understand the material they produce, rather than merely direct them to the therapist's own agenda, change will often begin to occur. When clients provide the momentum and direction for therapy, they *experience* acting more effectively and being more in charge of their own lives. Once clients have begun to initiate and lead with their own concerns, the therapist can actively participate by contributing his own interpretations, behavioral alternatives, and interpersonal feedback to the client. However, the information and understanding that the therapist offers will be far more useful if the therapist is responding to the client's own agenda, interests, or concerns. This process dimension is one of the most important characteristics of the therapeutic relationship.

Hierarchical Relationships Keep Clients Dependent. We have already noted how clients often resist the therapist's attempts to make them active participants in treatment. Many clients will be troubled by expressing their own wishes, acting on their own initiative, and achieving successes.

Because so many clients have not been supported in their own individuation and are threatened by self-direction, competence, or success, they continually elicit advice, direction, and explanations from the therapist. Therapy will not be productive if this helper-helpee mode is enacted. This will shift responsibility away from the client and onto the therapist, and create the hierarchical relationship discussed in Chapter 2. Clients will not be able to adopt a stronger stance in their own lives as long as this dependency is fostered.

Unfortunately, therapists often comply with the clients' subtle or overt request to tell them what to talk about in therapy and what to do in their lives. It is flattering to think that we know what is best and can tell others what to do; it appeals to the narcissism in every therapist. Although there will certainly be times when the therapist needs to take a directive stance, this cannot characterize the ongoing process of therapy. If it does, clients are passively healed by the powerful therapist, and remain dependent on helpers to manage their lives. Because this occurs so regularly, we need to examine further this *dependency-fostering* approach to therapy.

Supporting Clients' Own Autonomy and Initiative. Effective therapy fosters and encourages the client's own autonomy. Therapists cannot just *talk* with clients about independence and autonomy. They must create a relationship in which clients *behave* independently. To do this, the therapist must first give clients permission to follow their own interests and to introduce the material that is most relevant to them. Then it becomes critically important for the therapist to identify the meaning and feeling in their concern and to encourage the client to expand and elaborate it further. In response to the client's increasingly specific exploration, the therapist can help clarify the client's experience and, together, they can begin to generate more effective ways to respond. When this interchange spirals on throughout several sessions, clients will become committed to treatment and find that meaningful change has begun to occur. Facilitating this growth process may be the primary challenge and satisfaction of being a therapist.

The model of therapeutic interaction described above is an *independence-fostering* approach to psychotherapy. The client has the experience of sharing responsibility for the course of treatment by defining and addressing his own concerns and conflicts. The therapist encourages and supports the client in achieving this more assertive stance and secondarily contributes information and guidance to the client's own exploration.

A common misconception is that longer-term, dynamic, or relationship-based therapies are *dependency-fostering*, whereas short-term, problem-solving, or behavioral approaches are not. Actually, whether the therapy fosters dependence or independence is determined by the therapeutic process and not by the length of treatment or theoretical orientation of the clinician. In short- or long-term therapy, the client's dependency is inappropriately fostered when the therapist "cures" the client by repeatedly directing the course of therapy, giving advice, and prescribing solutions for the client. Let us examine an effective middle ground between the nonproductive extremes of directive and nondirective control.

Shared Control in the Therapist-Client Relationship. Therapy will be most successful when the therapist and client share control over the direction of therapy. It is overly controlling for the therapist to play the predominant role in structuring and directing the course of treatment, and it is ineffective to nondirectively abandon clients to their own confusion and frustration. In a more productive relationship, the therapist will encourage the client to take the lead but will contribute information, clarifications, and alternatives to the material the client has produced. It will be therapeutic for many clients to experience a relationship in which control is not competed over or held by one or the other party, but is shared by both participants. For example, in Chapter 2 we stressed that, in the beginning of treatment, the therapist should encourage the client to take the initiative and bring up whatever he would like to discuss. For example:

> I would like you to begin each session by bringing up what you want to talk about. I want to work on what is most important to you.

Some therapists will be frustrated by this approach because they feel an urgency to address problems and begin finding solutions. This practical, problem-solving orientation certainly has some very real advantages and is necessary in crisis situations. However, this approach has several important drawbacks. First, we have already seen how a directive approach prevents the therapist and client from uncovering conflicts that were not evident in the client's presenting problem. Second, the therapist is not to merely "fix" the client's presenting problem anyway. A much broader goal is desired, and the therapeutic approach suggested here facilitates it: *teaching clients that they possess the personal resources to resolve problems and effectively negotiate their own adult lives.* Working in this way, the client gains an increasing sense of autonomy and personal power, which does not occur when the client merely follows the therapist's lead.

Although personal power and autonomy are goals that most therapists would acclaim, the problem-solving therapist would assert: "What if you follow the client's lead and it takes you nowhere?" It is true that a nondirective approach requires an unrealistic amount of time and patience from the therapist, and often results in a disorganized and unfocused therapy. As stated earlier, however, there is an effective middle ground of shared therapist-client control that therapists miss when they adopt a purely directive or nondirective stance. Next, we will examine some therapeutic interventions that enact or express this middle ground of shared control.

Therapeutic Interventions That Place the Client at the Fulcrum of Change

We have already noted how therapists can encourage the client's lead while still participating actively in shaping the course of therapy. The critical technique is for the therapist to intervene without taking the impetus away from the client. Three different examples illustrate effective and ineffective ways to intervene successfully. In the first example, the therapist is ineffective because she takes responsibility for the continuing movement of therapy away from the client.

Ineffective Interventions That Leave the Therapist at the Fulcrum of Change. Suppose that the client is filling the therapy session with seemingly irrelevant storytelling. The therapist cannot find a common theme to any of the client's stories or understand the emotional connection and personal meaning the stories hold for her. It seems as if nothing significant is occurring. At that point, it is easy for the therapist to stop the client and direct her toward a specific topic that the therapist thinks would be more fruitful. Although this needs to be done sometimes, the therapist must be careful to revitalize their interaction without shifting the impetus for therapy away from the client and onto herself. In the dialogue below, the onus for therapy comes to rest with the therapist and the client loses an internal focus for change.

Therapist:
I don't think this is taking us anywhere.

Client:
Yeah, I'm not sure where I'm going with this either. What would you like me to talk about?

Therapist:
You have had trouble asserting yourself in the past, and I think we need to look at that problem. Last week you said you wanted to ask your boss for three weeks of vacation instead of two. How are you going to handle that confrontation?

Client:
I'm not sure, what do you think I should say?

Therapist:
To begin with, you need to arrange a face-to-face meeting with him. It is important that only the two of you are present so you can have his full attention. Then use the "I" statements we have practiced to directly state what you want.

Client:
Sounds good, but what would you say to him first?

This exchange will not be productive, even though the therapist has moved the client to a more salient topic and provided useful information about effective confrontations. The fulcrum of therapeutic movement has tipped from the client to the therapist and a hierarchical teacher-student exchange has resulted. Most clients will not be able to incorporate and act on the therapist's useful information until the client picks up the momentum and begins to actively participate again. Furthermore, because the client remained in a passive, following role as the therapist continued to explain and inform, the client does not gain the increasing sense of mastery or effectance that comes from participating in successful therapeutic movement. Thus a more productive intervention would be to direct the client to the new topic but wait for the client to become actively involved again before the therapist offers further information.

Effective Interventions That Place the Client at the Fulcrum of Change. Now we will see how the therapist can reorient the client toward more productive material, but do so in a way that keeps the momentum for therapy with the client. One way is to use a process comment that makes their current interaction overt and a topic for discussion. For example:

Therapist:
Are you using our time the way you want to right now? I don't have the feeling that what you're talking about is really very important to you.

Client:
Yeah, I'm not sure where I'm going with this either. What would you like me to talk about?

Therapist:
I think that we should try to identify what would be most important to you, and talk about that. What would that be right now?

Client:
I'm not really sure.

Therapist:
Let's just sit quietly for a moment, then, and see what comes to you.

This type of confrontation challenges the client to approach more substantial material, but does so in a way that does not take the impetus away from him. The therapist has directly intervened and confronted the client, but has left the client an active participant in revitalizing the discussion. *Clients produce far more significant material when they are encouraged to lead in this way rather than to follow.*

Effective Confrontations Reveal New Conflicts. The final example shows how new client conflicts can be identified for treatment when the therapist intervenes without taking the locus for change away from the client. Imagine the following situation: A nineteen-year-old client in a college counseling center had been telling his therapist about his attempts in early adolescence to observe his mother undressing. The client had been detailing his voyeuristic efforts at great lengths, but the therapist did not feel that this was really much of a concern for the client. Unless the therapist could find the relevant meaning for the client, he wanted to move on to other more salient issues. In the dialogue below, the therapist refocuses the client in a way that keeps the locus for change with the client and opens up an important new conflict area for therapy.

Therapist:
Does this feel like an important topic to you that you want to discuss with me? As I listen to you I don't get the feeling that you are really very interested in what you are telling me. Is that the case, or am I not understanding the meaning this holds for you?

Client:
I thought therapists were interested in this Oedipal stuff. I figured you would want to hear about it.

Therapist:
I'm struck by the fact that you are telling me what you think I want to hear, rather than working on what is most important to you. That's something we should look at in therapy. I wonder if you find yourself doing this in other relationships as well—trying to sense other people's needs at the expense of expressing your own?

This is another way in which the therapist has confronted the client and redirected therapy without taking the impetus away from the client. In this vignette, the therapist has also used their current interaction to uncover a potential new problem area for the client. Because this arose from their joint interaction and not from the therapist's private agenda or personal directive, most clients will be responsive to exploring this new issue. Thus, the therapist has effectively focused the client back upon himself, identified a new conflict area to be explored, and left the client a participant in directing the course of therapy.

As the client begins to work with the new problem areas that have developed out of the therapeutic relationship, important inroads will be made on the client's presenting problems as well. In most cases, significant progress cannot be made on the presenting problem until movement is made on other related conflicts that are not evident at the beginning of therapy. That is, clients have often been unable to resolve their presenting problem because they have not addressed other issues that interlock and impinge on the presenting problem. As noted above, adopting an internal focus will identify salient conflicts that clients did not realize were relevant to their presenting problem. We will return to this issue of expanding clients' conceptualizations of their problems in Chapter 7.

ENLIST CLIENTS IN UNDERSTANDING THEIR OWN CONFLICTS

In this final section, we will bring the internal focus into the therapeutic relationship. Once clients have begun to look within and express their inner world, the therapist can further clients' mastery over their own lives by engaging them in understanding their own conflicts. A common misconception about psychotherapy is that the therapist is completely responsible for figuring out what is wrong with the client. Many beginning therapists have unrealistic expectations that they must be very insightful and knowing, and then suffer under these performance demands. Here again, this places the impetus for change entirely in the therapist's lap and leaves the client a passive recipient, waiting to be enlightened. A more effective approach is to extend the collaborative alliance into the problem-solving phase of therapy as well.

Rather than setting the stage for therapists to announce interpretations and explanations, therapists will be more effective if they elicit clients' active involvement in understanding their own conflicts. Although change certainly depends on the therapist's conceptual understanding of the client, the client must participate in a collaborative alliance as well. This frees the therapist to respond more effectively to what the client produces and gives clients the opportunity to become more effective in managing their own lives. Rather than trying to provide answers, therapists should develop the skill to help clients exercise their own strengths and resources. Real change has occurred when psychotherapy has not only resolved the client's presenting problem, but has fostered the client's sense of effectance as well.

This third component of helping clients adopt an internal focus for change is illustrated by contrasting two different ways of responding to a client's dream. Although both of these therapists share a similar conceptual framework for understanding the dream, they enact a very different interpersonal process with the client.

The Process Can Recapitulate the Client's Conflict

Anna is a twenty-two-year-old client who lives at home with her embittered and chronically embattled parents. For several years, Anna has been struggling with the developmental transition of emancipating from her family of origin. She cannot leave home and establish her own adult life. Anna has few friendships, dates little, and has no serious educational or career involvements. Anna's mother and alcoholic father fight constantly, and Anna feels it is her responsibility to stay home and help her mother cope with her problematic marriage. Anna entered therapy complaining of depression.

After several sessions, Anna volunteered a dream to her therapist that was of great importance to her. As the dream began, Anna was riding a beautiful horse across an open, green savannah. She felt as one with this graceful and powerful animal as they glided effortlessly across the broad grasslands. Sunlit rivers, birds in flight, and herds of grazing elk flowed past as they sped toward a distant mountain. Anna felt strong and free as she urged the tireless animal onward.

The distant mountains held the promise of new life amidst green meadows and tall trees. Anna felt their promise quicken inside of her as she urged the horse onward. But as the mountains drew near, Anna and the horse began to slow. The horse's legs became her own and grew heavier with each step. Anna desperately tried to will them on, but their footing became unsure and they began to stumble. At that moment, menacing riders appeared on all sides, ready to overtake and capture her. Anna awoke with a scream.

"What do you think my dream means?" Anna asked.

Her bright and concerned young therapist offered a lengthy and insightful explanation. The gist of her interpretation concerned Anna's guilt over leaving home. The therapist suggested that if Anna went on with her life and pursued her own interests, she would feel powerful and alive—just as she had in the dream. But before Anna could reach her goal and experience the satisfactions of having her own independent life, she would have to free herself from the binding ties of responsibility that she felt for her mother and her parent's marriage. Her loyalty to her mother threatened to entrap her in guilt and prevent her from having her own adult life.

Anna responded enthusiastically to the therapist's explanation: "Yes, I do feel as if I am being bad whenever I leave my mother. Is that why I dreamed that?"

Again, the therapist provided a provocative answer: "We've been talking about whether you are going to move in to an apartment next month. I think the dream reflects your conflict over taking this big step on your own."

Anna:
I want to move out, but I can't leave my mother with my father. She says she will divorce him if I move out, and it'll be my fault. What should I do?

Therapist:
I can't make that decision for you. You have to be responsible for your own decisions.

Anna:
But I don't know what's best to do, and you always do. You're so much smarter than me—I thought about that dream all day and I didn't know that's what it meant.

Throughout the rest of the session, Anna continued to plead for advice and expressed her discouragement about being able to resolve her own problems. The therapist kept refusing to tell her what to do and gave her a lengthy explanation about autonomy, independence, and the need for her to find her own solutions. The hour ended with Anna feeling agitated and depressed and the therapist still explaining the need for Anna to make her own decisions.

Although the therapist was astute in linking Anna's dream to the current manifestation of her conflict over leaving home, this was an unproductive session. How did their therapeutic process go awry?

In this session, Anna metaphorically reexperienced the same conflict with her therapist that she is struggling with at home. In her family, Anna was trained to be dependent and believe that she didn't have the wherewithal to succeed on her own. She was made to feel guilty whenever she acted independently. In the first fifteen minutes of their session, the therapist acted as the knowing parent who gave all of the necessary answers to the needing child. This interaction *behaviorally* communicated the message that Anna will be dependent on the therapist's superior understanding. On another level, however, this message was contradicted by the therapist's *verbal* message about independence. This mixed message about independence from the well-intentioned therapist immobilized the client.

Anna reacted so intensely because she needed permission from the therapist to become more independent, yet simultaneously expected that the therapist needed her to remain dependent, just as her mother did. When the pattern of having to be dependent on the authority was reenacted with her therapist, Anna's fear that she was incapable of making her own decisions and having her own life was confirmed. Anna remained depressed for the next few sessions, and even made vague allusions to suicide before the therapist successfully reestablished a collaborative alliance.

The Process Must Enact a Corrective Emotional Experience

In contrast, let's examine a different type of response to Anna's dream. What would have been a more effective reply to Anna's question "What do you think the dream means?" Any response that engages the client in exploring the dream with the therapist will be more effective than the therapist providing explanations to the client (no matter how accurate). Within this approach, therapists can choose to respond in many different ways. For example, therapists can engage clients in exploring their own dreams in the following ways:

> It sounds like a very important dream to me, too. Let's work on it together. Where should we begin?

> What was the primary feeling you were left with from the dream? Can you connect that feeling to anything going on in your life now?

> What was the most important image in the dream for you? Tell me what that image suggests to you.

> I feel uncomfortable when you ask me to tell you what your dream means. It's as if you think I have all the knowledge and you don't have anything to contribute, and I know that isn't true!

Each of these responses encourages the client to participate actively with the therapist. The therapist may ultimately give the same interpretation to the client, but it will be more effective if it evolves out of their joint effort and is integrated into their continuing collaboration. This gives clients a relationship where they are not one-down or dependent on the therapist, but are encouraged to exercise their own abilities and resources. When this occurs, clients' motivation to work in therapy increases and their sense of effectance is fostered. Fostering independence is a corrective therapeutic experience. It gives clients like Anna the permission they need to grow out of their dependence and act capably in their relationship with the therapist, something they have not experienced in the past.

CLOSING

Clients will not be able to resolve their problems unless they act out a different and more satisfying solution to their conflict in their relationship with the therapist. Adopting an internal focus for change provides clients with the type of experience that can produce change. By determining what material will be covered and by participating in finding solutions to their problems, clients gain an increasing sense of their personal power and uncover the interrelated constellation of feelings and beliefs that make up their problems.

As clients begin to reflect on their own experience and become less preoccupied with others, their affective world opens up and becomes available in a way that produces change. This affective unfolding is a critical step in the process of clarifying and resolving problems. However, the intensity of the emotions that are aroused by adopting an internal focus can be frightening for clients and intimidating for therapists. Thus, the next chapter will examine how therapists can help clients master the deep-seated emotions that are aroused by looking within.

SUGGESTIONS FOR FURTHER READING

1. In his classic paper, "Motivation Reconsidered: The Concept of Competence" (*Psychology Review* 66 [1959], pp. 297–333), Robert White introduces the concept of *effectance motivation*, an innate drive that leads individuals to actively explore and master their environment.

2. In his book, *How People Change* (New York: Harper & Row, 1974), Alan Wheelis discusses the internal process of change. In particular, see the chapter "Freedom and Necessity," which uses the language of *responsibility* to clarify how clients must focus on themselves rather than others in order to change.

3. In a tour de force presentation, Albert Bandura argues that perceived self-efficacy is the underlying mechanism of change across all treatment approaches. In "Self Efficacy: Toward a Unifying Theory of Behavioral Change" (*Psychological Review* 84, No. 2 [1977], pp. 191–215), he emphasizes that little enduring and generalized change results from verbal suggestion or persuasion. Instead, clients change when they have authentic experiences of *enactive mastery*. This occurs when clients have the actual experience of performing adaptive new coping responses with the therapist.

4. In his informative book, *Helplessness* (Freeman, 1975), Martin Seligman discusses how learned helplessness operates in depression and anxiety. Seligman suggests that depression dissipates when clients can exert more control over their environment, and offers interesting suggestions for providing young children with experiences of control that teach them that they do have the power to influence their lives. Many of these ideas are readily applicable to helping clients gain greater mastery in their own lives.

5

Responding To Conflicted Emotions

CONCEPTUAL OVERVIEW

Conflicted feelings lie at the heart of enduring and pervasive problems. Change in therapy is a process of affective relearning, and this change occurs when the therapist responds effectively to the client's conflicted emotions. When the therapist focuses clients on themselves, the troubling feelings that are central to their problems will emerge. That is, looking within causes clients to feel more intensely, and express more directly, the emotions that accompany their problems.

This affective unfolding is a pivotal point in therapy because it brings the therapist and the client to the emotional basis of the client's problems. On the one hand, clients will welcome the promise and reassurance of having the therapist make contact with their problems on a deeper, more personal level. At the same time, however, clients also want to avoid feelings that are too painful, too intense, or that just seem hopelessly unresolvable. Thus the therapist's response to the client's emerging feelings is critical and will greatly influence the eventual outcome of therapy.

Clients will not be able to change unless the therapist provides a more satisfying response to their conflicted emotions than they have received from others in the past. Unless the therapist effectively approaches the client's emerging affect, the therapeutic relationship will lose its vitality and therapy will be reduced to an intellectual rendering. Thus the purpose of this chapter is to help therapists respond to the full range and intensity of feelings that are aroused when clients begin to look within.

74

We will see that the therapist's ability to help clients change is in direct relation to how the therapist responds to their emotions.

CHAPTER ORGANIZATION

The first section of this chapter provides intervention guidelines for responding to the client's affect. Therapists need to approach the client's feelings and help expand the affective component of the client's problems. The second section continues the theme of approaching the client's affect and focuses upon working with the predominant or characterological affect that the client experiences.

The third section introduces the therapist to the interrelated sequence of emotions that comprise the client's conflict. For many clients, three related feelings recur in an ordered sequence, and therapists must identify and respond to each feeling in the sequence. Too often, clients cannot resolve conflicted emotions because therapists do not address each of the distinct feelings that make up this affective constellation.

Finally, the fourth section discusses characteristics of the therapist that influence his ability to work with the client's emotions. This is one of the most important issues in clinical training since the therapist's own personality, needs, and current life situation will often keep him from responding to the strong emotions that clients present. All therapists need to seek consultation at times in order to manage their own emotional reactions to the material that clients present. If not, therapists will be less capable of responding to the full range and intensity of the client's emotions.

RESPONDING TO CLIENTS' CONFLICTED EMOTIONS

Many situational problems can readily be resolved by simply obtaining new information, trying out behavioral alternatives, or recasting problems in a new framework. In and of themselves, these brief interventions are sufficient to resolve many of the problems that clients present, and they comprise an important aspect of change for almost all problems. For many of the more enduring and pervasive problems that clients present, however, the conflicted emotions that accompany problems must be addressed as well.

In therapy, clients are often reluctant to work with the emotions that emerge for them. On the one hand, most clients hope that the therapist will be able to help with their emotional reactions but, at the same time, clients want to avoid the painful feelings that they have not been able to resolve alone. There are several reasons why clients may be reluctant to share these feelings with the therapist. To some clients, it may seem like reexperiencing the same hopeless pain for no reason, suffering needless shame or embarrassment for revealing their inadequacies or having to struggle with the fear of losing control of their unremitting rage or consuming need. As a result, clients will often resist the therapist's attempts to touch the emotional core of their conflicts, although they long for this contact as well.

It is understandable that clients have this resistance, but therapy will be reduced to an intellectual exercise—incapable of effecting enduring change that can be generalized to other situations—if the therapist complies and bypasses clients' emotions. Although conflicted emotions are the basis of most clients' problems, they also provide the avenue to resolution and change. Therapists can respond more effectively to their clients' emotions by using the following intervention guidelines.

Approach the Client's Affect

In their moment-to-moment interaction with clients, therapists are repeatedly confronted with choices of how to respond to what the client has just said or done. For example, the therapist can respond by seeking more information, clarifying what the client has just said, relating this material to other issues the client has discussed in the past, and so forth. As a general guideline, however, the most productive response is to *respond to the feeling that the client is currently experiencing.* That is, the therapist's first priority is to acknowledge and approach the affective component of the client's response.

The following dialogue illustrates this guideline. Imagine that the therapist and client have just sat down together to begin their first session:

Therapist:
Tell me, Mike, what is the difficulty that brings you to therapy?

Client:
I'm having a lot of problems with my fifteen-year-old son. We disagree about everything and can't seem to talk to each other anymore. He doesn't do what I ask him to, and I don't like his values. I guess I'm pretty angry at him. His mother and I are divorced, and I'm thinking it may be time for him to go live with her. Do you think it's okay for a teen-aged boy to live with his mother?

Therapist:
I don't think either of us understands what is going on between you two well enough to decide that yet. You said you were "pretty angry" at him. Tell me more about your anger.

In this example, the client has presented many different issues that the therapist could have chosen to pursue. Following the guideline above, however, the therapist approached the primary affect that the client presented. The therapist could have responded differently and inquired further about the issues that the father and son disagreed about, worked on values clarification with the father, obtained more background information about the father-son relationship or the divorce, provided research findings about the effects of mother-custody versus father-custody on boys, and so on. Although these and many other responses may work fine, responding to the client's feeling will usually produce the most information and intensify the therapist-client exchange.

In the dialogue above, the client spoke about his anger directly and the therapist responded to it immediately. In addition to responding to clients' overtly expressed feelings, therapists must also respond to the covert or unverbalized feelings that clients experience.

Strong feelings are usually aroused whenever clients discuss an issue that is conflicted for them. That is, overtly stated feelings or nonverbal affective signs such as tearing, grimacing, or blushing are signals that inform the therapist that the client is addressing a significant issue. Clients are often unaware of this, however, and therapists must help clients explore these emerging feelings more fully. In the example below, the therapist responds to the client's nonverbal cues and draws out the affect that this situation holds for the client. Imagine that the client has been discussing her marital problems with her therapist:

Client:
I don't know if I should stay married or not. I haven't been happy with him for a long time, but I can see how hard he's trying to make our relationship work. And our four-year-old son would be devastated if we ever broke up. I don't know what's right to do, and it's so important for everyone that I make the right decision.

Therapist:
As you speak about this your face tightens. What are you feeling right now?

When the therapist responds to the client's feeling in this way, whether it is overtly or subtly expressed, it often serves to clarify the client's central concern. For example, this client may express concerns such as:

I'm so sad about hurting the people I love.

I'm afraid everyone will think I'm selfish for leaving and they'll blame me for the divorce. They'll all hate me.

I don't want to be alone. I don't want to be married to him anymore, but I'm afraid I can't leave and make it on my own.

I'm furious that I'm the one who has to make this decision. I'm responsible for every decision we make, and I always pay for it. It's not fair.

Throughout every session, clients will have an emotional response to the issues and concerns that matter most to them. Sometimes the client's affect will be presented forthrightly; often it will be subtle and elusive. If the therapist can approach and draw out the client's affect, as in the example above, it will usually bring further disclosure from the client and clarify the content of the client's conflict.

Expand and Elaborate the Client's Affect

We must look further at how the therapist can best respond to the client's feelings. At times, it can be helpful to anticipate or label a client's emerging feeling (e.g., "You must have been furious" or "You're frightened"). As a general guideline, however, a more effective response is to give clients an *open-ended bid* to explore the feeling further. For example, an open-ended response is when the therapist encourages clients to explore or express *what they feel is central* in their affective experience. A simple response such as "What are you feeling right now?" or "Tell me more about that feeling" is remarkably effective in eliciting the client's affect. This open-ended bid to elaborate the feeling *in any way the client wishes* is also more effective than trying to label the client's feeling in an either-or fashion. For example, if the therapist were to say, "Were you feeling _____ or _____ in that situation," the choice may restrict the client rather than invite a free range of responses. The open-ended bid is more effective in drawing out just exactly what the client is feeling, especially as the client often experiences something that the therapist has not anticipated.

This type of open-ended response is also more effective than asking clients why they are experiencing a particular feeling. That is, more information is disclosed if the therapist replies, "Help me understand your anger better" or "Tell me about your anger" than if the therapist asks the client to explain his feeling by asking "Why were you angry about that." By inviting the client to express more fully whatever feeling he is having, therapists are giving the message that they are interested in the client's own subjective experience and they are comfortable sharing whatever the client is experiencing. Most clients have not had permission to share their emotions so freely or honestly in the past, which is why this is one of the most important responses therapists can give their clients.

Clarify the Client's Subjective Feeling. Giving clients an open-ended bid to explore their feelings will also help clients clarify what this particular feeling means to them. Too often, therapists erroneously assume that a particular affective word such as *angry* or *sad* means the same thing to their clients as it does to them. Therapists should not assume that they understand what a particular affective word means to a client without clarifying what it means to this particular client. Therapists must actively encourage clients to elaborate the personal meaning that this feeling holds for them. This is especially true if a client repeatedly uses the same affective word to describe herself, or if there is cross-cultural disparity between the therapist and the client. Finally, having every client elaborate her affect in this way will also safeguard therapists against becoming overidentified with the client and seeing the client's experience as being the same as their own.

Clients are often uncomfortable and, therefore, unfamiliar with many of their emotional reactions. As a result, clients also need to clarify the broad *undifferentiated feeling states* they often experience. For example, the following questions suggest several ways that therapists can help clients learn more about the emotional reactions that comprise their problems:

Can you bring that feeling to life for me, and help me understand what it is like for you when you are feeling that?

Do you have an image that captures that feeling, or is there a fantasy that goes along with it for you?

Is there a particular place in your body where you experience that feeling?

Is this a familiar or old feeling? When is the first time you can remember having it? Where were you? Who were you with? How did the other person respond to you?

How old do you feel that you are when you experience that feeling? Can you attach an age to it, such as being seven years old or thirteen years old?

Does this feeling have its own sound or movement? Can you make a sound that would let me hear what it's like, or a gesture that would help me see it?

Some of these exploratory questions will work well with a particular client, not at all with another. Therapists will need to find what works best for each client. In general, however, these responses are all ways of approaching the client's emotions and clarifying the subjective meaning they hold for the client. These types of responses also tell clients that the therapist is concerned about their feelings—who they are and what is important to them. Further, they tell clients that the therapist is different from many other people they have known and is comfortable with their emotions.

Exploring feelings in these ways also creates an opportunity for therapists to confirm the client's personal experience. Clients have often had their feelings and perceptions invalidated by others and these types of responses give the therapist a chance to validate their emotions. In sum, it is profoundly important for clients to receive each of these messages. Together, they comprise a caring, concerned response that reassures clients about the therapist's ability to understand and help with what is most important in their lives.

Experiencing versus Talking about Feelings. Another reason for approaching clients' feelings in these ways is to *intensify* the affect. The exploratory responses suggested above are also attempts to amplify the client's emotional reactions. Although many clients are adept at talking about their feelings (especially psychologically sophisticated clients), it is a very different matter to feel or experience one's emotions. Little change occurs until clients are able to stop talking about their emotions in an intellectualized or objective manner, and actually experience their conflicted emotions with the therapist. Let us examine the critical difference between talking about and experiencing feelings further.

As stated above, the previous ways of approaching feelings are also intended to intensify the client's immediate affective experience. These therapeutic responses will help clients experience or get in touch with the emotional content of what they are discussing. Another way to help clients experience their feelings more fully is to *mirror* the client's emerging affect. For example, if a client's feeling is on the verge of coming through, clients may blink back tears, open their eyes wide in terror, clench their jaw in anger, tighten their lips to keep them from trembling, shake their head from side to side in protest, rock or hold themselves for comfort, drop their head and cover their eyes in shame, hold their breath in fear, and so on. The therapist can mirror or match the client's posture and expression as a way to clarify, amplify, and invite the full intensity of the client's emotional reaction.

It is important to draw out the client's affect because the greatest opportunity to help clients change occurs at the moment clients are experiencing the full emotional impact of their problems. It is the therapist's ability to be available and compassionate to clients *while they are experiencing their conflicted emotions* that allows clients to move through their conflicted feelings. Clients cannot do this when they are alone with their feelings or when they are insulated from the full intensity of them, as the following case example illustrates.

Throughout the session Jean had been telling her therapist about her hopelessness and despair. She described her life as a merry-go-round of endless ups and downs that always returned to the same hopeless conflicts. This past week she had dropped out of school, as she had done "so many times before," and gave in to pressure from her abusive boyfriend to let him move back into her home again. Jean described her hopelessness about ever being able to do or have anything for herself. Sooner or later, she acknowledged, the only way out of her misery would probably be suicide.

The therapist could feel Jean's despair and was deeply moved by her pain. The therapist tried to work with Jean's feelings by acknowledging her pain and validating her experience ("Of course you feel hopeless and defeated—you haven't been able to do what you wanted to do for yourself again. Like so many times before, you felt that you had to meet someone else's needs rather than say no and do what you wanted for yourself").

Just as Jean had done in all of their previous sessions, however, she was not able to "feel" her feelings with the therapist. That is, Jean would not share her actual feeling with the therapist or let the therapist be emotionally connected to her *while she was experiencing the sadness*. Because this critical connection to the therapist was missing, Jean still felt helplessly alone with her feelings and hopelessly alone in her life. In part, because she could not allow herself to be comforted by or revealed to a caring other, Jean had not been able to resolve the helplessness and hopelessness that she felt in this crisis and that she had experienced throughout her life.

The upsetting setback of the previous week had intensified Jean's distress. The therapist recognized that this crisis provided an opportunity to make contact with Jean's feelings for the first time:

Therapist:
It just seems hopeless.

Jean:
[*long pause, nods*]

Therapist:
You don't want to try anymore. You don't want to hurt anymore. You just want it to stop hurting, and suicide seems like the only way out.

Jean:
[*nods*]

Therapist:
You are so sad. You have been sad inside all of your life.

Jean:
[*nods, looks at therapist*]

Therapist:
Show me, in your eyes, how sad you really are.

Jean:

[*looks away, puts hands over eyes*]

Therapist:

I want to be with you in your sadness. I can't take your sadness away, but you don't have to be alone with it anymore. Let your sadness come into your eyes, so I can see it and be with you while you feel it.

Jean:

[*looks at therapist, sorrowfully, and slowly begins to cry*]

Therapist:

Yes, I can see your sadness, and how much you have been hurt.

Jean:

[*begins sobbing, and reaches to the therapist*]

For the first time, Jean was able to let the therapist be available to her while she experienced her despondency. The therapist acknowledged the risk that Jean had taken and they discussed how it felt to share her sadness with the therapist. Later in the session, Jean volunteered that she felt "lighter" and her depression lifted for the next few days. We will return to Jean later in this chapter and see how this issue continued to unfold for her over the next few sessions.

IDENTIFY AND PUNCTUATE THE PREDOMINANT AFFECT

Clients often feel confused, trapped, or defeated by their emotions because they seem irrational or inappropriate to the current situation. Clients often think that their feelings seem to occur for no reason or are stronger or different than the situation calls for. This inability to understand their own emotional reactions is the source of tremendous insecurity and distress. One of the most important ways to help clients achieve a greater sense of adequacy and mastery in their lives is to help them make sense of their emotional reactions. Therapists can do this by working with the client's *predominant affect*.

Clients usually enter therapy in response to one of two situations. First, a current life crisis echoes or recaptures an earlier emotional conflict that originally occurred years ago. That is, the current stressor taps in to a preexisting vulnerability or *old wound*. Second, clients may enter therapy in response to feeling overwhelmed by *too many stressors* that have occurred in a short period of time. These stressors have overwhelmed the client's usual coping strategies and defense mechanisms. We will see below that the client's experience often revolves around a central affect and that therapists need to identify and punctuate this predominant feeling.

An Old Wound

The first reason many clients enter therapy is because of an old wound. This occurs, for example, when clients experience a painful loss such as through divorce or death. It is especially difficult for clients to cope with this current loss when it arouses unresolved feelings from other significant losses in their past. For example, clients may have a predominant feeling about the current loss such as emptiness, betrayal, abandonment terror, or intolerable sadness. The current feeling becomes both understandable and manageable when it can be linked to similar feelings that have been aroused by other losses in their lives. Thus the therapist needs to identify the central affect that the current crisis has aroused and link it to the original "wound." This is one way to help clients make sense of their seemingly irrational feelings and, thereby, gain greater mastery of them.

Multiple Stressors

Second, clients often enter therapy when they have suffered too many stressful events in a short period of time. Most individuals have adaptive coping mechanisms to help them manage a single crisis event unless the current stressor taps into a preexisting vulnerability. If a second or third stressful event closely follows the first, however, it becomes much harder for individuals to cope. The client's usual coping strategies fail and the cumulative stressors precipitate symptoms and maladaptive, defensive maneuvers.

When multiple stressors have occurred, clients often enter therapy describing themselves as overwhelmed, defeated, or broken. The stressful events that have precipitated the client's crisis and request for help often reflect a central theme and therapists are more effective if they can identify and articulate this unifying theme. For example, clients often repeat a *compacted phrase* that encapsulates their emotional responses to the stressful events that have occurred:

I want everyone to go away and leave me alone.

It's too much for me; I just can't stand it.

I don't care anymore; there's no point in trying.

As noted in Chapter 2, therapists must look for recurrent affective themes and try to unlock the emotional reactions that have become encapsulated in these compacted sentences. Underlying each repetitive, compacted sentence are one or two central feelings that capture the impact these stressors have had on the client. Like spokes around the hub of a wheel, the various problems and stresses that occurred are often connected by one or two central feelings. For example, in response to losing too many people or things, the client may have an overriding feeling of being despondent, empty and alone, powerless and hopeless, or afraid of any further losses, changes, or new commitments. When therapists articulate the underlying feeling that links the impact of several different crisis events, clients feel understood and invest further in the therapeutic relationship.

A Characterological Feeling

In the beginning of this chapter, therapists were encouraged to respond to the client's current affect. In addition to tracking the client's moment-to-moment affect, therapists can also listen for a recurrent feeling that pervades the client's life, a *characterological affect*.

Once therapy is underway and the therapist has learned more about the client, the therapist can often identify a predominant feeling that captures the client's current conflict and also characterizes his life. That is, if the therapist is empathic and sees things from the client's point of view, the therapist can usually find a central feeling that reflects the fabric of the client's life. Clients often have two or three core feelings that are familiar and continuous throughout their lives. When the therapist can identify these central feelings that capture the client's characterological conflict, the client often responds: "Yes, that's how it has always been for me," "That's what it's like to be me," or "That's who I really am." Clients experience these central feelings as their fate because they have "always been there and it seems like they always will be." One of the most significant interventions therapists can make is to accurately reflect these generic feelings to the client.

For example, after listening to the client for several sessions the therapist may respond: It seems as if you have always felt:

. . . *burdened* by all the demands you feel you have to meet.

. . . *afraid* that people are going to "find you out" and point up your true inadequacies.

. . . *resentful* that no matter how much you do, it's never enough.

. . . *wary* that others are trying to put you down or take advantage of you.

The therapist must be prepared to respond to all of the varying emotions that clients experience in the course of therapy. However, therapists will be most effective when they can identify the repetitive feelings that have recurred throughout the client's life and are seen by the client as central to his sense of self.

THE COMPLEXITY OF CLIENTS' FEELINGS

It is difficult and sometimes discouraging to work with clients' conflicted emotions. Some clients are adamant in wanting to avoid their emotions and others talk endlessly about the same feelings without any change resulting. One reason for these problems is that therapists have only responded to the client's single, presenting affect. To be effective, therapists must work with the three-tiered constellation of feelings that make up the client's emotional conflict.

If the therapist acknowledges the client's current affect and invites him to explore it further, a sequence of interrelated feelings, a constellation of emotional reactions that are central to the client's conflict, will often occur together as a predictable, patterned sequence. Although different variations occur for each client, a triad of interrelated feelings that repeat throughout the client's daily life can often be identified. The process of change involves mastering each of the feelings in this affective constellation. This section examines the two affective constellations that most commonly occur. We will see that therapists help clients change by responding to the entire sequence of feelings that occur, rather than just responding to the first feeling in the sequence—the client's primary, presenting affect.

Anger-Sadness-Shame

The first affective constellation we will examine consists of anger, sadness, and shame. The predominant feeling-state for many clients is anger. These clients often experience and readily express angry feelings including irritation, impatience, criticism, and cynicism. However, the client's anger is often a *reactive* feeling to an original or primary feeling of sadness, hurt, or vulnerability. That is, the anger is a secondary feeling that occurs in response to an original experience of sadness, hurt, or pain.

The therapist must acknowledge the client's anger, locate its source and target, and help the client find an appropriate way to express it. Therapists often stop at this point, however. If so, clients will remain obsessively "stuck" in their angry, blaming, or critical feeling-state and no change will result. Why does this occur?

Clients remain fixed in their angry stance because the anger response is a *reactive feeling to an original hurt that has not been expressed and to which no response has been given.* The therapist must help the client bring out the original emotional response of sadness or hurt that led to the reactive feeling of anger. Said again, the anger response is a secondary feeling that occurs in response to the primary feeling *that is more threatening or painful for the client to experience.*

One way to reach the original affect is to wait for clients to spontaneously ventilate their anger and, immediately afterwards, invite them to examine what they are feeling now. Following expression of the reactive feeling, there is often an *open window* to the original feeling of hurt or sadness. For example, the therapist might respond, "What are you feeling right now, after you have just expressed how angry you are?" The original feeling of sadness, hurt, vulnerability, or helplessness will often surface at this moment. The therapist can then acknowledge this feeling as well, which will often dislodge the client from the familiar reactive feeling of anger.

There is another way to approach the primary feeling underlying the predominant reactive feeling. If the client's original feeling is not accessible in the moment after expressing his anger, the therapist can inquire directly about the original experience that led to the client's anger. For example, "Something must have hurt you very much for you to remain so angry about that. Tell me how you felt when that happened." If the client again begins to express his anger, indignation, or sense of injustice about what occurred, focus the client back upon his own original experience: "Yes, I know how unfair that seemed to you, but how did it feel to you when . . . ?" This type of query also helps to elicit the original hurt that underlies the reactive response. As the client's original feeling of sadness or hurt is expressed and the therapist responds, the client *comes in contact with the internal aspect of his conflict*. It is this internal aspect of the conflict that has kept the client from being able to change.

Next, we will restate this reactive-primary sequence and take it one step further by bringing in the third feeling in the sequence. When this type of client experiences anger, sadness often follows. Although the anger is easily experienced, the client has learned that it is unsafe to experience and/or share the original sadness-hurt-vulnerability. To avoid the original painful feeling, the client defensively returns to the reactive feeling of anger in an obsessive or repetitive manner that could cause others to describe him as being "an angry person."

The therapist's task is to help these clients experience the sadness-hurt-vulnerability underneath their repetitive anger. But, as soon as the original hurt is activated, the client will defend against this feeling and reflexively return to the safer expression of anger. Thus the therapist must explore the client's resistance to the original painful affect. Although clients resist the original feeling for different reasons, it is often because *the original affect of pain or sadness arouses a third, aversive feeling of shame, anxiety, or guilt.*

For example, if the therapist inquires about the client's resistance to the original hurt or pain, clients will often say something like: "If I let the pain be there, it's admitting that she really did hurt me," "They won," or "I really am weak." As soon as clients who express these types of concerns experience the hurt that underlies their anger, they usually have painful feelings of shame or humiliation. To repeat, if the therapist draws out the original pain that underlies the anger, a third feeling of shame or humiliation that is associated with being hurt is aroused as well. The client will defend against both the original sadness and the shame associated with it by reflexively returning to the "stronger" anger.

Instead of shame, other clients will experience anxiety or guilt in response to feeling the original hurt. For example, some clients will say that if they let themselves feel sad/hurt/vulnerable, then "no one will be there," "others will go away," or "I will be empty and alone." These clients feel painful separation anxieties upon experiencing their hurt or pain and avoid this anxiety by reflexively returning to their anger. Still other clients will say that if they let their sadness be real, it is admitting that they really do have a need—which makes them feel selfish, bad, or unworthy. For these clients, a third accompanying feeling of guilt emerges as part of their regularly occurring affective constellation.

For many clients, a triad of feelings exists such as frequent anger, which defends against unexpressed sadness, which, in turn, is associated with shame, guilt, or anxiety. *Significant and enduring change results when clients can experience, express, and contain each feeling in the triad.* More specifically, clients resolve their internal conflicts when they can (1) let themselves experience the full intensity of each feeling, (2) express the feeling and share it with the therapist so that they are no longer alone with it or hiding it, and (3) contain, hold, or tolerate the difficult feeling rather than having to move away from it.

When clients can integrate their conflicted emotions in this way they have internally mastered their conflict. They no longer need the same maladaptive response patterns they have employed in the past. Clients are then prepared to adopt new, more adaptive responses that they could not incorporate previously. Although other steps are important, this is a pivotal experience in the process of change.

Sadness-Anger-Guilt

The other commonly occurring affective constellation consists of sadness, anger, and guilt. This time a case study will be used for illustration.

Whereas some clients lead with their anger and defend against their hurt, another type characteristically leads with their sadness and avoids their anger. This type of client presents with an undifferentiated feeling-state of sadness-helplessness-vulnerability-depression. These clients do not experience or express anger, avoid interpersonal conflict, and tend to respond to other's needs at the expense of their own. To illustrate this contrasting affective constellation, we return to Jean—the client in the previous case study.

Earlier we examined a sample dialogue in which the therapist invited Jean to share her sense of hopelessness: "Show me, in your eyes, how sad you really are." For the first time, the client was able to let someone respond to her pain and be emotionally connected to her *while she was experiencing it*.

Later in that session, the therapist explored why it had always been so difficult for Jean to share her pain with others. Jean responded that her painful feelings, memories, and needs were all sickeningly real if some-one else saw them. Jean had experienced these sad-empty-hopeless feel-ings all of her life, but they had always been ignored or invalidated in her family of origin. Jean had internalized her family's taboo against un-happy and angry feelings. As a result, she had denied to herself the reality of the deprivation and disparagement that she had suffered throughout her childhood. And, as so often occurs, as an adult Jean went on to reenact her childhood conflict through the abusive men with whom she chose to become involved.

When Jean returned to therapy the following week she had made a significant change. For the past several months she had been involved with another irresponsible, exploitative man. This week, when the boy-friend again borrowed her car and arrived two hours late to pick her up from work, she expressed her anger for the first time. Jean also told him that she deserved to be treated with more respect and that she had the right to have her own needs considered as well. Jean had remained in this relationship for several months because she was "afraid to be alone." At this point, though, she decided that this relationship was destructive to her and ended it.

Once the therapist was able to touch Jean's sadness and hurt, her anger was activated and subsequently expressed in an appropriate man-ner. Jean had remained locked in her sad and helpless victim role, in part, because the direct expression of anger and the assertive expression of her own needs were both unacceptable. As often occurs, *Jean began to claim her own personal power once her feelings were expressed and she received validating responses to them*. We must look more carefully, however, at the sequence of feelings that unfolded for Jean.

Although Jean began the next therapy session by sharing her good news about ending the destructive relationship, she had difficulty staying with this feeling of strength. Jean gradually retreated from her indigna-tion at how badly this man had treated her, began to feel concerned about how she "may have hurt him," and wondered if she had been selfish to end the relationship. The therapist anticipated that Jean would feel guilty upon experiencing her anger or responding to her own needs, however, and helped her explore her guilt.

Just as before in the anger-sadness-shame sequence, Jean defensively avoided her anger because it aroused a third aversive feeling. In Jean's affective constellation, a third affect of guilt served to reflexively return her to her characteristic affect of sadness/helplessness. As the therapist helped Jean integrate all three of these interrelated feelings, she was able to relinquish her victim stance for longer periods.

With the therapist providing a supportive, holding environment, Jean could let the deprivation that she originally experienced in her family become real to her. As this occurred, Jean stopped defending against these painful memories in her past by reenacting them in her current relationships. Jean could also accept her anger at the hurtful ways she had been treated and stopped feeling guilty when she asserted her own needs. Coming to terms with each component of this affective constellation eventually left Jean feeling stronger and more in control of her life than she had ever felt. As before, significant life changes followed from Jean's internal resolution of her conflicted emotions. In this way, therapists help clients resolve their conflicts by responding to each feeling in their affective constellation.

PERSONAL FACTORS THAT PREVENT THERAPISTS FROM RESPONDING TO CLIENTS' EMOTIONS

Finally, we must turn our attention away from the client and examine personal characteristics of the therapist that prevent therapists from responding to their clients' emotions. This is an especially important dimension of therapy, yet it often receives too little attention. Just as it is easier for clients to externalize and focus on others rather than themselves, it is also easier for therapists to focus on the client than it is to look within at the therapist's own issues and dynamics. If therapists are not prepared to work with their own emotional reactions to the feelings that clients present, however, they will tend to avoid or intellectually explain their clients' feelings. Thus the purpose of this section is to help therapists anticipate and manage their own reactions to the evocative material that clients present.

In the previous sections we have seen how therapists can elicit the client's affect and anticipate a sequence of interrelated feelings. In addition, an essential component of helping clients resolve their conflicted feelings is for them to receive a caring and accepting response from the therapist. No enduring change occurs without respect and compassion for the emotional conflicts with which clients are struggling. This is fundamental to helping clients change but, in actual practice, it is often difficult for therapists to respond to all of their clients' feelings. Why?

Every therapist brings her own personal conflicts, developmental history, and current life stressors to the consulting room. This section will show how these factors in the therapist's own life can keep the therapist from working effectively with the client's emotions.

The Therapist's Need to Be Liked

The first issue we will examine is the therapist's need to be liked. Most students who are drawn to clinical practice are genuinely kind people—sincerely concerned about others and ready to give of themselves. They are often nurturing, caring people who can readily respond to other's hurt and pain. At the same time, however, many therapists also have strong needs to be liked by others and may have difficulty accepting the anger, bitterness, and distrust that some clients will feel toward them. Or, some therapists have strong needs to nurture others who are dependent upon them. These therapists enter clinical practice, in part, in order to fulfill these needs and they may have difficulty supporting the client's healthy individuation at times. The following discussion encourages all therapists to assess their own motivations for becoming clinicians and to examine what needs of their own are being fulfilled by doing therapy. The issue is not whether therapists will have their own needs and countertransference propensities, but how they will deal with them. All therapists have certain countertransference reactions, and this self-examination is one way to manage them effectively.

Beginning therapists are often taken aback when their well-intended attempts to approach the client's affect meet with anger, rejection, or ridicule. Beginning therapists often absorb the client's rebuff, comply with the defensive side of the client's feelings, and stop approaching the client's conflicted emotions. This is most likely to occur when the therapist's own needs to nurture or to be liked have been frustrated. To be effective, however, the therapist must continue to work with the client's resistance and approach the conflicted feelings.

To do this, the therapist can adopt the same strategies for working with the client's resistance that were presented in Chapter 3. That is, the therapist should not push clients to express a feeling they are reluctant to share, but instead should explore what is the threat or danger for them if they do so (e.g., "What are you afraid will happen if you let yourself feel_____"). The therapist must forgo winning the client's approval and not be a "nice" person who does not approach difficult feelings or awkward interpersonal situations. Instead, if the therapist goes ahead and addresses the client's resistance, the client will often become able to share the feelings that have been held away.

In sum, the feelings that therapists are most likely to have difficulty working with are clients' angry and critical feelings toward them. However, these emotional reactions will occur at times if the therapist approaches each of the feelings in the client's affective constellation. Therapy is most likely to falter at the point at which the therapist cannot respond to a particular feeling that the client is struggling with. Because it is so important for therapists to be able to respond to all of the client's feelings, we will continue to address this in the examples that follow.

The Therapist Assumes Responsibility for the Client's Feelings

Another factor that keeps therapists from responding to their clients' feelings concerns the issue of responsibility. Too often, therapists erroneously believe that if they respond to a client's feeling it means that they are responsible for *causing* the feeling or for *taking the client's pain away*. Three related problems occur when therapists assume such inappropriate responsibility for clients' feelings.

The first problem with assuming such responsibility is that therapists tend to avoid their clients' feelings because they do not want to hurt them or make them feel bad. These therapists mistakenly believe that responding to a painful feeling in the client is the same as causing that feeling to exist in the client. Therapists must keep in mind that they did not cause the client to have this feeling originally—it was present before the client met the therapist. The therapist has simply responded to the feeling that the client was experiencing. The unrealistic belief that the therapist is to blame for causing the client's feeling leads the therapist to feel *guilty*. This guilt over "making the client hurt" will immobilize therapists and prevent them from responding effectively.

A second problem occurs when therapists confuse their legitimate responsibility to respond to the client's feelings with an inappropriate belief that they are responsible for causing the client's original feeling. If the therapist inappropriately accepts responsibility for causing the client's feeling, it follows that the therapist must also be afraid of the client's angry retaliation for having to reexperience the painful affect. Clients will hurt when painful feelings are aroused and anger often accompanies painful feelings. Thus, if the therapist accepts responsibility for causing the client's original feeling, both the therapist's guilt and fear of the client's retaliation may keep the therapist from approaching the client's conflicted emotions. The therapist can respond to clients' anger without accepting responsibility or blame for causing this pain, however.

A third problem results when therapists labor under the impossible burden of having to fix the hurt they have caused the client to feel. That is, when therapists take responsibility for causing the client's feeling, they also assume responsibility for making the client feel better. This is always a myth, however, as therapists can never take away clients' hurt or fix their pain.

If therapists should not shoulder this inappropriate responsibility, what should they do for their clients? The therapist's appropriate response to the client's feelings is threefold. First, the therapist must help clients identify, experience, and express more fully whatever feelings they are having. Second, the therapist must also be empathic or emotionally available to clients so that they can share their feelings with a concerned other rather than have to experience them alone as they often have in the past. Third, the therapist needs to confirm the validity of the client's feelings. The therapist does this by helping clients understand their feelings and make sense of why they are experiencing this particular feeling now. If the therapist accepts this challenge, but does not assume responsibility for causing or changing the client's feeling, the therapist will be able to respond effectively to whatever feelings the client presents.

Assuming responsibility for clients' feelings is one reason therapists may adopt the ineffective approaches of telling clients what to do, reassuring them, or explaining and interpreting their emotions before they can experience them. Even if the therapist is not prone to assuming too much responsibility for the client's feelings, however, most therapists will struggle with this issue when the client's affect becomes very intense.

For example, a therapist was treating a young boy who was dying of leukemia. The therapist would sit with the boy in the hospital and talk with him about his impending death: "What is the scariest thing about dying; what are you most afraid of?" The therapist approached the child's feelings in this direct way, and the boy responded by screaming, "I don't want to die, I don't want to die! I'm afraid to die, I want to live!" Sitting there feeling helpless, seeing the terror in this young child's eyes, the therapist felt like a sadistic, perverse monster to be making this child feel such anguish.

But the child went on to say, "I don't want to be alone, I'll be all alone if I die!" Inviting the child's feeling revealed his concern that he would be "all alone." As the therapist heard the separation anxieties and abandonment fears that were gripping this young boy, the therapist understood his primary concern and was able to talk with him in a helpful way. More important, the therapist was able to help his mother understand his central fear and reassure him that her love for him would last forever. Talking with the mother and son together about his fear of being left alone also allowed them to be closer during his illness. This closeness greatly alleviated the child's abandonment terror and subsequent fear of dying.

Working with such intense emotions as these will often lead therapists to feel that they are responsible for causing the client's pain. When this occurs, therapists tend to avoid these profound feelings. To keep this from occurring, therapists must consult with a supervisor or colleague to help them manage their own exaggerated feelings of responsibility that are aroused by the client. If not, these countertransference reactions will prevent therapists from responding effectively to the client. In the example above, the therapist could not have stayed with the intensity of the boy's fear or the mother's loss without a colleague to help manage the therapist's own emotional reactions.

Family Rules

Another reason why therapists may not be able to respond to certain feelings that clients present is because of *family rules* about emotional expression that were learned in the therapist's family of origin. Every family has unspoken rules that govern how emotions are dealt with. That is, emotional expression in families is governed by a rule-bound *homeostatic system* that prescribes what feelings can be expressed and which are unacceptable. The rule-bound system also prescribes when, how, and to whom certain feelings can be expressed. Further, the intensity or degree of emotional expression that is allowed is also gauged by the family homeostatic mechanism. For example, if too much conflict, independence, or closeness is expressed in the family, a corrective homeostatic mechanism automatically occurs to bring the level of emotional expression back within acceptable limits. The following example illustrates how homeostatic mechanisms operate to keep family emotional expression within prescribed limits.

Suppose that in the Smith family a moderate degree of hostility and conflict can exist between the older sister and the younger brother. A lesser degree of frustration and irritation can mutually be expressed between the father and both children. However, anger is rarely expressed between any family member and mother, and never between the father and the mother. What is the the homeostatic mechanism that serves to keep this system operating within these boundaries? Whenever a child begins to express angry feelings toward mother, or have direct conflict with her, mother stops the child's emotional expression by looking sad and hurt. If the child's anger continues, father then intervenes and says something like, "Don't talk to your mother that way," or mother figuratively brings father in as a regulatory influence by saying, "I'm going to tell your father about this when he comes home."

In contrast, when anger, conflict, or differences of opinion begin to escalate between mother and father, the children serve as homeostatic regulators and respond in predictable, patterned ways to terminate the parental conflict. For example, the oldest child, eight-year-old Mary, serves as a go-between in the parental relationship. She tries to make peace between her parents by carrying messages back and forth between them. This mechanism usually succeeds in terminating parental conflict except in periods of exceptional family stress. If the parental conflict continues, the younger son may then provide a diversion to the parental conflict by acting out in some predictable way, such as by breaking something or having an accident. By becoming a problem that mother and father must now jointly address, their rule-breaking level of conflict is terminated and the family's emotional equilibrium returns to within acceptable levels.

This example can be linked to the case study of Jean that we have been following throughout this chapter. Imagine that we have just turned the clock ahead 20 years. The oldest child in the Smith family, Mary, who was serving as the mediator to assuage parental conflict, is now a graduate student in clinical psychology. Mary is an intern at a community mental health agency and has been seeing Jean in therapy for the past four months. The family rules that Mary has learned in her family of origin will influence her ability to respond to Jean's emotions, just as the family rules that all therapists have learned in their families will influence how they respond to their clients.

Earlier, we observed the critical incident in which Jean was able to let Mary respond to her pain and share her sadness for the first time. Things had gotten somewhat better for Jean since then but her problems still continued. Jean was able to end the abusive relationship with her boyfriend and felt better for awhile, but she soon became depressed again and fell back into a victim role. Jean was still unable to say no to the demands of others or to follow through and act on her own wishes and interests. Frustrated by her continued depression, Jean angrily criticized Mary for the first time: "I keep coming here every week, but I'm not getting better. You make me have these awful feelings and it doesn't help like you said it would. I don't think you know what you're doing or care how I feel!"

Mary was stunned by Jean's angry outburst even though it was short-lived and Jean quickly apologized. Mary was especially surprised by this criticism because she thought they had been much closer in recent weeks. Throughout the rest of the session, Mary backed away from Jean's anger by offering Jean reassurances. Mary tried to convince Jean that she really did care for her, and that she would get better if she would continue to come to therapy and work with the difficult feelings they had been sharing. Mary felt terrible that Jean had gotten angry at her and anxiously sought help from her supervisor as soon as the session was over.

Mary's supervisor was responsive to her distress over Jean's anger and was able to help Mary understand what went on for her during the session. In reviewing a videotape recording of the session, the supervisor helped Mary recognize how she had tried to assuage Jean's anger with reassurances, rather than allowing Jean to feel angry with her or disappointed about her lack of progress. The supervisor explored with Mary why she tried to assuage Jean's anger, rather than encouraging Jean to express her concerns fully and responding to her frustration.

With her supervisor's help, Mary realized that she had been unable to tolerate Jean's anger. She had indeed tried to assuage it, just as she had always done before with her mother. Mary's old role was to "take care of" the conflict rather than allow others to express their dissatisfaction and listen to their concerns. In addition to clarifying Mary's old response pattern, the supervisor also helped Mary to generate working hypotheses about what this critical response may have meant for Jean. The supervisor noted that Jean's expression of anger followed sharing her hurt, and hypothesized that the anger may be part of her affective constellation, which needs to be addressed. That is, Jean needed the experience of being able to express her anger at someone who would take her concerns seriously and would not abandon her. In part, Jean may have been testing to see if she could be critical of Mary and still remain in relationship with her.

Without this helpful consultation, Mary and Jean probably would have become stuck in their relationship and therapy would not have progressed further. Jean could not move forward with her conflicts as long as Mary could not respond to the anger component of her affective constellation. In their next session, however, Mary was able to recover and asked Jean to discuss her frustration and anger. Although Mary still felt an anxious compulsion to reassure Jean and move on, Mary was able to contain her own discomfort and discuss Jean's concerns with her.

Clients will not be able to resolve long-standing conflicts unless the therapist can respond to each component of their conflicted affective constellation. As we noted before, therapy usually stops progressing at the point at which the therapist cannot respond to a particular feeling that the client is experiencing. Family rules about emotional expression are one important factor that influences how therapists respond to their clients' emotions. With this in mind, all therapists should examine the rules that governed how emotions were dealt with in their own families, and how they are bringing their own familial roles and rules for emotional expression to their clinical work. For many therapists, their own therapy will be the best way to change ineffective family rules that they are still enacting with their clients.

Situational Conflicts in the Therapist's Life

Another factor that may keep therapists from responding effectively to their clients' emotions is situational stresses in therapists' own lives. For example, when therapists are struggling with personal problems in their own lives that are similar to those their clients are experiencing, therapists may have difficulty approaching their clients' affect. Or, more likely, therapists will not be able to allow clients to experience fully the feelings they are struggling with. That is, if therapists are having difficulty coming to terms with the feelings aroused by a problem in their own lives, they may not be able to give the client permission to experience or express similar feelings. Here again, these countertransference reactions will occur for every therapist. The issue is not whether they occur but how they are dealt with.

Therapists' own reactions to their clients are the biggest obstacles to responding effectively to their clients' emotions. Therapy is a very human interchange. Although the personal availability of the therapist is the greatest asset in helping clients change, it will also be an obstacle at times. More specifically, the therapist's own countertransference issues are operating when the therapist fails to accurately identify the feelings that the client is presenting, avoids rather than approaches the client's feelings, or becomes personally invested in changing how the client responds or feels about an issue.

Countertransference reactions occur for every therapist. When they do, therapists must consult with a colleague or supervisor to better understand and manage their own reactions. When therapists find that they are repeatedly having difficulty with the same type of affect or supervision does not free them up to respond to the client's feelings, therapists should seek therapy for themselves. Because change is predicated on the relationship that the therapist provides the client, therapists must make an ongoing, lifelong commitment to working with their own dynamics. Without this willingness to work on their own personal reactions to clients, the help therapists can provide will be limited. Furthermore, those therapists who are unwilling to work on persistent countertransference reactions are those most at risk to be a danger to their clients. It is a privilege to be able to help people change, and therapists honor that privilege by acknowledging their own limitations and personal involvement in the therapeutic process.

CLOSING

As seen in Chapter 4, clients' conflicted emotions will not emerge in therapy unless the therapist focuses clients inward. An externalizing focus will lead therapists into a problem-solving and advice-giving mode that precludes the client's affective exploration. As the client talks about the problem out there with others, the therapist's complementary role is to give advice, reassure, or disclose what the therapist has done himself to solve similar problems. Although these responses can be helpful at times, little change will occur if they characterize the ongoing course of therapy.

But if the therapist does not tell the client what to do, what does the therapist really have to offer the client? The most important way to facilitate change is to help clients master their conflicted emotions by reexperiencing and integrating feelings that have been too painful to tolerate in the past. All clients have experienced tragedies in their lives that will be entwined with the symptoms and problems they present. The therapist helps clients resolve their presenting problems by sharing the full intensity of whatever feelings they are experiencing. The most important aspect of therapy is responding to clients in these deeply personal ways. Yet therapists must also be aware that their biggest obstacle to providing clients with a relationship that can produce change will be their own discomfort with certain client feelings. Thus therapists must make a lifelong commitment to working with their own dynamics and examining how their own personhood influences their clinical practice.

Part III will next show how therapists can use the client's conflicted emotions to help conceptualize the client's dynamics. Then, in Part IV, this conceptual formulation will be applied to helping clients resolve their conflicts and change.

SUGGESTIONS FOR FURTHER READING

1. One way for therapists to increase their effectiveness with clients is to explore their motivations for becoming therapists and to examine how their own dynamics are expressed in their clinical work. It is just as important to focus on the personhood of the therapist as it to focus on client dynamics and intervention strategies. Two sources that can help therapists explore these issues are: Chapter 21 of J. Bugental's *The Search for Authenticity* (New York: Holt, Rinehart & Winston, 1965) and A. Guggenbuhl-Craig, *Power in the Helping Professions*, (New York: Springer Publications, 1971). See especially the concept of the "wounded healer."

2. At times, techniques can be useful to elicit and clarify the client's affect. A book that describes Gestalt techniques for intensifying client affect is W. Passons, *Gestalt Approaches in Counseling* (New York: Holt, Rinehart & Winston, 1975).

Conceptualizing Client Dynamics

6

Familial and Historical Factors

CONCEPTUAL OVERVIEW

The previous chapters have focused on the interaction that occurs between the therapist and the client. The next three chapters step back from this intensive tracking of the therapeutic process and help therapists conceptualize their clients' dynamics. In order to be effective, therapists must be able to formulate a clear conceptualization of the client's personalty and problems. The fact that beginning therapists have had little training or experience, however, makes it difficult for them to conceptualize their clients' dynamics or to apply this conceptualization to treatment. Although no single book, supervisor, or theory is sufficient to teach therapists how to recognize the pattern that exists in their clients' dynamics, helpful guidelines are available.

How can therapists understand what their clients' problems mean and use this conceptual understanding to guide their treatment plans? One way to understand problematic development is to examine what occurs for offspring in families that function well. Once the basic familial processes that produce healthy offspring are identified, it is easier to understand how normal development can go awry and lead to the enduring personality conflicts that clients present. Thus, this chapter will help therapists recognize the familial antecedents of clients' problems. Family systems concepts that clarify the genesis of many characterological problems will be introduced in order to aid therapists in conceptualizing their clients' dynamics. The discussion in this chapter lays the foundation for the comprehensive conceptualization model presented in the next chapter.

101

CHAPTER ORGANIZATION

This chapter examines three fundamental dimensions of family life. The first part discusses the structure of family relations and the nature of the parental coalition. The second part examines the separateness-relatedness dialectic that was briefly introduced in Chapter 1. The third part explores childrearing practices. Problems in each of these areas lead to developmental conflicts that are central to the symptoms that clients present. Understanding how these familial factors shape personality development will enable therapists to respond more effectively to their clients.

STRUCTURAL FAMILY RELATIONS

Structural family relations are the basis for family organization and define how the family operates as a social system (Minuchin, 1974). This term refers to the relatively enduring patterns of alliances, coalitions, loyalties, and alignments that exist in the family. Structural family relations shape family communication patterns and the roles that family members adopt. Among the different structural family relationships that exist, the parental coalition is the pivotal axis of family life and shapes much of how the family functions (Teyber, 1981). In particular, the nature of the parental coalition primarily determines how well children adjust.

The Parental Coalition

In healthy families, the marital relationship is the primary two-person relationship in the family. That is, both spouses have a primary loyalty commitment to each other, and the marital coalition cannot be divided by grandparents, children, friends, employers, or others. Parents will still have differences and conflicts between themselves—and they will be committed to others as well—but the marital relationship is a stable alliance that cannot be disrupted by others. In contrast, families in which the primary emotional bond or involvement is not between mother and father often produce offspring with enduring personality conflicts. In these problematic families the primary alliance is between a grandparent and parent, a parent and a child, or within some other dyad.

How does a primary parental coalition develop? Both parents must have been able to psychologically separate from their families of origin, have achieved an autonomous identity in early adulthood, and have been able to make a primary loyalty commitment to a peer relationship.

Said differently, as young adults, these offspring have been able to transfer their primary loyalty commitment from their parents in the previous generation to a spouse in the same generation. The question here becomes who comes first? Do you choose the parent or the spouse? ✳

If young adult offspring have not been able to shift their primary loyalty commitment from their family of origin to their spouse, a primary marital coalition will not develop. The primary loyalty of one or both spouses will remain with their parent. When this occurs, the primary dyadic relationship in the family is a cross-generational alliance between a parent and the adult offspring, rather than a primary marital coalition between the husband and the wife. This cross-generational alliance (e.g., maternal grandmother-mother) usually repeats in the next generation with the birth of children and results in a primary parent-child coalition as well (e.g., mother-child). Before going on to see why these cross-generational alliances are so problematic for offspring, we must better understand the important psychological processes that are being enacted in forming a primary parental coalition. We will do this by examining the wedding ceremony as a cultural rite of passage.

The wedding ceremony is a familiar ritual for illustrating these concepts about shifting loyalty bonds from the family of origin to the spouse and forming a primary marital coalition. A central purpose of the wedding ceremony is to publicly mark a transition in loyalty bonds from the parents and family of origin to the new spouse. How does this occur? Once family, friends, and clergy are all assembled for the ceremony, the father walks the bride down the center aisle to the front of the church. In front of all, the father symbolically gives the bride away by placing her hand in the hand of the waiting groom. The father then leaves the couple by stepping back from the front of the church and sitting down beside his own wife. The bride and groom, who have now been separated from the parental generation, turn away and step forward to be married. In this ceremony, the bride and groom are shifting their primary loyalty commitments and publicly defining themselves to family and friends as an enduring marital couple.

This shifting of primary loyalties from the previous generation to the new spouse is a major developmental task. Although this transition is usually difficult for most families, it becomes especially conflict-laden in families that have not had a primary marital coalition. The question of who comes first, parent or spouse, may be painfully enacted in conflicts that surround planning for the wedding day. Offspring embroiled in cross-generational alliances often find that their wedding day, and the preparations for it, are a wrenching battle between conducting the ceremony the way the couple being married want it done and doing it the parent's way. The underlying conflict is over shifting loyalties from the previous generation to the spouse, but it is played out in arguments over who will be invited to the wedding, where it will be held, how it will be conducted, who is financially responsible, and so on. In contrast, young adults who enjoy their wedding day have been able to switch their primary loyalty from parents to each other. These couples are not being pulled apart by competing loyalty ties that induce guilt. With this background in mind, we now turn to how the parental coalition influences child development and examine why primary marital coalitions are better than cross-generational alliances.

How the Parental Coalition Influences Child Adjustment

Why is the nature of the parental coalition so crucial for family functioning and child adjustment? This section examines four reasons why children are better adjusted if the primary coalition in the family is between mother and father rather than between any other dyad.

First, when mother and father have a stable alliance, children cannot come between their parents and play one parent off against the other. For example, if a primary coalition exists between mother and eight-year-old daughter, father will have trouble setting and enforcing limits with his daughter. If father tries to put his daughter to bed at 8:00, or have her pick up her room, she can often defy these attempts at discipline by appealing to her mother. The daughter learns that she does not have to do what dad says because mom is likely to take her side against dad. When children can play one parent off against the other in this way, children learn that rules do not apply to them. That is, these children learn that they do not have to conform to adult rules in general, and they will often disobey teachers and try to manipulate other authority figures in their lives. These problems with limits and authority will carry over into adulthood and are especially likely to lead to problems in the work sphere where adults must be able to conform to rules and cooperate with others. A tragic illustration of this principle is found in Woodward's (1984) biography of the late comedian, John Belushi.

A second type of problem develops for children when the primary coalition is between a parent and a child rather than between the mother and father. Cross-generational alliances frequently result in the *parentification* of children. That is, a role reversal occurs in which children take on the role of meeting their parent's emotional needs rather than the parent responding to the child's needs. When certain emotional needs of these parents are not met by their spouse, they inappropriately turn to one or more of their children to meet their own adult needs for affection and intimacy, for approval and reassurance, or for stability, direction, and control. These parents will often describe their parentified children as their best friend, lifeline, or confidant (Teyber, 1985). It is problematic for children when they become responsible for, or take care of, the emotional needs of their parent. The problem with this role reversal is that offspring must give to their parents rather than receive. The natural flow of nurturing from parent to child is reversed and children's age-appropriate dependency needs go unmet. These parentified children grow up to feel overly responsible for others, afraid of depending on others, and guilty about having their own needs met. As adults, parentified offspring often describe themselves as feeling empty or "having a hole inside of me" as a result of having given rather than having received throughout their childhoods. Parentified children initially enjoy having such a special and powerful role vis-à-vis their parent. As adults, however, they ultimately come to resent having been used by their parent and having been deprived of their own childhoods.

A third problem for many children caught in cross-generational alliances is emancipation conflicts. If the mother and father have a primary marital coalition, children are free to grow up and become successful young adults who can leave home. Why? Parents do not need the child to remain dependent on them in order to fulfill their own lives. In contrast, if the primary coalition is between parent and child, these offspring may feel guilty about forsaking their parent to the unfulfilling relationship with the other spouse. As a result, they associate anxiety and guilt with achievements and outside commitments. In this regard, guilt over emancipation frequently underlies academic failure in college, as well as many other symptoms and problems that students present in college counseling centers (Teyber, 1983). Thus, cross-generational alliances impose binding loyalty ties that make young adults feel guilty about leaving home, successfully pursuing their own career interests, and establishing satisfying love relationships in adulthood.

Fourth, children in families with a primary marital coalition are more likely to gain a realistic sense of their own power and control than are children raised in cross-generational alliances. When children form the primary emotional bond with a parent, they become too important to the parent and exert too much influence over the parent's well-being. As a result, these children gain an exaggerated sense of their own importance and a grandiose sense of their own ability to influence others. Children cannot gain a realistic sense of their own limits and capabilities when they are encouraged in the illusion that they can prop up a parent's sagging self-esteem, maintain their parent's emotional equilibrium, or make important decisions for the parent. It is highly reinforcing for children to feel so powerful vis-à-vis their parent and they will be extremely reluctant to give up their special role. However, the other side of their grandiosity is a parallel sense of inadequacy, arising because children are never capable of actually meeting such adult needs.

These are just four of the many ways in which children are better adjusted in families with a primary marital coalition than with cross-generational alliances. Therapists will see the consequences of these structural family relationships operating with many of their clients. As we will see, the nature of the parental coalition also influences two other basic dimensions of family life, the separateness-relatedness dialectic and childrearing practices.

THE SEPARATENESS-RELATEDNESS DIALECTIC

The second basic dimension of family life that informs therapists about the nature and source of client conficts is the *separateness-relatedness dialectic*. This term refers, in part, to the family's ability to respond to both the child's need for closeness and for autonomy. Recall the dialectic of separateness-relatedness that was introduced in Chapter 1. As children develop, each family faces the task of having to provide both intimacy and individuation—to be close and separate at the same time. Infants and very young children must be provided with a symbiotic union with a nurturing parent. Children progressively become more independent and, by adolescence, must be supported in their further individuation and emancipation from the family. In healthy families, there is an *experiential ranging* between the poles of symbiotic union and individuation (Farley, 1979). That is, parents in these families have the breadth and flexibility to range back and forth along this continuum of separateness-relatedness and meet children's needs both for closeness and for autonomy.

In contrast, less effective families are more restricted in their experiential ranging. That is, they do not have the flexibility and personal resources to function well at both ends of the continuum. These less effective parents cannot move back and forth along this continuum to meet the changing needs that children present at different developmental stages. As noted in Chapter 1, enmeshed families cannot support the child's developmental movement toward individuation whereas disengaged families cannot meet offspring's needs for closeness.

How does the separateness-relatedness continuum relate to the parental coalition? The following example shows how families without a primary marital coalition are more restricted in their experiential ranges.

Suppose that a young married couple has not separated psychologically from their families of origin. Such newlyweds are likely to have a high degree of conflict in their marriage that they are both unable to resolve. In many cases, the couple will attempt to deal with their relationship problems by having children. Without being aware of it, the parents will experience the children as extensions of themelves and project their own conflicts onto the children. That is, rather than address their own internal conflicts and marital problems, they attempt to control their conflicts by externalizing them onto their children.

To illustrate, if the mother's need for closeness cannot be met by the father, she may turn to the child to have her emotional needs met. This solution will work well in the short run but it establishes the basis for long-term family problems. Typically, the mother could not emancipate psychologically from her own parents and she is made anxious by individuation. As long as the child remains dependent on her, her need for closeness is met and her anxiety over individuation is managed. On the other hand, the father is made anxious by closeness. The primary mother-child coalition allows him to gain greater distance from the anxiety-arousing demands of closeness from both the spouse and the child. In this way, the child becomes both a wedge that holds the marriage together and, at the same time, ensures distance between the couple.

This type of solution eventually poses a dilemma for the child's continuing development, however. The child's innate push for growth will disrupt the neutralizing wedge in the marital relationship, and this will arouse each parent's conflict. Thus, these parents need to encourage nongrowth, dependency, or incompetence in the child in order to maintain the marital status quo. At the same time, however, parents will also express anger and frustration to the child about the child's refusal to grow up and act responsibly. This family's limited experiential ranging is most likely to come to a head during adolescence when offspring face the developmental hurdle of emancipating from the family of origin. The mixed messages the child has received about growing up and remaining dependent will often erupt in psychological symptoms and acting-out behavior at this time. Furthermore, these underlying conflicts have been internalized by the child and often continue to be expressed in symptoms and problems throughout adulthood as well.

This example is just one illustration of how the parental coalition and the family's experiential range shape the personality conflicts that clients present in therapy. Exploring these two dimensions will help therapists better understand their clients. Childrearing practices are a third dimension of family life that influence child adjustment, and we will see that they can be readily integrated with the previous two dimensions.

CHILDREARING PRACTICES

Three Styles of Parenting

The third dimension of family life that is relevant to understanding how personality conflicts develop is childrearing practices. Most families employ one of three parenting styles: *authoritarian, permissive,* or *authoritative.* This section examines these three styles of childrearing and shows how each is related to the problems that clients present in therapy. Part of this discussion draws on research by Baumrind on the effects of childrearing practices (1967, 1971).

Authoritarian parents are firm disciplinarians. Children are given unambiguous prescriptions for acceptable and unacceptable behavior. Parental rules are clearly explained and the consequences for violating them are consistently enforced. Authoritarian parents also hold high expectations for their children to behave in a responsible and mature manner. Children are expected to perform up to their abilities and to be competent and contributing family members.

Authoritarian parents do not give children reasons or explanations for the rules they set, however. Compromises or alternatives are not discussed with children. Children of authoritarian parents cannot ask why a rule is set—they must simply obey. Furthermore, although authoritarian parents discipline their children and expect much of them, they do not provide their children with much warmth or affection.

In contrast, permissive parents are lax disciplinarians. Children often do not know what behavior is expected of them and they do not know what consequences will occur if they violate parental norms. Most important, permissive parents do not consistently enforce the rules that they do set. As a result, children of permissive parents learn that they do not have to obey because parents will not follow through and enforce the rules they set anyway.

Thus, authoritarian parents exert a high degree of control over their children. However, these limits and rules are not coupled with warmth and affection, with parental explanations for why the rules have been set, or with opportunities for the children to discuss compromises and alternatives with their parents. In contrast, permissive parents are often expressive, loving, and communicative with their children, but their children are not disciplined nor are they expected to behave in a mature, responsible manner. Before looking at the problems that result from these two ineffective childrearing styles, let us contrast them with the more effective, but less well-known, authoritative style.

The authoritative childrearing style produces the most healthy, well adjusted children. Authoritative parents possess a wide range of parenting skills that allows them to combine firm discipline with nurturant child care. Although authoritative parents set and enforce firm limits, they also communicate with their children. Authoritative parents give reasons and explanations for the rules they set, and they will negotiate compromises and discuss alternatives with their children. While authoritative parents expect mature, responsible behavior from their children, they also provide a great deal of physical affection and spoken approval. In short, authoritative parents combine the most effective features of the other two parenting styles. They are nurturing parents who communicate with their children, but they are also firm disciplinarians who place high demands for maturity on children. Research has found that authoritative parents produce children who are independent, self-controlled, successful with peers, and generally have a positive, happy mood.

Therapists will find that most of their clients have been reared by authoritarian or permissive parents. The first section below examines how these childrearing practices are reflected in the conflicts that clients present in therapy. The second section relates childrearing practices to the other two dimensions of family life presented earlier—structural family relations and the separateness-relatedness dialectic.

Consequences of Childrearing Practices

In socialization, young children gradually give up their own immediate demands for gratification in order to maintain parental approval. It is the threat of parental punishment and withdrawal of parental love that leads young children to inhibit their own impulses and conform to parental standards. If all goes well, the child's conflict between the desire to gratify her own impulses and the fear of parental punishment will be successfully resolved. A successful resolution is one in which children learn to obey, but without sacrificing their own initiative and positive self-regard. That is, healthy children can become self-controlled and self-reliant without inhibiting their own initiative or losing their sense of being prized by their parents (Wenar, 1982).

For children of authoritarian parents, however, the trade-off between giving up their own wishes to maintain parental approval is too severe. Because authoritarian parents provide too little nurturance and affection, too much of the child's own initiative and positive self-regard is forsaken in order to secure parental approval. These children are obedient but they are also anxious and insecure—complying with parents out of fear.

This interpersonal conflict between the authoritarian parent and young child has been internalized by the time the child is school-aged. What was originally an interpersonal conflict becomes an internal or intrapsychic conflict. These well-behaved, insecure children become harsh, critical, and demanding toward themselves, just as their parents have been toward them. Many of these offspring will seek therapy as adults and they are likely to present with symptoms involving guilt, depression, unassertiveness, anxiety, and low self-esteem.

Offspring of permissive parents will also have adjustment problems but their symptoms are different. These offspring are more likely to develop acting-out or externalizing problems and they are less likely to seek therapy as adults. Why? Children of permissive parents learn that they can avoid the consequences of their own behavior by manipulating others. Rules and limits do not apply to them and wishes can be gratified without delay. Research has found these children to be dependent, immature, demanding, and unhappy. They have little self-control, low frustration tolerances, and do poorly with their peers. As adults, these offspring tend to be impulsive and to avoid taking responsibility for their own behavior. As a result, they are more likely to develop acting-out disorders such as alcohol and substance abuse. They also tend to be more self-centered and demanding in their interpersonal relations, and less capable of making commitments and following through on obligations.

Relating the Three Dimensions of Family Life

This section draws some relationships between the three basic dimensions of family life: the nature of the parental coalition, the separateness-relatedness dialectic, and childrearing practices. Authoritative parents have the emotional flexibility and range of parenting skills necessary to meet both children's needs for closeness and for individuation. Authoritarian and permissive parents have a more limited experiential range than authoritative parents. Specifically, the experiential range of authoritarian and permissive parents is limited to opposing halves of the separateness-relatedness continuum. For example, the range of authoritarian parents does not extend to include intimacy and closeness. These parents do not meet children's age-appropriate dependency needs for warmth and affection, although their emphasis on mature, responsible behavior does allow children to individuate.

In contrast, permissive parents meet children's emotional needs better, but they do not foster their children's individuation by expecting competent and independent behavior from them. Children of permissive parents are further stifled in their individuation because permissive parents are especially likely to embroil children in cross-generational, parent-child alliances. Of the three parenting styles, permissive parents are least likely to establish a primary marital coalition, most likely to embroil children in cross-generational alliances, and most likely to parentify children.

The family dynamics presented in this chapter offer a parallel to the relationship between the therapist and the client. Therapists, like authoritative parents, must develop their own abilities to respond at both ends of the separateness-relatedness continuum. On the one hand, effective therapists are those who have a flexible experiential range that allows them to nurture and care for clients. On the other hand, therapists must also be able to set limits with clients, challenge and confront them when necessary, and tolerate clients' anger and disapproval at times. For example, therapists need to be able to respond to the deprivation and emotional needs of clients who have been reared by highly authoritarian parents. At the same time, therapists must also be able to set clear rules and limits with the provocative, demanding, or testing behavior of clients who have been reared by permissive parents.

Thus, the personal challenge for therapists is to examine their own experiential range that has been shaped in their families of origin. Therapists must identify their own limitations and work to develop a flexible interpersonal range that allows them to respond to the diversity of problems that clients present.

CLOSING

This chapter has provided an introduction to three basic dimensions of family functioning: structural family relations and the parental coalition, the separateness-relatedness dialectic, and childrearing practices. These three aspects of family life will help therapists understand the genesis of clients' personality and emotional problems. The next chapter leaves this general discussion of how normal development goes awry in families and provides a detailed model for conceptualizing client dynamics.

SUGGESTIONS FOR FURTHER READING

1. Basic information on child development and child psychopathology will help therapists understand their clients' personalities and problems. One outstanding text is: C. Wenar, *Psychopathology from Infancy through Adolescence: A Developmental Approach* (New York: Random House, 1982). (See especially chapters 5 through 8.)

2. Structural family relations provide an illuminating road map for understanding family functioning. Seminal work in this area has been provided by Salvadore Minuchin in his book, *Families and Family Therapy* (Cambridge, Mass: Harvard University Press, 1974). (See especially chapters 3 and 5.) For a general review of structural family relations and how the parental coalition serves as the principal axis of family functioning, see E. Teyber, "Structural Family Relations: A Review," *Family Therapy* 1, pp. 39–48. An empirical study of these structural concepts is also found in E. Teyber, "Effects of the Parental Coalition on Adolescent Emancipation From the Family," *Journal of Marital and Family Therapy* No. 1, pp. 89–99. Finally, Bob Woodward's biography of the

late comedian, John Belushi, also illustrates the effects of cross-generational alliances on child development. See chapter 2 of: B. Woodward, *Wired* (New York: Simon and Schuster, 1984).

3. *Parentification* is an important concept for therapists to understand since so many clients have been scripted into this familial role. Further information about this far-reaching concept can be found in chapter 9 of E. Teyber, *Helping Your Children with Divorce* (New York: Pocket Books, 1985).

4. The terms *separateness-relatedness dialectic* and *experiential range* are useful family systems concepts that are readily applicable to individual psychotherapy. One informative article that can also lead to further reading in this area is J. Farley, "Family Separation—Individuation Tolerance: A Developmental Conceptualization of the Nuclear Family," *Journal of Marital and Family Therapy*, January, 1979, pp. 61–67.

7

A Model for Conceptualizing Client Dynamics

CONCEPTUAL OVERVIEW

This chapter provides a model for helping therapists conceptualize how client conflicts are expressed, maintained, and resolved. This model for conceptualizing client dynamics is based upon the client's generic conflict and interpersonal strategy for coping with this conflict. The term *generic conflict* refers to a central or underlying conflict that pervades the client's life and links together the different problems that the client presents. Therapists will be far more effective when they can identify the client's central conflict, understand how the client defends against this conflict, and recognize how this conflict is expressed in current relationships. If the therapist can formulate the client's generic conflict and interpersonal adaptation to it, this conceptualization will lend structure and organization to the disparate material that clients present. In turn, this conceptualization will effectively guide the therapist's intervention and treatment strategy.

If formulating a conceptual understanding of the client's dynamics is essential to change, why has discussion of it been delayed to this point? Shouldn't the therapist be formulating a conceptual picture of the client's personality and problems earlier? As noted in Chapter 2, client conceptualization is an ongoing process that begins with the initial client contact. General hypotheses about client dynamics are formulated early in treatment and these tentative working hypotheses are further refined or discarded as the therapist learns more about each particular client. It is not until the client's conflicted emotions emerge, however, that the central conflict underlying the client's problems becomes clear. That is, the therapist often cannot identify the client's generic conflict until the client's conflicted emotions emerge. Just as initially focusing clients inward elicits affect, clients' emotions now serve as guideposts to signal generic conflicts.

CHAPTER ORGANIZATION

The first section of this chapter provides a model for conceptualizing the client's generic conflict—how it originally developed, the client's interpersonal adaptation for coping with it, and how it is being expressed in current symptoms and problems. This model of conflict expression includes: (1) the client's unmet developmental needs, (2) the original environmental block that created the conflict, (3) the client's intrapsychic defenses against her blocked need, (4) the client's interpersonal strategy to rise above or overcome her blocked need, and (5) an interpersonal resolution of the generic conflict. Together, these five components of the conflict model provide an initial framework for conceptualizing client dynamics.

This model for conceptualizing clients is an integrated system composed of numerous, complex psychological processes. In the second section, an extended case study illustrates how this model can be used to guide treatment plans and intervention strategies.

A CONCEPTUAL MODEL

This section presents a model for conceptualizing how client conflicts are expressed, maintained, and resolved. This discussion does not suggest how therapists can intervene with their clients but, instead, gives therapists a framework for conceptualizing their clients' conflicts and adaptation to them. Much of the discussion that follows is derived from the interpersonal theory of Karen Horney (1945, 1950). The five components to this model are schematized in Figure 7−1. We begin by examining how enduring personality problems result when one or more of a child's basic developmental needs go unmet.

The Child's Need Is Blocked

This conceptual model begins with a child's basic needs for succor. Part 1 of Figure 7−1 refers in the broadest sense to young children's

FIGURE 7-1

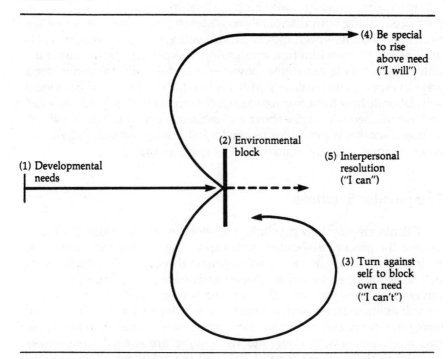

(4) Be special
to rise
above need
("I will")

(2) Environmental
block

(1) Developmental
needs

(5) Interpersonal
resolution
("I can")

(3) Turn against
self to block
own need
("I can't")

The author wishes to thank Dr. Robert Hilton for this schematization.

dependency needs on their parents and, in particular, to children's need for attachment. If parenting figures are consistently responsive to the child's bids for affection and attention, the child will be able to freely experience and express this need. Of course, as the child develops he will have to learn to accept limitations on the parent's ability to respond and to tolerate delay in parental response. If the parent is not responsive, however, anxiety will soon become associated with the child's need.

To illustrate, suppose that a young child's need for warmth and affection goes unmet from his authoritarian parents. When the preschool-aged child approaches his parents for comfort or "emotional refueling," his need is rejected (e.g., "What do you want now? Leave me alone!") or rebuffed (e.g., "You don't need to kiss and hug other people like that; that's sissy stuff"). If this type of interchange occurs repeatedly, the child will soon learn to anticipate rejection, and feel anxious whenever his need for affection is aroused. As indicated when the arrow hits the perpendicular line in part 2 of Figure 7-1, the child still experiences his need, but the expression of it is blocked by the parent's cold response.

Most enduring psychological problems begin when a basic childhood need such as this is blocked. Although clients may struggle with many different unmet needs, the source of most generic conflicts involves a failure to provide children with both the nurturing and emotional contact they need, along with discipline, consistency, and structure. Once the need is blocked, however, the child constructs a *compromise solution* that is designed to prevent him from continuing to experience anxiety over the unmet need. At the same time, however, the child will also find indirect ways to express and partially gratify the need. Parts 3 and 4 of this model will elaborate how this compromise solution works both to block the need and, simultaneously, to rise above and indirectly gratify it. The rest of this section discusses the complex psychological maneuvers that individuals adopt to cope with this unmet need or generic conflict.

Compromise Solutions

Clients employ two psychological mechanisms in order to defend against the anxiety associated with expressing, or even experiencing, their blocked needs. First, we will examine three ways in which clients defend against their unmet developmental needs by responding to themselves in the same way that others originally responded to them. Second, we will examine three ways in which clients adopt a general *interpersonal coping style* to try and rise above their unmet need. Taken together, these two mechanisms of *blocking* and *rising above* are clients' compromise solution to their generic conflict. We will see below how this complex defensive system works.

Clients Block Their Own Need. Consider the child in the beginning of this discussion who was unsuccessful in getting his parents to respond to his emotional needs. The child tried desperately with the limited skills and means that are available to a child but he was unable to stop the parental rejection and elicit the nurturing and support he needed. In order to gain some active mastery over his helplessness, and to ward off the anxiety-arousing need, the child began blocking his own need in the same way that the environment originally blocked it. That is, clients turn against themselves and block their own needs by adopting the same hurtful responses toward themselves that others in the environment originally gave to them. This attempt at mastery may be referred to as identification with the aggressor or, as some clinicians colloquially refer to it, "using the devil's tools to fight the devil." Part 3 of Figure 7−1 reflects how the child begins to do to himself what was originally done to him. There are three ways that this can occur.

First, clients block their own need *intrapsychically* and respond to themselves in the same hurtful, rejecting ways that others have responded to them. That is, when the child in our example feels a need for reassurance or affection, he will block his need by feeling critical or contemptuous of himself and his own need. For example, when his own unacceptable dependency needs are aroused as an adult, he will often say to himself the same critical things he heard from others years ago. Furthermore, the critical, shaming, or rejecting affect that clients feel toward themselves is the same affect that parenting figures originally expressed toward the child's need years ago.

Second, clients block their anxiety-arousing need by reenacting in current relationships the same conflict that was originally experienced in earlier, formative relationships. That is, on an *interpersonal* level, clients will say and do to others what was originally done to them. For example, the child in our example will likely grow up to be a parent who similarly disparages dependency needs in one of his own children. Especially in the arena of parenting, clients will reenact the same conflicts and hurtful messages that they received in their own childhoods. As parents, many clients feel helplessly dismayed as they watch themselves respond to their children in the same hurtful ways that their parents responded to them. Despite sincere pledges that "I will never do to my children what my parents did to me," this occurs with clocklike regularity. Here again, adult offspring gain some mastery and defend against their own conflicts by reenacting what was originally done to them, rather than allowing themselves to reexperience the original hurt, deprivation, or powerlessness.

Third, clients block the experience and expression of their own conflicted need by *eliciting* the same unsatisfying response from others in current relationships that they originally received in the past. For example, the child in our example is likely to grow up and select a marital partner who cannot respond to his needs for affection, closeness, or intimacy. Or, if the spouse is capable of responding to this need, he will not be able to accept her emotional responsiveness. Why? The possibility of having a response to his old, unmet need will arouse too much anxiety. The spouse's affection will arouse the pain of the original deprivation, and the client will anticipate that his spouse will reject his need as others have in the past. Thus, this client may simultaneously elicit and reject nurturance from his spouse, which will certainly frustrate and confuse her.

In sum, clients defend against their unmet needs by (1) intrapsychically responding to themselves in the same rejecting ways that parenting figures did, (2) identifying with the rejecting parent and responding to others in the same hurtful way that they were responded to, and (3) selecting to become involved with others who provide the same hurtful response to them that they originally received as children. Although one of these three modes may be predominant for a particular client, most clients will employ all three mechanisms at different times in order to defend against their anxiety-arousing need.

At the same time as clients are blocking their needs on each of these levels, they are simultaneously trying to get them met in an indirect way. Next, we will turn to the top half of Figure 7—1 (part 4) and see how clients make a lifestyle out of rising above their unmet need, and turning this defensive adaptation into a virtue.

Rising Above the Unmet Need. Parts 1 through 3 of Figure 7—1 show that when clients have had a primary need blocked throughout their development they employ three strategies to defend against it. Clients do to themselves what others originally did to them, and they try to master this conflict by turning a passive experience that originally happened to them into an active experience over which they now have some control. The key element is how the same hurtful affect that was originally expressed toward the child is taken up by individuals and actively turned against themselves to block their own unmet need. This is only half of the conflict, however. Paradoxically, just as the client defends against the anxiety of reexperiencing the unmet need, the client simultaneously tries to rise above it and have it met indirectly. Part 4 of Figure 7—1 shows the other side of the client's compromise solution—the client's attempts not to block the need but to rise above and indirectly gratify it.

The client's unmet childhood need does not dissipate or go away as he grows up. The need may be repressed or defended against, but it continues to seek expression. As a result, clients do not give up trying to have the need met. At the same time, the unmet need remains too anxiety-arousing to be expressed directly. So clients try to rise above the unmet need and indirectly fulfill it by adopting one of three interpersonal coping styles. Horney has labeled these lifestyle adaptations *moving toward*, *moving away*, and *moving against* others.

Moving Toward, Moving Away, and Moving Against. Clients adopt a fixed interpersonal style both to reduce the anxiety associated with the unmet need and to find some partial, indirect gratification of it. For example, in their families of origin some clients learned to cope with their conflict by *moving toward*, or pleasing people. These clients could earn some needed approval and diminish the threat of further rejection by complying with their parents and being unfailingly nice or good. Their primary mode of relating to others became one of submitting, accommodating, or pleasing others and never asserting their own wishes. Thus, these clients have learned to defend against their unmet need, and to win some needed approval to indirectly gratify the need, by consistently moving toward others in a pleasing, servile way.

Other clients have learned that aggressiveness and resistance to parental wishes, if pursued long enough, will ward off the pain of an unmet need. These individuals *move against* others and expansively seek to be in control of themselves and others. They approach life and relationships with the attitude that they will win what they deserve. Thus a repetitive interpersonal style of moving against others has been adopted in order to protect these clients from their generic conflict.

The third interpersonal style is to *move away* from others. These clients have learned that the best way to reduce their anxiety and defend against their unmet needs is through physical avoidance, withdrawal, and self-sufficiency. Although clients may employ all three of these interpersonal coping styles at different times, one style usually becomes predominant or characterological.

To review, we have seen that clients use three ways to defend against the unmet need that are similar to the ways the need was originally blocked by parents or others in the environment. Next, we turned to the top half of Figure 7–1 to see how clients also try to rise above their blocked need and indirectly have it met. First, we introduced the interpersonal styles of moving toward, against, or away from others that clients adopt to cope with their generic conflict. Now we are ready to examine how clients use their characterological interpersonal style to try to rise above their unmet need and gratify it. As we will see below, however, even though clients earn many rewards from their interpersonal coping style, it remains a defensive adaptation that does not resolve their real conflict or meet their original unmet need.

Being "Special" to Rise Above the Need. Most clients will adopt one of the three interpersonal styles as a general lifestyle to cope with their generic conflict. Clients turn this defensive coping style into a virtue and use it to feel special and rise above their need. That is, clients do not experience their interpersonal strategy as a defensive coping system but as a virtuous way of relating to others that makes them feel superior. However, this unrealistic sense of being special actually reflects the low self-esteem and damaged sense of self that results from the original unmet need and environmental block. Often, clients' only sense of worth or value comes from their ability to rise above their unmet need and either please others, achieve and succeed, or withdraw and feel cynically superior. The following discussion shows how clients convert their defensive, interpersonal coping style into a virtue.

Although moving-toward clients are compliant and submissive, they will not experience themselves as servile. Instead, these clients will convert this defensive coping strategy into a virtue that makes them special or secretly better than others. How is this done? The moving-toward client will become a selflessly and endlessly loving person. She will become someone who is always sensitive to the needs of others and committed to the ideals of peace and harmony. In this way, the defensive interpersonal style becomes a source of self-esteem—a virtuous quality that wins needed approval from others.

Similarly, moving-against clients do not see themselves as angry, competitive, self-centered, or demanding although they frequently behave this way. Instead, they see themselves as heroes—strong leaders entitled to direct others who are inferior and less capable. Or, the moving-away client rises above her need through aloofness, and glorifies this stance by feeling self-righteously self-sufficient. The moving-away client is cynical and feels better than the ordinary masses who are so mundane as to be caught up in everyday happenings.

What was originally a way to lessen anxiety has become a fixed and pervasive interpersonal style for these clients. This broad interpersonal style has also become a way for clients to become special, gain a sense of identity and self-esteem, and rise above their unmet needs. The process of turning their defensive coping style into a virtue, gift, or talent that is prized as evidence of their specialness is part of Horney's *neurotic pride system*. The client's self-esteem is brittle and vulnerable, however, since it is based on being special and rising above rather than on valuing one's own feelings that have been valued by significant others.

We now have the two sides of the client's conflict. On the one hand, clients block their own needs and respond to themselves in the same critical or rejecting ways that adult care-givers originally responded to them. Clients will internalize and feel toward themselves the same affect that the parent originally communicated toward their need (e.g., disappointment, contempt, resentment, indifference, and so on). This affect will usually be evidenced as low self-esteem when clients enter therapy. Clients are often seeking treatment to be rid of this intrapunitive feeling.

In contrast to the blocking response, the side of the client's conflict that leaves him feeling special is usually more covert and is harder for the therapist to work with. Yet the therapist must address this side of the client's conflict as well. Clients are reluctant to let go of their attempts to rise above their need by being special. Why? The interpersonal coping style they have adopted has provided them with relief from the anxiety of the unmet need; it has allowed them to earn some indirect gratification of the original need, and it has become the primary source of their self-esteem. For example, moving-toward clients have often been able to make others like them. In like fashion, moving-against clients have often been able to achieve a great deal of success and power, and moving-away clients have often been able to become safely aloof.

Thus the manner in which clients have turned their defensive interpersonal adaptation into a sense of being special provides tremendous secondary gains. No wonder then that clients will be reluctant to explore this rising above adaptation with the therapist. It has become the basis of their identity, the primary source of their self-esteem, and the only way they have of defending against their seemingly unresolvable conflict. Understandably, the client will not want to risk giving all of this up without having something better to replace it with. As we will see below, however, the client never really succeeds in rising above the original conflict through these compensatory lifestyle adaptations.

"Shoulds" for the Self, "Entitlement" from Others.   Clients both gain something and lose something by their compromise solutions. As a result of their feeling special and virtuous, the client gains what Horney terms *false pride* and a sense of *entitlement* from others. For example, the self-effacing, moving-toward client expects unrealistic adulation and approval from others and often demands constant reassurances. The expansive, moving-against client claims leadership, respect, and allegiance from others. And, although it may look as if detached, moving-away clients have no claims, they demand that others never criticize them or make requests of them. These neurotic claims leave clients exposed to continuing frustration and conflict, however, as others frequently do not accept these unrealistic demands and expectations.

Just as the sense of being special entitles clients to make unrealistic claims or demands of others, clients also have to demand a lot of themselves in order to maintain their specialness. Accompanying clients' excessive demands upon others is a harsh and uncompromising set of "shoulds" they place upon themselves. For example, moving-toward clients suffer under the self-imposed demands that they should be the perfect lover, teacher, spouse, and so forth. They must always be calm, caring, sensitive, and responsive to the needs of others and never feel angry, be critical, or act selfishly. Moving-against clients demand of themselves that they should be able to quickly overcome all difficulties and obstacles. They must be able to control all of their feelings at all times and overcome bad moods simply by an act of will. Moving-away clients pay for their specialness by believing that they should be able to work tirelessly and always be productive. They demand that they should be able to endure anything without becoming ruffled or upset and they must never need help or reassurance from anyone.

Thus the *tyranny of the shoulds* is an exacting price to pay for the client's sense of specialness. The therapist must keep in mind, however, that the "shoulds" clients place on themselves and the neurotic claims they place on others reflect their damaged self-esteem and impoverished sense of self.

Resolving the Generic Conflict

Part 5 of Figure 7–1 illustrates how the client's generic conflict can be resolved. Ultimately, the client's compromise solution to her original conflict will never succeed. The client can block the anxiety-arousing need and try to rise above it in the ways described above. However, these compensatory maneuvers will not release the client from her conflict. Furthermore, not only will the lifestyle adaptation of moving towards, away, or against others never allow the client to resolve the original conflict, this defensive adaptation will expose the client to continual frustration. First, we will examine three reasons why the client's compromise solution will not succeed, and then explore what can be done to help the client successfully resolve her generic conflict.

First, the tyranny of the shoulds places unrealistic and unrelenting demands on the client. These can be heard, for example, when clients enter therapy exclaiming, "I can't do all of this anymore! I can't be a giving mother, a loving wife, and successful professional. I can't be everything to everybody anymore." The quality of life is diminished by these harsh and fatiguing expectations on self, even if they do not lead to a crisis that brings the client to therapy.

Second, the client's sense of entitlement and being special will usually fail as well. That is, self-effacing clients will not be able to win the love of everyone they need. Expansive clients will not always succeed or be able to make others defer to their demands, and others will criticize detached clients or force them to compete. Inevitably, clients' attempts to become special and rise above their conflict will lead to repeated interpersonal conflicts, failure, and frustration. Clients usually enter therapy when situational life stressors, developmental transitions in adulthood, or aging have caused their interpersonal coping strategies to fail.

The therapist must be empathic to the narcissistic wound that clients suffer when their attempts to be special and rise above their conflict fail. Even though the demands that clients place upon themselves and others are unrealistic, it is excruciatingly painful when their interpersonal adaptation fails. As noted earlier, the interpersonal coping style that clients have adopted is the basis of their identity and their primary source of self worth—a brittle substitute for the genuine self-esteem they lack. From clients' point of view, they *are* their ability to please, to achieve, or to remain superior and aloof. Clients overreact to certain seemingly insignificant events because their entire sense of self is threatened when their interpersonal coping strategy fails.

Furthermore, it is shattering for clients when their interpersonal coping style fails because it arouses the original helplessness, vulnerability, and shame that accompany their unmet need. Eventually, the therapist must respond to the unmet need beneath the client's compensatory attempt to obtain security through winning other's approval, achieving power and success, or withdrawing and going away. Before the therapist can do this, however, the therapist must first respond to the intense anxiety or depression aroused by clients' beliefs that they are of no value if they can no longer successfully please, achieve, or remain aloof.

Third, the most important reason the client's compromise solution cannot succeed is because the client can never rise above her original conflict or unmet need. No matter how saint-like or loving, how successful or accomplished, or how self-contained and independent, the client is still defending against the original conflict. All of these interpersonal maneuvers are attempts to avoid the problem by blocking and trying to rise above it rather than addressing it directly.

Let us review this sequence and take it one step further to show how the client's generic conflict can be resolved. If the child's developmental need is blocked by the environment, the individual will adopt a compromise solution that temporarily relieves the anxiety of the unmet need but does not resolve the underlying conflict. On the one hand, clients try to block their own needs just as they were originally blocked by significant others. The arrow turning back against the block in part 3 of Figure 7–1 illustrates how clients turn against themselves. The arrow turning back refers to the client's intrapunitive feelings, belief that "I can't," and sense of helplessness and hopelessness.

At the same time, however, clients also try to rise above the old unmet need by becoming special, turning their defensive lifestyle adaptation into a virtue, and obtaining some indirect gratification of the original need. *All clients will be intensely invested in trying to overcome and rise above their generic conflict as it will feel like defeat to have to come to terms with the original need or conflict.* Thus the arrow moving out over the block in part 4 of Figure 7–1 refers to the client's grandiose sense of being special and defiant attempt to rise above the conflict (e.g., "I will never let them hurt me again"). This rigid, defensive stance reflects an act of will to overcome the client's need and rise above her conflict rather than to try and resolve it by addressing it directly.

In order to resolve the generic conflict, clients must relinquish their compromise solutions. Clients must stop trying to block the original need and to rise above it. Instead of avoiding the conflict in these two ways, clients must approach it by allowing themselves to experience the original unmet need and the reactive feelings that accompany it. It is more adaptive now as an adult to incorporate the original hurt and vulnerability—by reexperiencing what was once dreaded—than it is to continue to try and defend against it. Said differently, the client must allow the unmet need to come through the old block and be expressed to the therapist, as shown in part 5 of Figure 7–1. Once the original hurt or need begins to emerge in therapy, the therapist must provide a more satisfying response than the client has received in the past. As we will see more fully later, this is where the *corrective emotional experience* that produces change occurs.

If clients receive a more effective response from the therapist than they have received from others in the past, they will not need to block their need or attempt to rise above it anymore. The therapist's more accepting and understanding response to the old need and the conflicted feelings that accompany it will alleviate the anxiety that the original need aroused. Once this occurs, clients will be able to adopt new and more effective behavioral alternatives, and expand the limited interpersonal style that they have adopted to cope with their conflict. In Chapter 9 we will examine more fully how the therapeutic relationship can be utilized to help clients resolve their generic conflict. For now, an extended case study will help therapists apply this conceptual model to therapeutic interventions.

CASE STUDY OF PETER: MOVING TOWARD OTHERS

Developmental History and Precipitating Crisis

In order to illustrate this model, we will return to the child in the beginning of this chapter and call him Peter. Throughout his childhood, Peter's authoritarian parents left his age-appropriate dependency needs for affection, warmth, and caring profoundly unmet. In addition, Peter's parents divorced when he was six years of age and his father did not take an active parenting role after the divorce. Peter saw his father infrequently and their contacts were superficial and inconsequential when they were together.

Peter's mother was overburdened by the demands of raising three children on her own, working full time, and trying to make some kind of personal life for herself. She was involved with several men in the years following the divorce but she was never able to establish an enduring love relationship. Frustrated by the many demands and few pleasures in her life, she often made Peter the target of her resentment. She was often irritable toward Peter, criticized him when things went wrong in her life, and felt resentful of his needs. Although she tried her best to be fair to the children and give them a good home, she could not provide Peter with a dependable source of love and affection.

After his father left, Peter quickly learned that taking care of his mother was the best way to ward off her anger and disapproval, and to win whatever affection he could. By ten years of age, Peter had adopted a pervasive personality style of moving toward people. His teachers described him as an especially responsible and well-behaved boy who was a pleasure to have in class. We will now turn the clock ahead fifteen years to see how these developmental conflicts are expressed in Peter's early adulthood.

Peter is now a graduate student in clinical psychology. Becoming a therapist felt like a perfect career choice to Peter. He prided himself on his sensitivity and concern for others and took pleasure in being able to help those in need. And now that he was carrying his own client caseload, it was great to find that he enjoyed being a therapist as much as he thought he would. Best of all, Peter was finding that he was often able to help his new clients. At least all of his clients seemed to like him and they kept returning to their therapy sessions each week. As his second semester practicum got underway, Peter felt that he was hitting his stride and on his way.

Later that semester, though, Peter's good feeling about himself as a therapist took a hard blow. After presenting a videotaped recording of one of his therapy sessions in group supervision, Peter received some unexpected feedback. The practicum instructor confronted Peter and said that he was being too nice to be helpful to his clients and that he seemed to need his clients' approval too much. The instructor went on to say that Peter was afraid of confrontations and was avoiding conflicts in the therapist-client relationship that should be addressed.

Peter was shocked by this unexpected feedback. He had no idea what the instructor was talking about and he felt hurt and confused by the criticism. It was important to Peter that his supervisor like him and approve of his clinical work. Peter tried to explain to the instructor that he didn't understand the close relationship that Peter was developing with his clients or recognize all of the important personal issues that his clients had been revealing. The instructor did not agree with Peter, however, and continued to confront him with these critical observations. To make matters worse, two students in the practicum group chimed in and agreed with the instructor's comments. With that, Peter's anxiety became so high that he could no longer even try to defend or explain himself, let alone try to understand or learn from their comments. Peter finally stopped arguing with them and quietly nodded agreement throughout the rest of the supervision session.

The next few days Peter felt sickened. He was confused and dismayed by the criticism that he was too nice and always trying to make people like him. His thoughts and feelings raced uncontrollably. For awhile, he thought that he should drop out of the practicum group, but then decided that if he only tried hard enough he could make the instructor see that his critical comments were inaccurate. Peter's mind kept racing to find a way to discount the feedback and stop the anxiety that was churning inside.

When it rains, it pours. One week later, Peter found out that his girlfriend was having an affair with another student in the program. Although he tried to be understanding at first, he felt shocked and betrayed. Peter alternated between angrily telling her that their relationship was over and desperately trying to win her back. Peter felt shattered. He became so anxious that he was unable to eat or sleep, let alone study. It felt as if a motor were racing inside of him—accelerating out of control. Peter began hyperventilating and having panic attacks. By the end of the week, he was so anxious that he was unable to drive his car.

To make matters worse, Peter tried to keep all of this to himself. He thought he should remain calm and together, and he was afraid that his supervisors would not want him to see clients if he was "so messed up" that he was having anxiety attacks himself. But despite his attempts to cover up his distress, his individual supervisor soon asked him what was wrong.

Although he could not ask for it, Peter desperately wanted his individual supervisor's support and he was greatly relieved to receive it. Peter explained how his practicum group was becoming one of the worst failure experiences of his life, and how hard it was to accept what his girlfriend had done. The supervisor was supportive but he did say that the practicum instructor's comments fit with some of his own observations. Because he knew that the individual supervisor liked him, Peter was able to consider the feedback this time. The supervisor suggested that these were important issues for Peter to work with, but that they were more than they could handle in supervision. They both agreed that Peter should begin seeing his own therapist at the student counseling center.

It helped that his supervisor knew about his panic attacks and still thought he could be a fine therapist, but Peter's anxiety was paralyzing as he began his own treatment. Fortunately, Peter was assigned to a skilled therapist who quickly recognized the generic conflict that precipitated his crisis. Peter's coping strategy of moving toward people in an accommodating and pleasing manner had worked well for him up to this point. However, both of the crises that Peter had just experienced ran headlong into the heart of his generic conflict. As Peter's ability to rise above his old unmet need by pleasing others failed, the anxiety associated with his developmental conflict broke through and panic attacks resulted. We must examine closely why Peter developed these symptoms.

Precipitating Crises, Generic Conflicts, and Symptom Development

Many people would have coped with the two stressful events that Peter experienced without developing such significant symptoms. We will use Peter to illustrate how symptoms develop when situational stressors tap into the client's generic conflict.

The first stressor for Peter was his practicum instructor's critical feedback. In general, criticism from a respected authority figure would be unsettling for most people but something they could cope with. For someone like Peter, however, such disapproval carries far more weight. Because of Peter's strong unmet needs for approval, his history of receiving excessive criticism, and his lifestyle adaptation of trying to win approval by being helpful and responsive, the supervisor's criticism was devastating.

Second, the practicum instructor specifically challenged Peter's interpersonal coping style of moving toward others. This confrontation not only aroused the anxiety of receiving criticism, but undermined Peter's primary means of warding off this anxiety (i.e., pleasing others and accommodating himself to their needs). Thus the instructor's feedback intensified Peter's generic conflict and, simultaneously, weakened his defenses against it.

If not for the subsequent crisis with his girlfriend, Peter probably could have recovered from the first setback without developing symptoms. Most likely, he would have reconstituted his interpersonal coping style and been successful in winning the approval he needed from others in his life—such as other instructors, friends, and perhaps clients. As we will see below, however, the subsequent stressor with his girlfriend also struck at the same generic conflict. At that point, his moving-toward coping style failed. The anxiety associated with his old, unmet need became too intense to be blocked and broke through in anxiety attacks and symptom formation.

A partner's infidelity will be highly stressful for almost everyone. Here again, though, this particular stressor held far greater significance for Peter when viewed within the context of his generic conflict. Peter had to cope with far more than just the loss of trust with his girlfriend. He also suffered a blow to his identity and basic sense of self-worth. As in Horney's *neurotic pride system*, Peter's coping style of moving toward entitled him to be special, so that others would love and prize him inordinately. Although Peter was hardly aware of these unrealistic claims, he expected his girlfriend to idealize him as the most sensitive and loving man there possibly could be. It was impossible for Peter to believe that his girlfriend could actually be interested in someone else. Peter's neurotic pride system was painfully shattered when he found that he was not the commanding center of his girlfriend's life that he felt entitled to be.

Multiple stressors occurred for Peter in a short period of time. In and of themselves, these would precipitate a crisis for many people and lead them to therapy. If these situational stressors do not tap into a preexisting generic conflict in the client's personality, however, such strong symptoms as panic attacks usually will not develop. The client will often be able to recover in a relatively short time with crisis intervention or short-term supportive therapy. In contrast, when life stresses tap into a preexisting generic conflict, a client such as Peter has to cope with far more than just the demands of the current situational stressors.

Thus, when Peter's girlfriend became sexually involved with another man, he had to cope with much more than just the pain of this loss or betrayal. He also had to cope with his old unmet dependency needs that were aroused by her loss, and with the wound to his vulnerable self-esteem when his sense of being special was shattered. Clients such as Peter do not have a secure sense of self-esteem to act as a safety net to fall back upon in times of crisis. As unrealistic as it is, the sense of being special and the secondary gains clients can earn by rising above their need is all that many clients have for a sense of self-worth. It is understandable, then, that Peter's anxiety became overwhelming and broke through in panic attacks. Both of the situational stressors intensified Peter's old unmet need, and they both took away his lifestyle adaptation for defending against his generic conflict. In this way, clients' presenting symptoms will make sense once they are conceptualized in the context of the client's generic conflict.

The Course of Treatment

Peter's therapist was skilled and experienced. He was empathic to the pain that these situational crises brought on for Peter but he also understood the generic conflict that constituted the real problem. The therapist recognized that the current crisis provided an opportunity to resolve the more important, developmental conflict that left Peter prone to reexperience crises such as these whenever others rejected or disapproved of him. In the months that followed, Peter was able to resolve the precipitating crisis and, for the first time, come to terms with his generic conflict and defenses against it. As a result, Peter was able to step back somewhat from his rigid moving-toward coping style and adopt a more flexible and varied interpersonal repertoire. Below, we will review the course of therapeutic events that allowed Peter to make these far-reaching changes.

Peter entered therapy in crisis and the therapist was able to respond effectively to his anxiety and hurt. From the first session, Peter felt understood and cared for by the therapist. In just a few weeks his anxiety became manageable and the panic attacks stopped. Although Peter remained anxious and upset, the shock and confusion that had been so disorganizing for him subsided as the therapist continued to understand his experience and respond to his feelings. As the initial crisis ended and

Peter began to feel better, however, Peter began to be resistant to the feelings he had been sharing with the therapist and talked about ending treatment.

The therapist observed that as Peter felt understood and supported by him, Peter's unmet need for emotional contact was assuaged and its attendant anxiety diminished. As that occurred, Peter began to reconstitute his old defenses against his generic conflict and reemploy his interpersonal style of moving toward others. Rather than terminate therapy at this point, however, the therapist was able to help Peter identify this habitual coping pattern and understand how it served to keep him from resolving his underlying conflict. The therapist continued to focus Peter inward and to explore the feelings that accompanied his generic conflict and defensive adaptation to it. Gradually, Peter began to experience and share with the therapist the deprivation he had suffered as a child. He also began to understand how he had coped with his emotional needs by taking care of and pleasing first his mother, and then others as well. As this progress occurred, therapy moved into a new phase in which Peter again felt anxious and insecure.

A host of contradictory feelings emerged for Peter in the next few months. Peter began to recognize how unloved and alone he had felt as a child, and how he had always believed that he wasn't loved because he was somehow lacking or unworthy. As Peter continued to feel the therapist's support, his long withheld feelings of sadness and longing came through the old block and were shared with the therapist.

As Peter began to mourn his childhood loss, two reactive feelings followed closely behind. Peter found himself feeling furious at his father for abandoning him and angry at his mother for forcing him to try and earn her love and approval. As soon as this anger emerged, however, the third feeling in Peter's affective constellation was aroused. Peter also became exceedingly anxious—afraid of being left helplessly on his own by the therapist, his girlfriend, and his father. Each of these three feelings in Peter's affective constellation was repeatedly aroused, and the therapist was gradually able to help Peter experience, express, and contain them. This was not a smooth or even process, however. As the primary feeling of sadness emerged, Peter's own internal blocking defenses were also activated (see part 3 of Figure 7−1). First, we will examine how the blocking side of Peter's compromise solution was expressed in therapy.

The rising-above defense was broken for Peter by his situational crises. He could no longer be special and win the approval he needed from either his practicum supervisor or his girlfriend. As his coping system failed, it opened the way for his original unmet need—and its accompanying emotional reactions—to come through the block and be expressed to the therapist. In addition to trying to rise above their generic conflict, however, clients also block their own experience of the original need. That is, the block that was originally imposed by the environment is taken up by the individual to defend against the painful feelings associated with the unmet need. Thus, Peter still blocked his own need with the therapist in both the intrapsychic and interpersonal ways discussed earlier. This side of Peter's compromise solution still needed to be worked through in therapy.

Peter tried to block the subjective experience and the interpersonal expression of his conflict by resisting each feeling in his affective constellation. For example, as the sadness of his emotional deprivation as a child emerged, Peter thought the therapist would be critical and rejecting of him. Peter was afraid that the therapist would want him to "stop crying, grow up, and act like a man." This *transference reaction* again served to block his sadness until Peter and the therapist were able to talk through Peter's misperception of the therapist.

Next, as Peter's anger toward his girlfriend, and then his parents emerged, Peter felt guilty; he felt that he *should* be understanding, accepting, and forgiving of them. This intrapsychic defense also reflected his moving-toward character and served to block his unmet need again. With the therapist's support, however, Peter was finally able to experience the anger that had always been taboo for him. Why was it so threatening for Peter to experience his anger or share it with the therapist? While growing up in his family, Peter had learned that relationships were not resilient, his anger was unacceptable, and he could easily destroy the little emotional support that he had won. Thus, Peter's anger threatened to break the already insecure emotional attachments he had and this, in turn, further aggravated his generic conflict. As a result, Peter's anger aroused his anxiety, which he tried to block by telling himself that he should be calm and together—especially if he were going to be a therapist.

Fortunately, the therapist was able to approach each of these feelings and work with Peter's resistance to them. Over the course of that school year, Peter was able to accept the reality and pain of his childhood loss, and allow the therapist to respond to the conflicted feelings that accompanied his generic conflict. As a result, Peter no longer needed to ward off his unmet need and its attendant anxiety so strongly. Peter felt less urgent about making others like him, more comfortable with interpersonal conflict, and more confident as his obsessive concern about pleasing others diminished. Finally, Peter was also able to keep the best parts of his moving-toward style. That is, he remained a sensitive, caring, and responsive person, although this was no longer the compulsive, unidimensional response pattern that it had been in the past.

Peter will certainly have further crises in his life, especially when life circumstances again tap into his old generic conflict. Peter has grown through this crisis, however, and therapy has helped immunize him against his predisposing vulnerability to rejection, criticism, and loss. By coming to terms with his generic conflict, the therapist helped Peter to stop carrying emotional baggage from his past into his present relationships. The internal changes that occurred for Peter will enable him to respond to future problems in a more adult, present-centered manner.

CLOSING

In this chapter, we studied a model for conceptualizing clients' dynamics. An extended case study of a moving-toward client illustrated how this model can be applied to treatment. We will also look at case studies of moving-against and moving-away clients after discussing additional information about conceptualizing clients and the process of change. At this point, however, two issues still remain incomplete.

First, we need further guidelines to be able to conceptualize clients' dynamics and use this conceptualization to guide clinical interventions. Chapter 8 provides further information about clients' current interpersonal functioning that will help therapists conceptualize their clients.

Second, as the compromise solution fails and the client's generic conflict emerges in therapy, the relationship that the therapist provides the client determines whether the client will be able to resolve the conflict and change. This pivotal juncture was identified in this chapter but specific guidelines for negotiating this phase of treatment were not provided. In Part IV, Chapters 9 and 10 will discuss more fully how the therapist can best respond to the client's emerging conflict.

SUGGESTIONS FOR FURTHER READING

1. Karen Horney's work has remained the touchstone for many interpersonally-oriented clinicians throughout their careers. Her writings are essential reading, especially *Neurosis and Human Growth* (New York: W. W. Norton, 1950). The reader may also be interested in two other books by Horney: *Self Analysis* (New York: W. W. Norton, 1942) and *Our Inner Conflicts* (New York: W. W. Norton, 1945).

2. Therapists in training need to be exposed to case examples that illustrate how theory guides clinical practice. Unfortunately, such effective illustrations are not plentiful. One of the most effective examples of integrating theory with practice is James Masterson's trilogy on using a developmental, object relations approach for treating borderline disorders. Masterson's books will be illuminating for many readers. See especially: *Psychotherapy of the Borderline Adult: A Developmental Approach* (New York: Brunner/Mazel, 1976), and *Treatment of the Borderline Adolescent: A Developmental Approach* (New York: John Wiley & Sons, 1972).

8

Current Interpersonal Factors

CONCEPTUAL OVERVIEW

The conceptual formulation presented here has three components. The first includes the three basic dimensions of family life introduced in Chapter 6. Most clients who enter therapy have experienced problems along each of these dimensions. Clients have usually come from families without a primary parental coalition, are often emotionally bound in cross-generational alliances and loyalty conflicts, and/or have not had their developmental needs for nurturance and discipline met. When development goes awry along these dimensions, children are likely to develop enduring personality conflicts.

The second component of our conceptualization is the schematic model for understanding how client problems are expressed, maintained, and resolved that we built on this familial/developmental perspective in Chapter 7. One important component of this conceptual model is clients' characteristic interpersonal style for coping with their generic conflict.

Now, in the third part of this conceptual formulation, we can expand the framework for examining clients' interpersonal functioning. This chapter shows how clients' current interpersonal relations provide the most important information for conceptualizing their dynamics. Furthermore, the therapist's own feelings and reactions toward the client are the therapist's best source of data for understanding the client's generic conflict and interpersonal defenses. Thus, this chapter shows how the therapist can systematically utilize the client's current interpersonal functioning and the therapist's own experience of the client to conceptualize the client's dynamics.

CHAPTER ORGANIZATION

The first factor we will examine in this chapter is the *circumplex* or range of interpersonal behavior that clients express. In the second section, we will see how therapists can be alerted to the client's generic conflict by tracking the client's anxiety. The third section helps therapists understand clients' problems by recognizing the ambivalent nature of their conflicts. The fourth section examines transference reactions. All four aspects of clients' current interpersonal functioning will be used to help therapists conceptualize their clients' dynamics.

THE INTERPERSONAL CIRCUMPLEX

The first interpersonal factor to help therapists conceptualize their clients is a schema for identifying clients' predominant interpersonal style. One effective definition of mental health or personal adjustment is that an individual has a broad range of feelings and interpersonal responses available and can flexibly adapt to changing situational demands. Better functioning individuals have a wide range of responses that they can employ in different settings. For example, healthier individuals can experience a full range of human emotions and interact in different ways to meet the varying demands of changing situations.

In contrast, more conflicted individuals are less flexible and adaptive. For example, the rigidly fixed interpersonal coping styles that clients adopt of moving toward, away, or against others presented in Chapter 7 are examples of ways in which most clients are inflexible in their perception of others, constricted in their range of emotions, and limited in the range of interpersonal responses they can enact.

Based on Sullivan's interpersonal theory, Leary (1957) developed a diagnostic coding scheme to describe the range, type, and flexibility of interpersonal responses that clients utilize. The first section below describes relevant components of Leary's circumplex model of interpersonal behavior. The second section shows how the circumplex model can be used to aid therapists in conceptualizing client dynamics. Specifically, the second section will show how the circumplex model can be used to identify the client's generic conflict and predominant interpersonal style.

Leary's Circumplex Model of Interpersonal Behavior

Like many other theorists, Leary observed that most interpersonal behavior has some reference to a power dimension such as dominance-submission or to an affiliation dimension such as love-hostility. Leary's circumplex is built upon this two-factor model shown in Figure 8-1. The

FIGURE 8-1 The Interpersonal Circumplex

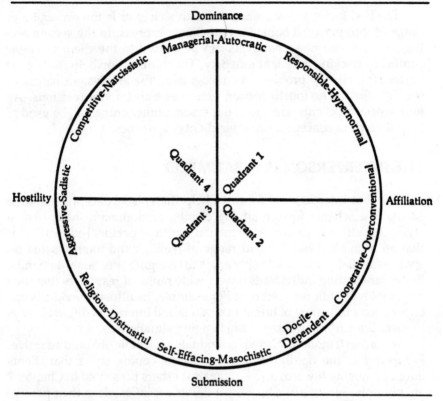

SOURCE: Adapted from T. Leary, *Interpersonal Diagnosis of Personality* (New York: The Ronald Press, 1957).

vertical axis of the circumplex is the dominance-submission dimension and the horizontal axis is the hostility-affiliation dimension. The two axes of the circumplex reflect four nodal points, and most interpersonal behavior can be mapped out by moving along a continuum between these four nodal points.

The circumplex has four quadrants that comprise blends of the nodal dichotomies of affiliation versus hostility and dominance versus submission. Quadrant 1 combines the dimensions of strength and affection. This quadrant describes behavior that ranges along a continuum from the dominance or power node (e.g., to manage, direct, lead) toward the affiliation node (e.g., to agree, cooperate, support). The various types of nurturant behavior, such as to teach, guide, or advise, reflect blends of strong and affectionate orientations toward others and fill in the continuum between the power and affiliation nodes.

Quadrant 2 describes behavior that ranges along a continuum from the affiliation node toward the submission node. The submission node encompasses behavior such as to obey, conform, ask for help, or be shy. The middle range that combines these two nodes is docile-dependent behavior, such as to admire, trust, depend, and agree.

Quadrant 3 describes behavior that ranges from the submission node to the hostility or assertiveness node. These behaviors range from anxious or shy behavior at the submissive node to aggressive, angry, critical, or firm behavior at the hostility node. In between these two nodes, distrustful behaviors such as being wary, skeptical, bitter, or suspicious reflect a blend of hostility and weakness.

Finally, quadrant 4 ranges from the hostile or aggressive node to the dominance or power node. This quadrant includes behavior that ranges from frank, critical, or aggressive at the hostile node, through the middle range of competitive and assertive behavior, and back up to the starting point of confident and independent behavior at the dominant node.

Leary further divided the four quadrants of the circumplex into 16 interpersonal themes or modes. His circumplex model included ratings for the intensity of behavior and feelings, such as the continuum of being irritated, angry, furious, and enraged. The circumplex also included ratings for the adaptive-maladaptive quality of each type of response, such as assert-attack, obey-submit, lead-dominate, or support-pity. Much of this complex model is beyond the scope of this discussion, but the circumplex does aid the therapist by providing a schema for picturing the client's recurrent interpersonal behavior. Below, we will see how this schema for describing the range of interpersonal behavior can be used to help conceptualize client dynamics.

Using the Circumplex to Conceptualize Clients

How can the circumplex model of interpersonal behavior be used to help therapists conceptualize their clients? The model is a conceptual aid to help therapists organize their perceptions and observations of client behavior. The circumplex does this by (1) clarifying the client's predominant interpersonal style and (2) identifying the types of responses that each interpersonal style tends to *elicit* from others. Knowing this will help therapists identify the client's generic conflict and understand how the client's interpersonal style is used to defend against his generic conflict.

The Circumplex Reveals Interpersonal Styles. The first way the circumplex model can help therapists conceptualize clients is by clarifying their predominant interpersonal styles. Thinking about the client's behavior in terms of how it would be mapped on the circumplex may reveal important patterns. Oftentimes, the client's behavior reflects a repetitive interpersonal style that is coded onto only one or perhaps two of the four quadrants. To illustrate, we will return to the case study of Peter, the moving-toward client in the last chapter.

If an observer sat behind a one-way mirror and coded everything Peter said to his therapist during the first two months of therapy, the vast majority of what Peter said and did would be rated near the affiliation node in quadrants 1 and 2. As a general lifestyle, Peter was helpful. He sympathized, agreed, and cooperated with people. In therapy, Peter tried to understand his girlfriend's infidelity and win his supervisor's approval. In contrast, virtually none of his behavior would have been coded in quadrants 3 or 4. Peter was never appropriately critical, forthright, assertive, angry, skeptical, or any of the other behaviors represented in the left half of the circumplex. Like Peter, most clients will try to reduce their anxiety and avoid their generic conflict by adopting a repetitive interpersonal coping style.

In this way, the circumplex can be used as a conceptual aid to help therapists identify the client's predominant interpersonal style. Just as important, it can also help therapists *identify the types of feelings and behaviors that the client systematically eschews.* That is, the unexpressed quadrants of the circumplex orient the therapist to conflict areas that need to be addressed in therapy. For example, the therapist would want to explore why Peter was not angry with his girlfriend or did not assertively set limits with his practicum instructor regarding how much critical feedback he could incorporate at one time. As clients improve in therapy, the range of feelings and interpersonal responses they can express should expand to include the entire range of the circumplex.

The Circumplex Reveals Eliciting Behaviors. The second way therapists can use the circumplex to conceptualize their clients is to observe the type of responses that the client's interpersonal style tends to elicit from others. Clients have developed their interpersonal style to systematically elicit certain desired responses from others and to systematically preclude responses that arouse their generic conflict. For example, Peter's moving-toward style will usually elicit from others similar responses near the affiliation node. His pleasing interpersonal style will also discourage angry-confrontive responses from quadrants 3 and 4 that arouse anxiety for him.

Eliciting behaviors serve to defend other types of clients against their generic conflicts as well. For example, clients who predominantly present quadrant 2 and 3 responses near the submissive node may be shy, self-effacing, passive, or dependent. These types of responses tend to elicit quadrant 1 and 4 responses near the dominant node. That is, these shy or self-effacing clients tend to elicit guidance, directives, or leadership from others they interact with. Similarly, a moving-against client who is frequently angry or dominating may sometimes elicit symmetrical, challenging-combative quadrant 4 responses from others, but they are more likely to elicit complementary quadrant 2 and 3 responses near the submissive node.

How does identifying the interpersonal responses that the client tends to elicit from others help the therapist recognize the client's generic conflict? Again, the case study of Peter provides a good illustration. Peter's moving-toward interpersonal style tended to elicit approval, acceptance, kindness, and trust from others. If Peter's therapist had reflexively responded to what Peter's interpersonal style elicited from him and others, Peter would not have changed in therapy. That is, if the therapist had merely supported Peter and met his need for approval—as Peter had always elicited from others—Peter would have only reenacted in therapy the same rising-above defense that he had used throughout his life. Instead, Peter's therapist *confronted* his moving-toward style and focused on it as a part of Peter's problem that needed to be addressed in therapy.

Eventually, the therapist helped Peter understand how his fixed interpersonal style of moving toward others served to protect him from his generic conflict. This fixed interpersonal style elicited from others the approval, support, and nurturance that Peter missed as a child. In addition, his pleasing style discouraged the critical, angry, or rejecting responses that were so threatening for him. As Peter mastered his developmental conflict in therapy, he became less in need of compulsively winning others' approval. Peter was able to expand his interpersonal repertoire and utilize quadrant 3 and 4 responses when they were appropriate as well. Once he no longer needed others to regard him as ever kind, loving, and gentle, Peter could also become appropriately assertive, frank, independent, and confident for the first time.

Thus, the therapist must be aware of what the client systematically tends to elicit from others, and hypothesize how this interpersonal strategy protects the client from his central conflict. In addition, *therapists must attend to the feelings and reactions that the client tends to elicit in them.* In fact, this is one of the therapist's most important sources of information about the client. If therapists can observe what the client elicits in them, it will inform therapists about the nature of the client's conflict and interpersonal defenses, and about how the client's conflict is being brought into the therapeutic relationship. For example, therapists must generate working hypotheses to understand why a particular client elicits certain responses in them such as reassurance, disinterest, competition, confusion, irritability, nurturance, and so forth. The therapist's task, then, is to keep from reflexively responding to what the client is eliciting. Instead, the therapist must try to find a different response that does not reenact clients' conflicts, but helps clients recognize their interpersonal coping style and understand how it serves to protect them from their generic conflict.

TRACK THE CLIENT'S ANXIETY

The second interpersonal factor to help therapists conceptualize their clients is to *track the client's anxiety*. Although the subjective experience of anxiety is always uncomfortable, and may be intensely painful, anxiety is the therapist's ally. Anxiety serves as a signal to help the therapist identify and focus on the client's central conflict. The therapist does not understand the client's problem or what needs to occur in therapy to resolve it until the therapist understands what makes the client anxious. That is, in order to understand the client's generic conflict, the therapist first must be able to understand why certain situations or interactions make the client anxious and how the client has learned to defend against this anxiety.

This section provides a four-step sequence that therapists can use to track the client's anxiety to clarify the nature and source of the client's conflicts. The sequence (1) identifies manifest and covert signs of client anxiety, (2) approaches directly all signs of client anxiety, (3) observes the issues being discussed and the interpersonal process occurring between the therapist and the client that precipitate the client's anxiety, and (4) focuses the client inward to explore the source and meaning of her anxiety.

Identify Signs of Client Anxiety

Clients will become anxious in the session when the material they are discussing touches upon their generic conflicts. As we saw in Chapter 7, clients develop complex interpersonal coping strategies and defense mechanisms to ward off the anxiety associated with their generic conflicts. If the therapist can identify the interpersonal transactions, subjective needs, or situational demands that make the client anxious, the therapist is better prepared to recognize the underlying conflict that has triggered the client's anxiety. Thus, throughout the course of therapy, therapists are continually asking themselves: What makes this client anxious? When does she become uncomfortable? Where do her insecurities lie? In order to conceptualize the underlying conflict that is troubling the client, the therapist must actively attend to the anxiety (or anxiety equivalents) that the client manifests. For example, the therapist must be alert for signs indicating that the client is now experiencing something that is making her anxious. There are a thousand different ways for clients to express their anxiety, such as nervous laughter, nail biting, hand gesticulation, agitated movement, stuttering, hair pulling, speech blockage, and so on. These anxiety equivalents will be expressed in endlessly varied ways across clients and therapists will have to learn how each particular client tends to express her anxiety. The first step in tracking the client's anxiety, however, is simply to observe when the client becomes anxious.

Approach the Client's Anxiety Directly

In Chapter 5, we suggested that therapists approach and draw out the feelings that emerge for clients in the session. In a similarly forthright manner, the therapist should also approach client anxiety about an issue being discussed or about what is going on between the therapist and client at that moment. As before, the therapist can focus clients on their experience in an open-ended way (e.g., "What are you feeling right now?") or by labeling the anxiety more directly (e.g., "Something is making you anxious right now. What do you think that is?").

By focusing clients on their anxiety *as they are experiencing it*, and inviting them to explore it further, the therapist is leading clients closer to the conflict that is the source of their problems. This is why clients are often ambivalent about the therapist's request to explore their anxiety. On the one hand, clients may welcome the opportunity to share their anxiety with the therapist—and the confusion and pain that often follows closely behind. On the other hand, clients also recognize that approaching their anxiety will bring them closer to their underlying conflict, which is threatening for them to experience. As a result, therapists can anticipate that if they approach their clients' anxiety, it may intensify their anxiety and arouse their resistance.

As we discussed in Chapter 3, the therapist must respond to the client's resistance by exploring why it is threatening or dangerous for the client to approach her anxiety. This approach will be far more effective than ignoring the client's resistance or trying to push through it and persuading the client to talk about the conflict. Before the therapist and client can address the conflict itself, they must explore why it is threatening for the client to share it with the therapist. As emphasized before, the therapist must honor the client's resistance. The therapist does this by trying to understand the original, aversive experiences with others that led the client to be resistant in this particular way, and then providing the client with a different and more satisfying response than she has received in the past.

Observe What Precipitates the Client's Anxiety

To review, the therapist first observes when the client is anxious, and then helps the client focus more directly on the experience. At the same time, the therapist must also carry out a third task. The therapist must try to recognize (1) what issue was just being discussed or (2) what type of interaction was occurring with the therapist that *precipitated* the client's anxiety. If the therapist can identify what has just occurred to make the client anxious, the therapist will be better able to identify the underlying conflict that has generated the anxiety. We must examine this precipitant closely.

Clients will be able to discuss many different issues comfortably with the therapist. When clients enter a topic area that makes them anxious, however, the therapist must try to identify the issue or theme that has just precipitated the anxiety. Was the client just talking about sex, death, money, success, divorce, inadequacy. . . ? What is the issue that seems to be disturbing for the client? Answering this question will show the therapist what issues are linked to the client's central conflict and need to be explored further. As we will see below, the therapist can help the client explore this more effectively if the therapist has already formulated working hypotheses about the possible conflicts that may be generating the anxiety.

The second way to understand the potential meaning of the client's anxiety is to hypothesize how the interaction occurring between the therapist and the client may have triggered the client's anxiety. That is, the interpersonal process transpiring between the therapist and client may be reenacting a historical conflict for the client. For example, the therapist may observe that as the client became anxious, the therapist was:

＊ Expressing confusion about what was going on in the session at that point. The client then became anxious, perhaps because his volatile, alcoholic father would act confused and then start insulting him and attacking him for something that went wrong.

or

＊ The client had just made an important insight and the therapist acknowledged her achievement. The client then became anxious, perhaps because she believed that she would always have to be so insightful and perform so well, as a parent had always expected of her.

or

＊ The therapist had just been supportive, and perhaps the client felt anxious because strings had always been attached to what he had been given in the past. The client may have become concerned that the therapist would make him pay for his support in some way, just as his parent always used to do.

The therapist should generate working hypotheses such as these about how the current therapist-client interaction may have aroused a historical conflict for the client. These hypotheses can then be used to help the therapist and client explore the client's anxiety and understand the underlying conflict that is the source of it.

Focus Clients Inward to Explore Their Anxiety

Restating this sequence, the therapist is alert for signs of client anxiety and approaches it whenever it occurs. Simultaneously, the therapist tries to identify what precipitated the client's anxiety and begins to generate working hypotheses about the underlying conflict that is the source of it. Finally, the therapist must focus the client inward to explore what the anxiety means. If the therapist can work through the client's resistance to approach his anxiety, and help the client express the thoughts, feelings, and memories that are associated with the anxiety, the client's internal conflict will usually emerge. The following dialogue illustrates this process.

Client:
You know, this sounds awful to say, but I don't think my mother really wants me to change very much in therapy. I don't think she's a bad person or anything, but I do think I'm getting better, and she's sort of bothered by that.
Therapist:
How so?
Client:
Well, I haven't been depressed for awhile now, and I've actually been pretty happy and outgoing the last month or so. Maybe it's just coincidence, but it seems that as I've gotten better, my mother has withdrawn and been harder to talk to. I think that might have gone on between us for a long time.
Therapist:
Yes, I think so too. You know, you have been understanding some very difficult and important things in the past few weeks. It's a pleasure to see you doing so well.
Client:
[fidgets, begins picking at her nail, and starts talking about another topic]
Therapist:
Did something just make you feel uncomfortable?
Client:
I don't know, how much time is left?

Therapist:
What are we talking about, or what is going on between us right now, that is making you anxious?

Client:
[long pause] I think I'm afraid you're going to go away or something.

Therapist:
Uh-huh. Well, we were just talking about how your mother goes away when you are feeling stronger, and I just told you that I thought you were doing very good work in here.

Client:
Yeah, but you're not going to stay with me either if I get better.

Therapist:
What do you mean?

Client:
If I get better, then we stop. I won't be able to come see you anymore, and then I won't have my mother, or you or anybody!

Therapist:
I think the conflict that you and I are having together right now is central to many of your problems. To be strong and happy and independent, you feel you have to be alone. And if you want to be close to others, then you have learned that you have to be sad and depressed and needy. I think you have had to struggle with that awful choice all of your life.

Client:
[crying] Yeah, maybe I have.

In this way, tracking the client's anxiety can help the therapist conceptualize the client's generic conflict. It can also lead the therapist and client to the internal conflict that is the basis of the client's problems. We will return to this issue and explore it further in the following section.

THE AMBIVALENT NATURE OF CONFLICT

The Two-Sided Structure of Clients' Conflicts

The third interpersonal factor for conceptualizing client dynamics is to recognize the ambivalent nature of conflict. There are two sides to the client's generic conflict and therapists must respond to both sides before problems can be resolved. What is meant by "both sides" of the client's conflict? The word *conflict* refers to two opposing impulses. Often, therapists fail to recognize both sides of the conflict that underlies clients' problems and only respond to one side of the conflict. Therapists can better understand their clients' problems when they can identify the two conflicting needs, wishes, or impulses that comprise the conflict. Recognizing the two-sided structure of conflicts will enable therapists to respond to the *ambivalence* that has immobilized the client and prevented change from occurring.

Colloquial expressions convey the two-sided nature of conflict. For example, we often say that someone is "stuck between a rock and a hard place," that someone has grabbed "both horns of the dilemma," or that a difficult relationship is "like a two-edged sword." These expressions capture the push-pull nature of conflict—that you are "damned if you do and damned if you don't." Below, two previous case studies are reexamined in order to highlight the two-sided conflict that comprises the client's problem. Once the therapist is able to recognize the structure of the conflict and articulate the ambivalent feelings that result from having this conflict, seemingly irrational and self-defeating behavior becomes understandable.

The young adult client in the sample therapist-client dialogue that ended the previous section wanted to get better—to end her chronic depression, become more outgoing and involved with friends, and find a career path that she could pursue. Until the last few weeks, however, the client had not been able to accomplish any of these goals. Although she had expressed these wishes for many years, she could not follow through and realize them. For example, she rarely initiated activities with peers and often declined the invitations she received from others. She repeatedly enrolled in college but would eventually lose interest and drop out after one or two semesters. Without recognizing the two-sided conflict that immobilized this client, her behavior seems irrational.

On the surface, it does not make sense that a client such as this will not do what she says she wants to do unless she really is just lazy, sick, masochistic, unmotivated or receiving too many secondary gains from being home and depressed. Therapists and others in clients' lives often attribute such pejorative labels to clients when their underlying conflict is not understood. Clients' contradictory behavior does make sense, however, once the two-sided, push-pull nature of their conflict is recognized.

In the preceeding dialogue, the client and therapist had just brought into focus how the client is immobilized between two aversive consequences that prevent her from resolving her problem. On the one hand, she wants to grow up and have her own life, friends, career, independence, and identity. But, at the same time, she also feels a need to be close to her mother and feel her mother's continuing support and availability. The client's conflict is that her mother will withdraw and induce guilt if she starts to pursue her own goals and succeed with friends, in school, or with life in general. Unable to break this "tie that binds," the client repeatedly fails and has to return home. Only upon her return home and failure to emancipate does her mother again become available to her. Having to sacrifice her own independence to secure the support she also needs, the client becomes depressed over her inability to do what she wants and over her internalized resentment toward her mother's binding control. An informative discussion of these family dynamics is found in Jay Haley's book, Leaving Home.

After a few months, the same cycle will be reenacted again. That is, the frustrated client will start to act on her own need for autonomy, seek peer contacts, and reenroll in school. Just as before, however, her mother will withdraw and the client will not be able to emancipate without her mother's support. In a few months, the client will return home again feeling hopeless and a failure. Completing the cycle, the mother will again become comforting and supportive of the daughter in her defeat. This type of cyclic transactional pattern can continue for decades, until both sides of the client's conflict are made overt and worked through in therapy.

Another illustration of conflict was provided by Jean, the client in Chapter 5. Recall that she was the client who began to change only when she experienced her conflicted feelings with the therapist, rather than merely talking about them. Without recognizing her underlying conflict, Jean's behavior also seems irrational and self-defeating. Jean's primary symptom was her continuous involvement with selfish, demanding, and abusive men. Jean complained that she felt unhappy, used, and afraid in these destructive relationships but she was unable to disengage from them. She remained in the relationship no matter how bad things got for her. Paradoxically, when the man decided to leave her she would feel panicked, not relieved, and would quickly become reinvolved in a similar type of relationship. This pattern had continued throughout her twenties and thirties, and finally led her to seek help for her agitated depression.

At the time Jean entered therapy, she was applying the same pejorative labels to herself of masochistic and stupid that were noted earlier. Jean's friends also described her as crazy and hopeless for continually reinvolving herself in the same type of destructive relationship. As before, however, Jean's seemingly irrational and self-destructive behavior does make sense once the two-sided, push-pull nature of her conflict is recognized.

For years, Jean had said she wanted to be able to meet her own needs, set limits and say no sometimes, and leave relationships that were not supportive. But, year after year, she continued to meet a man's need at the expense of her own well-being. She could not say no and set self-preservative limits, even though she had learned the skills to do so in assertion training classes. Nor would she leave relationships in which she was dominated, manipulated, and exploited. Next we will examine the conflict that prevented Jean from doing what she wanted for herself and that makes her seemingly irrational behavior understandable.

A countervailing force covertly opposed all of Jean's attempts to change. As soon as Jean started to act on her own needs, set limits, or try to leave a relationship she felt cold, small, and alone to the point of panic. In other words, she was gripped by intense separation anxieties whenever she made any movement toward her own individuation. Thus, as soon as Jean started to do what she wanted for herself these painful feelings were activated. Her only means of abating these separation anxieties and feeling related to others again was to retreat to the familiar dependent/victim role.

This paralyzing conflict developed in Jean's family of origin. Growing up, Jean was an extremely parentified child. She was expected to respond only to her parents' needs and she was harshly rebuffed or painfully shamed for expressing her own "selfish will." Throughout her childhood, she received so much criticism from her parents, and so little emotional support, that she desperately needed whatever thin threads of approval she could earn by devoting herself to them. Whenever she tried to express her own wishes or ask for what she would like, she was told that she was selfish and demanding. As a little girl, Jean clearly was left starving for the approval she could not receive but desperately needed. Afraid of receiving further rejection from her parents, she was eager to serve them and comply with whatever they asked of her. Thus, as a child, Jean became a captive of her own need for relatedness that she could neither relinquish nor fulfill. In her book *Prisoners of Childhood*, Alice Miller elucidates this type of poignant conflict.

Ultimately, in order to maintain some minimal sense of relatedness to others, Jean *identified* with her parent's critical rejection of her. That is, she internalized her parents' contempt for her and began hating herself for being "bad" and "selfish." As an adult, she recapitulated the feelings and experiences of her childhood by selecting punitive, selfish men who confirmed and fostered her own internalized feelings of self-loathing and worthlessness.

With this developmental background in mind, it is easier to see how Jean's seemingly irrational behavior does in fact make sense. Her only sense of herself as a person, and her only means of being in relationship, is to meet another person's need. When she finally becomes depleted by this role and begins to respond to her own needs (i.e., set limits, ask for what she wants, leave a hurtful relationship), panic results. Her separation anxieties, unmet dependency needs, and self-hatred becomes overwhelming, just as they were for her when she was a child. In order to diminish the panic, she becomes connected to others again by retreating to the abusive relationship and reenacting the same pattern. She again responds to the boyfriend's demeaning demands and suffocates her own needs, feelings, and life. The same cycle will soon start again, however, as her frustration and resentment over having her own life denied begin to reemerge. Temporarily, she will start to respond to herself and her own needs, only to be immobilized again by the same separation anxieties and guilt.

A cyclic dynamic such as this is difficult to change. As Jean illustrates, however, change is possible if two things occur. First, Jean began to change this pattern when she experienced a relationship with the therapist in which her own needs were listened to, responded to, and valued for the first time. This was difficult to provide, however, because Jean was adept at rejecting the care and concern that she desperately wanted from the therapist. Second, the therapist was also able to help Jean understand the two-sided structure of the conflict that had bewildered and immobilized her throughout her life. Understanding the conflict helped Jean change by allowing her to feel more compassionate toward herself and her own predicament, and more accepting of the choices and compromises that she had been forced to make throughout her life in order to survive. This acceptance, in turn, helped her to disengage from her own self-hatred and value herself and her own needs for the first time. Soon after this internal change occurred, Jean became involved with a supportive and responsive man for the first time.

Ambivalent Feelings

The two clients above illustrate the push-pull nature of conflict—that there are two opposing forces that the client has not been able to reconcile. Therapists cannot conceptualize the client's dynamics until they can articulate "both horns of the client's dilemma" and recognize its two-sided structure. In addition to framing the client's problem as a conflict, therapists must be able to *respond to the opposing feelings that accompany both sides of the client's conflict*. Too often, therapists are ineffective because they only respond to one-half of the client's ambivalent feelings. The case vignette below illustrates that the client cannot change unless the therapist acknowledges both sides of the client's ambivalent feelings.

Marie is a twenty-five-year-old female client. During the course of therapy Marie discovered how angry she was at her mother. To this day, her mother expected Marie to be perfect, insisted that Marie never had any problems, and always needed Marie to be happy. In therapy, Marie began to realize how much she resented her mother for denying so many of her true feelings and for having so many expectations of how she *should* be. Marie's therapist resonated with her new awareness and actively supported her anger.

At first, it was liberating for Marie to be able to express her long-suppressed anger. She was both excited and relieved to realize that she no longer needed to fulfill her mother's unrealistic expectations. This good feeling was short-lived, however. In the following weeks, Marie's new-found freedom gave way to a growing sense of futility and pessimism. The therapist thought that Marie must be guilty about defying her mother's expectations and was depressed because she was defensively turning the anger she felt toward her mother back on herself.

While repeatedly offering this interpretation, the therapist continued to draw out and encourage Marie's anger. Moving in a different direction than the therapist, however, Marie began to share fond memories about her mother and recalled with longing special times they had spent together making cookies after school. The therapist was not very responsive to Marie's positive feelings toward her mother, however. The therapist thought that Marie's positive feelings were part of denying her anger toward her mother, avoiding the conflicts in their relationship, continuing to idealize her mother and thereby remaining committed to meeting her mother's expectations.

Marie's therapist only recognized one side of her ambivalence and failed to respond to the feelings on both sides of her conflict. Yes, Marie was angry at her mother and these suppressed feelings needed to be explored, expressed, and validated. But, at the same time, Marie also knew that her mother had offered her many fine things as a parent and she did not want to forego the good things they had shared. Marie's conflict was not knowing how she could keep the good things she had experienced with her mother without having to internalize the problematic aspects of their relationship as well. Thus, on the one hand, Marie wanted to reject the unrealistic demands to be perfect and happy that her mother placed on her. But, at the same time, Marie became depressed when it seemed like the only way to do this was to give up her identification with her mother altogether. Rightly so, Marie did not want to lose her most important female role model and risk losing the feminine parts of herself as well.

Therapy stagnated as Marie remained depressed so her therapist sought consultation from a colleague. The colleague quickly recognized both sides of Marie's conflict and encouraged the therapist to allow Marie to simultaneously have contradictory feelings of appreciation and anger toward her mother. As a result of this consultation, the therapist began responding to the other side of Marie's feelings as well. For example, the therapist soon responded, "You feel two different ways toward your mother at the same time. You're angry at her for expecting you to be perfect, but you also treasure many of the fond times you've had together. Tell me about both your angry and your loving feelings toward her." As the therapist encouraged Marie to explore and express both sides of her feelings, her depression lifted. Marie began to clarify what parts of her mother she wanted to keep and make a part of herself, and what parts of her mother and her mother's expectations she wanted to discard. This process of differentiation also allowed Marie to clarify which issues she wanted to confront and try to change in her current relationship with her mother and which issues she preferred to let go of and simply accommodate herself to. Marie spurted forward in therapy as soon as the therapist helped her come to terms with both sides of her ambivalent feelings. Therapy was soon successfully terminated as Marie better integrated parts of her own identify as a woman and initiated a rapprochement with her mother.

In sum, clients change when the therapist recognizes the two-sided structure of their conflicts and responds to both sides of their ambivalent feelings.

TRANSFERENCE REACTIONS REVEAL CLIENT CONFLICTS

The final interpersonal factor for conceptualizing clients is *transference reactions*. Transference is one of the most important concepts in psychotherapy. Therapists use this term in different ways, however, and over the years competing definitions have evolved. For some, transference has come to refer to all of the thoughts, feelings, and perceptions that the client has toward the therapist. For others, transference just refers to those reactions that have been inappropriately displaced onto the therapist from someone in the client's past. In other words, transference occurs when emotional reactions that actually belong to a person in the client's past are inaccurately *transferred* to the present relationship with the therapist. Such transference reactions systematically distort the client's perceptions of and reactions to the therapist. Therapists can use transference reactions both to conceptualize client dynamics and to help clients resolve their conflicts within the therapeutic relationship.

Transference Is an Everyday Occurrence

To some degree, everybody transfers in their daily lives and everyday interactions. That is, everyone systematically misperceives others based on previous learning that is overgeneralized to the present situation. For example, imagine that a university professor is standing in front of a large lecture hall about to convene the first class meeting of Psych. 100. Before he has even begun to lecture, many students will be transferring expectations from significant male authority figures in their own lives onto the professor. Thus, eighteen-year-old Mary sits in the first row of the lecture hall and looks up to the professor admiringly. Just as she still somewhat idealizes her father, Mary similarly respects the middle-aged professor even though she actually knows little about him.

In contrast, from high up and far away in the last row of seats, Joe looks down on the professor disparagingly. Joe anticipates that the professor does not know as much as he thinks he does and that he will not be very well prepared for class. Just like his own father who always had to be right and on top, this professor was probably going to try and get away with putting a lot over on them in class. Joe had already decided that this "know-it-all" professor was not going to get away with much if he could help it.

Hopefully, the professor will be aware of the fact that people tend to transfer onto authority figures who hold power and onto those who have high public visibility (e.g., movie *stars*, sports *heroes*, and political *leaders*). If the professor is not sensitized to transference reactions, however, his self-confidence as a teacher will take a roller-coaster ride this semester. One day, Mary will follow him out of class and tell him what an interesting lecture he gave, while the next day, Joe will drop his books when he starts to speak and demand that he defend half of what he says.

Transference reactions such as Mary and Joe have toward the professor are everyday occurrences. The more conflicted or disturbed one is, however, the more one distorts the current reality by inaccurately displacing reactions from the past onto the present. For example, Joe and Mary have strong initial reactions to the professor that are based on little real-life experience with him. If Joe and Mary function fairly well psychologically, they will become more realistic in their assessment of the professor as they have more exposure to his teaching. In contrast, the more Mary idealizes her father and the more Joe disparages his father, the more likely it is that they will not be able to perceive the strengths and limitations of the professor accurately. Instead, they will maintain their initial perceptions and expectations despite the fact that they are inaccurate or overdetermined.

Just as transference reactions are more intense and pervasive the more disturbed one is, transference reactions are also more likely to occur in emotion-laden situations. For example, transference reactions are especially pronounced when two people are falling in love. In this regard, many married couples recall their courtship as the happiest time in their lives. The couple is so elated during this time because each member systematically misperceives the partner as someone who can fulfill unmet developmental needs and make one feel lovable, capable, or worthy when one has not felt this way before. This romantic period is usually short-lived, however. The transference projections soon break down as they both realize that the partner cannot satisfy all of their original needs as they had hoped. If the underlying unmet needs and resulting transference distortions have been especially strong, it will often result in dashed dreams and angry feelings of betrayal. In contrast, if the transference distortions of the partner have not been extreme, they can readily be shed to allow a more realistic and enduring relationship to develop. Relinquishing these transference distortions of the new spouse is the major psychological task of early marriage.

In therapy, the therapist can systematically utilize the client's transference reactions to better understand the client's conflicts. In fact, *one of the most effective ways to learn about the client's central conflicts is to note how the client perceives and reacts to the therapist.* Almost without exception, the client's conflicts will be reenacted in the therapeutic relationship. If the therapist is alert for when these transference reactions occur, they provide an invaluable tool for conceptualizing the client's conflicts.

Utilizing Transference Reactions to Conceptualize Clients

Some therapists are uninterested in the client's transference reactions because they do not see them occurring in therapy. The therapist will often miss the client's transference reactions, and the important information they provide, unless the therapist actively attempts to draw them out. How can the therapist elicit the client's transference reactions so they can be utilized in therapy? Two ways of accomplishing this are suggested below.

First, the therapist must ask the client to express whatever she is feeling toward the therapist. That is, throughout the course of treatment, the therapist should repeatedly ask the following types of questions:

What are you feeling toward me right now?

When you find yourself thinking about therapy, what kind of thoughts or feelings do you have about me?

As you were driving to our session today, how did you feel about coming to see me?

Second, the therapist should also explore what the client projects onto the therapist. That is, the therapist should ask:

What do you think I am feeling toward you as you tell me that?

How do you think I am going to respond to you if you do that?

What do you think I expect you to do in that situation?

These two types of questioning will make the client's transference reactions overt and allow the therapist to work with them in therapy. As the therapist draws out the client's subjective reactions toward the therapist, and elicits what the client projects onto the therapist, information about the client's central conflicts is revealed. In Chapter 4, we discussed how adopting an internal focus will uncover new conflicts that would not have surfaced otherwise. In the same way, exploring clients' reactions toward the therapist will also reveal new issues that need to be dealt with in treatment. Furthermore, this approach will also show how the same problems that clients are having with others, and that they originally experienced in formative family relationships, are being recapitulated in the therapeutic relationship. Thus, transference reactions reveal clients' generic conflicts and, as we will see in the following chapters, provide an opportunity to resolve them in the therapeutic relationship.

In addition to clarifying conflicts, transference reactions also reflect the fact that the client's feelings are trustworthy. The client's emotional reactions may not make sense at first because they often do not fit the current situation in which they are aroused. As a result, many clients experience their emotions as irrational and do not trust their own internal processes. This is especially likely to occur in the therapeutic relationship in which clients have many emotional reactions toward the therapist that seem uncalled for, exaggerated, inappropriate, or unrealistic.

The client's emotional reactions in general, and toward the therapist in particular, are not irrational. Many times they do not fit the present circumstances, but they do make sense when they can be placed within their original learning context. That is, real life events have legitimately caused clients to feel the way they do. If the therapist helps clients trace back their feelings to their original learning source, they will prove to be an *appropriate* reaction to someone else in another time and place. Although this may seem paradoxical at first, *transference reactions ultimately reveal that the client's feelings always make sense.*

In sum, clients transfer emotional reactions from past formative relationships onto the current relationship with the therapist. Helping clients understand where their emotional reactions originally stem from is a powerful intervention that leaves clients feeling in control of themselves. Finding that their feelings do make sense, even though in another time and place, is validating and empowers clients. Furthermore, making this connection between the past and the present is one way to leave the past behind so that new ways of responding can emerge.

CLOSING

In this chapter we examined four dimensions of clients' current interpersonal functioning: the range of interpersonal behavior and feel-

ings they encompass and the types of interpersonal responses they tend
to elicit from others, tracking clients' anxiety, the two-sided structure of
clients' conflicts, and transference reactions. This discussion may help
therapists better understand their clients' self-defeating or contradictory
behavior and their seemingly irrational feelings. In turn, this greater
understanding may enable therapists to be more patient and compassionate toward the conflicts with which clients struggle. These interpersonal
factors, together with the familial perspective and conceptual model
presented in the previous two chapters, will enable therapists to better
understand and intervene with the problems clients present. With these
conceptual guidelines in mind, we will now return to process and relationship issues and examine how the therapeutic relationship can be
utilized to resolve clients' problems.

SUGGESTIONS FOR FURTHER READING

1. Sullivan originally emphasized how clients' anxiety served to inform the
   therapist about their conflicts. His classic primer on interviewing, *The Psychiatric Interview* (New York: W.W. Norton, 1970), is still an illuminating clinical
   guide. Sullivan's interpersonal theory is presented in his book, *An Interpersonal
   Theory of Psychiatry* (New York: W.W. Norton, 1968). Both of these works
   are recommended to interpersonally-oriented therapists.

2. Alice Miller's book, *Prisoners of Childhood* (New York: Basic Books, 1981), is also
   highly recommended. It will sensitize therapists to the developmental arrests
   and internalized conflicts that interfere with adult functioning.

3. Chapter two of Jay Haley's book, *Leaving Home* (New York: McGraw-Hill,
   1980), elucidates the family dynamics and structural family relationships that
   impede individuation and emancipation for certain adult clients.

PART FOUR

Resolution and Change

9

An Interpersonal Solution

CONCEPTUAL OVERVIEW

Once the therapist has conceptualized the client's dynamics, how does change occur? Is the client's generic conflict resolved through an emotional catharsis of childhood traumas or from illuminating insights delved from the past? No. Valuable information about client dynamics can be obtained from familial experience but a consistent focus on past experiences will not produce change. In fact, this often serves only to defend clients against the anxiety of confronting current conflicts. In order to change, the past can be brought to bear on current problems but clients must enact a resolution of their conflicts in their current relationship with the therapist.

If the fulcrum of change is the current relationship with the therapist, what must the therapist do to help clients change? Does the therapist need to provide clients with "the love they never received?" Is the therapist's role to "reparent" the client? No, the therapist can never satisfy clients' unmet developmental needs, although this fantasy will be activated for many clients. Instead, the therapist has a more modest, but attainable, goal. The therapist must provide a relationship that allows the client to undergo as an adult those feelings, needs, and experiences that were too threatening to confront as a child. When this occurs, and therapists provide clients with a more satisfying response to their conflicts than they have received in the past, enduring change occurs.

Furthermore, the client's developmental conflicts are not just talked about abstractly in therapy—they are brought into the present by being reenacted in the therapeutic relationship. In order to change, the therapist and client must not recapitulate the client's conflict in their interpersonal process, as so commonly occurs. Instead, they must mutually work out a resolution to the client's conflict in their real-life relationship. If this corrective emotional experience occurs, the therapist will be able to help the client generalize this emotional relearning to other arenas in the client's life in which the same conflicts are being enacted. Conversely, if the therapist and client only talk about issues and dynamics, but their interpersonal process does not enact a resolution of the conflicts they are discussing, change will not occur. The purpose of this chapter is to clarify this process dimension and show how the therapeutic relationship can be used to resolve client conflicts.

CHAPTER ORGANIZATION

The first section of this chapter addresses how the interpersonal process that therapists enact with clients can be used to resolve clients' conflicts. The first part of this section reviews the course of therapy up to this point in treatment and summarizes three ways in which client conflicts are brought into the treatment setting and reenacted with the therapist. The primary focus of this chapter then shows how therapists can use the process dimension to help clients resolve these conflicts. Four case studies illustrate this approach.

In the second section, a set of guidelines are given to help therapists enact an interpersonal process that does not recapitulate the client's conflict in the therapeutic relationship. An effective, middle ground of appropriate involvement is described that therapists can establish with their clients. This optimal interpersonal distance will help keep therapists from becoming inappropriately overinvolved or underinvolved with their clients and, thereby, from recapitulating the client's conflict in the therapy relationship.

THE INTERPERSONAL PROCESS MUST ENACT A RESOLUTION OF THE CLIENT'S CONFLICT

Client Conflicts Are Reenacted in the Therapeutic Relationship

Whereas the previous chapters in Part III focused on conceptualizing client dynamics, we now return to intervention strategies. Before going on to examine how therapists can use the process dimension to resolve conflicts, we will look at a brief overview of the course of therapy. This review serves to introduce the next stage of therapy, and to place it within the overall context of the developmentally unfolding course of therapy.

Clients have unmet developmental needs that result in feelings that are too painful to be tolerated and integrated. Symptoms and problems develop as clients try to gain control of these emotions by manipulating or controlling their environment. The therapist's task is to identify these underlying conflicts and draw clients' attention to the compromise solutions they have adopted to avoid their internal conflicts. The therapist must then provide a supportive holding environment that allows clients to reexperience and integrate these threatening emotions rather than continuing to defend against them.

During the course of therapy, the therapist encourages clients to bring up for discussion the issues they feel are most important. The therapist's primary role is not to give advice, explain, reassure, self-disclose, or focus on the behavior or motives of others. Instead, the therapist follows the client's lead, and listens for patterns, themes, and feelings that recur throughout the material she presents. The therapist continues to focus the client inward, responds to the client's affect, and works to keep the client an active participant in the change process. As the therapist learns more about each client, the therapist will be able to conceptualize the generic conflicts and interpersonal coping styles that are expressed in the different issues and concerns that each client presents.

The therapist will be able to use this conceptual formulation to provide structure and direction to the course of therapy. For example, the therapist will be able to point out when and how clients employ their interpersonal coping strategy to rise above their conflicts. The therapist will also be able to help clients become aware of how they block their own needs and feelings by responding to themselves in the same way that others orginally responded to them. The therapist will also be able to help clients explore why they become anxious at a particular time, what types of responses they tend to elicit from others, and how they systematically avoid a particular interpersonal mode or affect. In these ways, the therapist helps clients become aware of their underlying conflicts and the maladaptive ways they have learned to cope with them. Although this conceptual awareness will be an important part of helping clients change, something more is needed.

At the same time the therapist and client explore the *content* of the client's dynamics, the therapist and client will also play out these same dynamics in their *interpersonal process*. As stated before, the client and therapist don't just talk about conflicts in therapy, they actually relive them in the therapeutic relationship. This occurs in three ways.

First, *transference reactions* bring the client's generic conflict into the current relationship with the therapist. As the client's unmet developmental needs begin to emerge in therapy, the client will become concerned that the therapist has been responding, or is going to respond, in the same frustrating way that significant others have in the past. These fears and misperceptions of the therapist predictably occur, and therapy will reach an impasse until the therapist can differentiate her own current response from the frustrating responses that the client has received in the past.

Second, clients will systematically *elicit* responses from the therapist that recapitulate their conflict. That is, clients do not merely misperceive the therapist, they actually elicit responses from the therapist that metaphorically reenact their generic conflict. When therapy fails, clients have usually recapitulated their generic conflict in the therapeutic relationship by eliciting responses from the therapist that are dynamically similar to responses they have received from significant others in the past. These include responses from the therapist that may be rejecting, idealizing, sexualizing, competitive, controlling, abandoning, critical, hopeless, and so forth.

Third, the *process* or manner in which therapists respond to clients may unwittingly reenact their conflicts in the therapeutic relationship. The relationship with the therapist must provide a more satisfying response to the client's conflict than the client has received in the past. It is difficult to provide this corrective emotional experience, however. Clients will expect, and often successfully elicit, the same hurtful responses from the therapist that they have received in the past. The therapist's task, then is to identify how their interpersonal process may be reenacting the client's conflict, and use a process comment to make this interaction overt and a topic for discussion. The therapist and client can then work together to establish a different pattern of interaction that does not recapitulate the client's conflict. As stated before, however, it is far easier to understand this intellectually than it is to enact with clients.

Thus, in order to lead to change, the therapeutic process must enact a resolution of the client's conflict rather than a repetition of it. When this occurs, clients have received far more than just an explanation for their problems. They have *experienced* a meaningful relationship in which their old conflicts have been aroused, but they have received a more satisfying response from the therapist that provides a resolution of their conflict.

Once the client has the real-life experience that change can occur, the therapist can help the client generalize this corrective emotional experience to other arenas in which similar conflicts are being enacted. This is the final *working through* phase of treatment and it will be discussed in the next chapter. With this overview of the change process in mind, we will now examine more closely how therapists can use the interpersonal process they enact with their clients to resolve conflicts.

Using the Process Dimension to Resolve Conflicts

Clients must experience a new and more satisfying response to their conflicts in their relationship with the therapist. To provide this, it is not enough for therapists to listen empathically, give interpretations, or facilitate client insights about the historical roots of problems. Nor is it enough to train and direct clients to try out new, more adaptive responses in their environment. Although these and other interventions are certainly useful, they are often insufficient to produce enduring change.

In addition, clients must experience a relationship with the therapist in which their old conflicts are aroused but the therapist does not respond in the same problematic way that others have in the past. This is easy to say but deceptively difficult to do. Therapists commonly fail to recognize how they are reenacting the client's conflict in their interpersonal process. In the three ways noted above, clients do not just talk about their problems in the abstract, they actually reenact the same conflicts they are discussing with the therapist in their interpersonal process. When therapy fails, the therapeutic process has usually reenacted the same conflict that the client has been struggling with in other relationships, and that originally brought the client to therapy.

Especially through transference reactions and eliciting phenomenon, there is a strong propensity for the therapeutic process to recapitulate the client's generic conflict. As we will see below, it challenges the therapist's own personhood to enact a solution to the client's conflict rather than a repetition of it. Below, four different types of case examples highlight the process dimension.

Example 1: It Is Difficult for Therapists to Recognize the Process When They Are Participating in It. The first example below summarizes an ineffective therapeutic relationship. This brief case summary illustrates how difficult it can be for therapists to recognize the interpersonal process they enact with their own clients. It is easy for therapists to understand the process dimension conceptually, and relatively easy to identify when the client's conflict is being reenacted between other therapists and their clients. In contrast, with their own clients, it is far more difficult to recognize how the interpersonal process is recapitulating the conflict.

An alcoholic client began therapy by expressing how much pain he was in as a result of his drinking problem. His wife was threatening to leave him and he was on probation at work. His eight-year-old son had recently seen him in an embarrassing situation while intoxicated and had asked him not to drink anymore. The client was distraught that even though the structure of his life was collapsing, he could not stop drinking.

During their first session the client sobbed, "Nothing ever works out; everything I try to do falls apart in the end."

The therapist was moved by the client's plight but, unfortunately, she became overinvested in helping him change. The therapist found it difficult to listen to how hopeless he sounded and she kept reassuring him that things would get better. The therapist disclosed that she had had a serious drinking problem of her own many years ago and that she knew just what he needed to do in order to stop drinking. The therapist and client quickly established a friendly relationship in which the client successfully elicited a great deal of nurturance from the responsive therapist. The client enjoyed this support immensely and sincerely tried to follow the therapist's advice and suggestions.

Things went better for about a month but then the client fell off the wagon and began drinking heavily again. When he started arriving late for his therapy sessions, and then missing several of them, the therapist began to feel let down. The final straw broke for the therapist when the client arrived for therapy intoxicated. The therapist felt angry and betrayed because she had extended herself to him more than she usually did with other clients. She felt that he was letting them both down, and told him so. In this way, the therapist became punitive toward the client and she also induced guilt over the impact of his "irresponsible" drinking on his family. The client was contrite and tried, unsuccessfully, to elicit her sympathy and support again. The client did not show up for his next appointment, however, and did not return to therapy.

This interaction recapitulated the client's conflict in two ways. First, the client initially elicited a promise of love and support from the therapist, but the therapist eventually turned to criticism and control. This confirmed the client's disillusionment that "nothing ever works out; relationships all go bad," about which he had forewarned the therapist during their first session. Second, the therapist benevolently tried to rescue this client who was behaving as a victim. The caretaking, advice-giving response from the therapist inadvertently defined the client as being incapable of managing his own life. Unfortunately, this response paralleled a similarly diminishing attitude that the client had received from his indulgent, but belittling, parent. The rescuer-victim process that was enacted in therapy prevented the client from addressing his real conflicts over adequacy, achievement, and commitment that he defended against, in part, through drinking.

In reviewing this case several weeks later, the therapist reported that "the client just wasn't ready to stop drinking yet. He's going to have to get worse and really hit bottom before he'll be able to admit there's a problem and do something about it." The well-intentioned therapist did not recognize that the interpersonal process they had enacted in their relationship unwittingly recapitulated the client's conflict and prevented change from occurring. As often occurs when therapy fails, the therapist only attended to the content of what they talked about and not to how their process might be recapitulating the client's conflicts.

From an emotionally neutral vantage point—such as that of supervising a student or looking at a colleague's therapy session on videotape—it is relatively easy to see how the client's conflicts have been reenacted in the interpersonal process. In humble contrast, it can be exasperatingly difficult to see one's own interpersonal process while engaged in an intense, affect-laden relationship. This is true for the well-seasoned expert and especially apt for the novice clinician. Beginning therapists will repeatedly reenact the client's conflict in their interpersonal process without realizing that this is occurring. It is difficult to learn to shift one's perceptions from the content level to the process level. Beginning therapists must be patient with themselves and know that the ability to recognize and respond to the process level is acquired slowly. In the second section of this chapter, specific guidelines will be offered to help therapists recognize when the process is recapitulating the conflict.

Example 2: How Process Comments Can Keep Therapists from Recapitulating the Conflict. In the previous example, the therapeutic process recapitulated the client's conflict. In the next example, a similar dynamic begins. Initially, a depressed client elicits the same critical and rejecting responses from the therapist that he has received in earlier formative relationships. In this case, however, the therapist recognizes their interpersonal process. By using a process comment to describe their current interaction, the therapist effectively realigns this maladaptive pattern of interaction.

Many clients enter therapy because of depression. These clients feel sad, believe they are bad, and act powerless to change their circumstances. In many cases, these clients communicate their very real suffering to the therapist with emotional pleas for help. Yet whatever the therapist tries to do or suggest does not work. Often, the therapist's efforts to meet the client's request for help are met with "Yes, but . . . ." A problematic cycle begins in which the client feels increasingly desperate and intensifies his emotional pleas for help. For example, the client might exclaim, "I can't go on living if things don't change soon!" In response to the client's escalating distress, the concerned therapist becomes more active and tries even harder to respond in some helpful way. However, nothing the therapist does has any impact or provides any relief for the client.

As the client rejects the help that he is eliciting, the therapist's own needs to help are frustrated. In some cases, the therapist's own sense of adequacy as a helping person will be threatened. When this occurs, *the client's eliciting behavior has tapped into the therapist's own issues and dynamics.* In response to this, some therapists will become punitive and critical toward the client whereas others will withdraw and emotionally disengage. When this occurs, the therapeutic process thematically repeats similar conflicted interactions that the client has experienced in the past and has not been able to resolve in other current relationships.

When therapy is unsuccessful, the therapist usually remains critical toward or disengaged from this "impossible" client. The depressed client's conflict is recapitulated as he again feels dependent on a relationship with someone who is critical, inconsistently available, or threatening to terminate the relationship and abandon him. What is the alternative? In successful therapy, the therapist is able to make a process comment and describe or inquire about what is going on between them in their present interaction. Rather than focus on the *content* of what they are talking about (e.g., depression), the therapist can point out *how* they are responding to each other. This is a very effective way to see and change the maladaptive, repetitive pattern of interaction. For example, the therapist might respond:

> Let's talk about what is going on between us right now and see if we can understand what's happening in our relationship. It seems to me that you keep asking me for help, but keep saying "Yes, but . . ." and don't ever allow me to help you. I think that I get frustrated with you then, and become more demanding of you. What do you see going on between us?

With a process comment of this type, the therapist is joining with the client in trying to understand their mutual interaction. The therapist is responding to the client's need by helping him look at his depression and how he expresses it to others. The process comment has also allowed the therapist to break the cycle of escalating client need and therapist frustration, at least temporarily.

How does this help clients change? In this example the client is *experiencing* a relationship with the therapist that provides a new and different solution to an old and problematic pattern of interaction. The client is not rejected or abandoned as he has been in the past, but remains engaged in a relationship with someone who consistently responds to his concerns. The client has not experienced this consistency, availability, or acceptance in past relationships. If this *corrective emotional experience* is repeated in many other big and small ways throughout the course of treatment, the client is experiencing a resolution of his conflict in his relationship with the therapist. When clients have the *experience* of change, rather than being advised what to do, being reassured, or having their behavior interpreted, they are better prepared to make enduring changes.

A key concept in the interpersonal process approach is that the capacity for change is fueled by the personal significance that the therapeutic relationship holds for the client. When an interpersonal solution is enacted in a meaningful relationship with the therapist, change is facilitated in two ways. First, in the context of this new type of relationship, clients can now approach the conflicted feelings that accompany their original unmet needs. In other words, clients have the supportive relationship necessary to undergo those experiences that were too threatening to be dealt with in childhood, rather than having to continue to defend against them. Second, the experience of change with the therapist *shows* clients, rather than merely telling them, that current relationships can be different and more satisfying than formative relationships have been in the past.

Continuing the previous dialogue with the depressed client gives an example:

Client:

Yeah, I do keep saying "Yes, but . . ." to you. That's terrible—if I'm doing that with you too, then there's no way I can get better. Should we just stop now?

Therapist:

Oh no! It makes sense that you are having the same problems in here with me that you have with other people. In a way, it is a problem, but in another way, it gives us the opportunity to resolve your problem right here in our relationship.

Client:

How?

Therapist:

If you and I can work out a different kind of relationship than you have had in the past, one that doesn't repeat this same old pattern, I think it will go a long way toward helping you change.

Client:

Do you think we can do that now if we haven't been able to up to this point?

Therapist:

Yes, I think it's very possible. In fact, I think we are breaking that pattern right now, just by talking about the way we interact together. Tell me, how is it to be talking with me about our relationship and the way we respond to each other?

Client:

I like it. It's different.

Therapist:

I like it too. I feel like I'm working with you, rather than being pushed away as I was feeling before.

In this example, the therapist has used a process comment to effectively alter the current interaction with the client. For the moment, the process comment has kept their interaction from recapitulating the client's conflict. Some variation on the old "Yes, but . . ." pattern will probably soon reappear and the therapist will have to make another process comment and work through a similar cycle again. In this way, however, the therapist is temporarily providing the client with a different response that does not recapitulate his conflict. The next example shifts from this single, time-limited interaction to a macroperspective that tracks the process dimension over the course of therapy.

Example 3: The Process Dimension Bridges Differing Theoretical Orientations. Therapists with different personalities and therapists working from different theoretical orientations can all help clients change. Every theoretical approach clarifies some important aspects of client problems. The greater component of change, therefore, is less the personality and theoretical orientation of the therapist than the nature of the relationship that the therapist provides the client. Change is likely to occur whenever the way in which the therapist and client interact provides a resolution of the client's conflicts rather than a repetition of them.

After two years in analytically-oriented therapy, Mrs. Jones still couldn't take charge of her life. She was always complying with her husband's demands and it was impossible for her to tell her children what to do and have them obey her. She also complained of her stultifying daily routine as a housewife yet she was never able to do anything to improve it. At her husband's behest, she would periodically enroll in a class or interview for an office job, but she was never able to follow through on any of his suggestions.

In therapy, Mrs. Jones had spent many hours reviewing her childhood. Her therapist had an uncanny ability to see the same unifying themes in many of the memories and recollections she shared with him. For example, her therapist repeatedly observed how she was subtly discouraged from initiating activities on her own or was not allowed to feel good about a success experience during childhood. Anytime she did something well as a child, her parents didn't notice it or didn't seem very happy about it if they did.

Mrs. Jones's therapist once explained to her, in a sensitive and informative way, that she had a passive-dependent personality style. Mrs. Jones was impressed that her therapist seemed to understand her so well. He knew so many things about her without her even having to tell him. Although her problems hadn't changed much yet, she still believed her therapist would cure her. He was so bright and insightful, and he genuinely seemed to care about her as well. And even though he didn't like to tell her what to do, when things became too much, he could usually help by explaining what the problem really meant. It was so comforting to be with him, Mrs. Jones didn't know what she would do without him.

It was Mrs. Jones's husband who finally ran out of patience with the slow course of treatment. After two years he was fed up with the big therapy bills and his wife's unremitting discontent. His wife's helpless dissatisfaction felt like a subtle but unending demand for him to love her more, give her more, or somehow fill up her life. He was tired of these subtle, nagging demands and he wanted it to change now.

Mr. Jones was a man of action in his work and he was not going to acquiesce to this way of life any longer. He obtained the name of a behaviorally-oriented therapist on the faculty of a nearby college. A friend had told Mr. Jones that this therapist was a "problem-solving realist" who could make things happen fast. This sounded like just the right approach to him. Mr. Jones insisted that his wife stop treatment with her present therapist and begin immediately with the new therapist. Mrs. Jones was panicked at the thought of leaving her therapist, but she sensed that her husband was truly at the end of his rope. Although she still believed in her therapist and felt very close to him, she was afraid that her husband might actually leave her if she didn't do what he said.

After her first few sessions with the new therapist, Mrs. Jones was surprised to think that perhaps her husband had been right after all. The new therapist wasted no time in taking charge of the situation. It was exciting to have the therapist outline specific steps for her to follow and it was sensible to have a specific plan laid out for how she was going to change. The therapist discussed a list of treatment goals with her and they planned a set of graduated steps for meeting these goals on a scheduled timetable.

In their first hour together, the therapist had Mrs. Jones role play how she responded to her children when they disobeyed her. Then with the therapist serving as a model and coach, they rehearsed more assertive responses that Mrs. Jones could try with her children. The therapist also had Mrs. Jones enroll in an assertion training class she was running for some of her other female clients. Each week Mrs. Jones was also to complete a homework assignment—this week she was to call up one new person she might like to develop a friendship with and ask her to lunch. She was supposed to report back to the therapist on this assignment at the beginning of their next appointment.

Mr. Jones was encouraged by this practical, problem-solving approach to his wife's problems. He began to think that something might change after all. Mrs. Jones was hopeful too. She felt reassured by her new therapist's goal-oriented, problem-solving approach. In fact, Mrs. Jones became determined to be the best client her therapist ever had and promised herself that she was going to do *everything* the therapist asked her to do.

Therapy progressed well for the first few weeks, but then things started to slow down again. Although she didn't really know why, Mrs. Jones began to find it hard to muster the energy to attend the new class she had signed up for. She knew her therapist would be disapointed in her for not doing what she was "supposed to do," but she just couldn't help it. Although she felt guilty about it, Mrs. Jones began missing her therapy sessions.

Although both of these therapists were capable of helping Mrs. Jones, they both failed to have a significant impact on her problems. They were both unsuccessful even though they seemingly used very different treatment approaches. Theoretically, the analytically-oriented therapist might attribute the unsuccessful outcome to the great difficulty in restructuring the passive, dependency needs of a basic oral character. The behaviorist might note that Mrs. Jones was not sufficiently motivated to change because she was receiving too many secondary gains from her help-seeking behavior. If we look at the interpersonal process that transpired between both therapists and the client, however, a very different picture emerges. These two therapists actually responded in a very similar (and problematic) way to Mrs. Jones.

We must look carefully at what Mrs. Jones *experienced* in therapy. With both therapists, Mrs. Jones reenacted the same maladaptive pattern that she had with her children and with her husband. Her presenting problem was that her children ran over her and she could not make them listen to her or obey her. Her compliance with her take-charge husband was a profound example of the same problem. Therapy failed in this case because her pattern of being passive and compliant recurred in the process that was enacted with both therapists. Unwittingly, both therapists provided a relationship in which she remained the passive helpee vis-a-vis the leader-helper. This interpersonal process reinforced her feeling that the source of strength and problem resolution did not reside in her but in the therapist.

In order for Mrs. Jones to change, she would need to experience a therapeutic relationship in which she did not feel one-down to a benevolent authority who held the power to solve her problems. Rather, she had to feel that the ability rested within herself to initiate, gain control over her own life, and resolve conflicts. Then her own strengths and resources could be utilized, along with the therapist's skill, in a more collaborative relationship.

Unfortunately, both of her therapists were comfortable with this relational process and did not bring it up as a focus for treatment. Neither therapist made the process comment that, in certain ways, their interaction repeated the same conflict and interpersonal style that was problematic for Mrs. Jones in other relationships. A process comment like this would have allowed Mrs. Jones to look at her problematic behavior in a supportive environment. More important, it would have given her permission to change her passive-compliant style and become more forceful and autonomous *in her relationship with the therapist.*

As long as the therapists were telling her what to do, Mrs. Jones could not set limits with her children, take a more assertive stance with her husband, or follow through and do what she wanted to do for herself. That is, the content of what she discussed with both therapists (issues about autonomy, independence, assertiveness) was not matched by the interpersonal process they enacted. Unless Mrs. Jones has the actual experience of behaving as an active, strong participant in her relationship with the therapist, she will not be able to adopt this healthy, stronger stance in other areas of her life. *This is what is meant by saying that the process must be congruent with the content.*

This is not a simple task for the therapist, however. It requires therapeutic skill and careful monitoring of the process to enact a more egalitarian, collaborative relationship with someone like Mrs. Jones. Mrs. Jones is an accomplished master at getting therapists, husbands, children, and others to lead, direct, and control her. If Mrs. Jones and the therapist had enacted a different process in their relationship, however, both the behaviorally and analytically oriented therapists could have been helpful to her. If they had encouraged her to initiate and lead—rather than directing her—her central conflict would have emerged in the therapeutic relationship. That is, Mrs. Jones would have become anxious as soon as either of the therapists encouraged her to behave more assertively and competently *in the therapeutic relationship.* Both therapists could have focused her inward on this anxiety and examined why it was threatening for her to step out of her dependent-compliant mode. Simultaneously, the therapists could have given her permission to act more assertively and competently within their relationship, and worked with her in a way that facilitated this new behavior in their sessions. Instead, Mrs. Jones continued to defend against her anxiety over being assertive/effective by retreating to her dependent, help-seeking role, and both therapists reenacted this conflict with her.

In most therapeutic relationships, the therapist and client will temporarily reenact the client's generic conflict in their interpersonal process. In successful therapy of every theoretical orientation, however, the therapist and client do not continue to reenact the old pattern. Instead, they are able to identify this process and work out a different type of relationship that resolves, rather than reenacts, the client's conflict. Once clients find that their old conflicts can be confronted, but that they do not have to result in the same hurtful or frustrating outcomes, clients are able to generalize this relearning to other relationships as well.

Example 4: The Process Dimension Shapes All Interpersonal Relations. As we have seen, the most likely reason for therapy to fail is because the therapist and client reenact the client's conflict in their interpersonal process. Because beginning therapists are not used to tracking the process dimension, it is difficult to recognize how the process may be reenacting the client's conflict. In order to highlight the process dimension and help discriminate the process that is enacted from the content that is discussed, the next illustration utilizes an example from outside of the arena of psychotherapy. The following example is taken from an athletic event that actually occurred. In this very different setting, however, we will see that the interpersonal process dimension can still be observed.

It is the championship game and two basketball teams are competing fiercely for the league title. One team is the defending champion from last year—a mature and confident team. The opposing team is the underdog—made up of talented but younger players who are far less experienced. The defending champions are heavily favored to win this game and repeat as champions. They have been here before and have already proven that they can withstand the pressure necessary to win championship games.

It is late in the fourth quarter and the game is tied. The fans are on their feet cheering at the prospect of an upset. The coach of the young team can feel that the game is about to slip away, however. His players are becoming rattled by the screaming fans, the advancing clock that now makes every mistake critical, and the unrelenting play of the opponents. To help compose his inexperienced players, the coach calls a two-minute time-out. His team has played well up to this point, but the seasoned coach knows that it is in these closing, pressure-packed minutes that the other team's experience is likely to make the difference.

Crouched with one knee on the sideline, the coach positions his five players in a semicircle in front of him. With the roaring crowd only a few feet away, the coach quietly makes eye-contact with the first player on his left. Without speaking, he calmly holds the first player's gaze for about twelve to fifteen seconds (a very long time amidst such pandemonium). Having compelled the first player's attention, the coach turns to the second player and maintains eye contact with him for another twelve to fifteen seconds, and so on with each of the five players. Each time, as he turns to engage the next player, the previous player's attention remains riveted on the coach. Finally, after making contact with each player in this way, the coach holds up a chalk board with one word written on it: "POISE."

The players and coach sit together silently for the remaining seconds of the time-out. The referee blows his whistle, the players return to the court, and they defeat the defending champions. The players did not make mental or emotional errors in the closing minutes of the game: they did not turn the ball over to the other team, they made clutch free throws in the final seconds of the game, and they smoothly executed the plays that they had practiced all year. In a word, they played with "poise."

This coach astutely identified the central issue that could defeat his team in the final minutes—being intimidated by a more confident and experienced team, losing their composure, and making mental mistakes that would cost them the game. Having recognized the central issue, however, the coach did not just *tell* his team that they had to remain poised in the final minutes in order to win. Instead of telling them what they should feel, he gave them the *experience* of composure during the time-out. The players were able to finish the game with such composure because the coach used the relationship he had developed with each of his players to give them the experience of composure during the final, tense minutes. Having felt composed during the time-out, the players were able to generalize this experience to their performance on the court and play with "poise."

Similarly, it is far more effective if the therapist-client interaction provides an experience of change than if the therapist merely tells the client what to do or explains what something means. It is often difficult to provide a relationship that enacts a resolution of clients' conflicts, however, and there are no easy formulas that tell the therapist how to enact this with different clients, all of whom are unique. Thus, the therapist must take the personal risk of entering into a significant emotional relationship with each client, and have the flexibility to provide the interpersonal experience that each client needs in order to change.

OPTIMUM INTERPERSONAL DISTANCE

The primary theme in the interpersonal process approach is that the therapeutic process must enact a resolution of the client's conflict. As noted above, it is easier to understand this conceptually than it is to implement in intense, affect-laden relationships. The best way to keep from recapitulating the client's conflict in the therapeutic relationship is to maintain an optimum interpersonal distance between the therapist and the client.

In order to establish a relationship that is capable of producing change, therapists must have an effective degree of involvement with their clients. If the therapist is inappropriately close, it will not be safe for clients to take the risk of letting the therapist influence them. Similarly, if the therapist is too distant or removed, the relationship will not be significant enough to effect change. Thus, one of the most important process dimensions for therapists to monitor is the balance of separateness versus relatedness in the therapeutic relationship. We will see below that, at times, all therapists will have difficulty maintaining an optimum interpersonal distance with some clients. However, the single biggest problem facing most beginning therapists is finding an effective degree of closeness or involvement with their clients.

Enmeshment

At times, all therapists will become inappropriately overidentified with certain clients who hold particular symbolic meaning for them and who tap into the therapists' own issues and dynamics. Because of their own personality dynamics, however, some therapists will consistently become overinvolved with many of their clients. How can therapists recognize when they have become inappropriately overinvolved with a client rather than being appropriately involved in a concerned and available way? Whenever therapists find that they are angry or critical of a client for not changing, they are overly invested in the client. Therapists are also enmeshed when they have dreams about a client, often think about a client outside of the therapy session, feel depressed when a client is not changing, see the client as being just like themselves, or become envious or elated over positive changes in the client's life. This overinvolvement is different from care and concern for the client, which is appropriate and necessary. When enmeshment occurs, therapists usually need the client to change in order to meet their own needs, such as to shore up their own feelings of adequacy as a therapist or to manage their own internal conflicts that have been aroused by the client.

Substantial problems occur when therapists become overinvolved with a client. They tend to become controlling of the client and to inappropriately project their own personal conflicts onto the client. It is easy to see how this tends to recapitulate the client's conflict in the therapeutic relationship. For example, many clients have grown up in families with overly controlling or intrusive parents. When the therapist cannot encourage clients' own autonomy and allow them to experience their own controls and personal boundaries, the therapist is responding in the same problematic way as the parents. This reenactment with the therapist will prevent clients from being able to resolve their conflicts around intimacy and control.

Furthermore, when therapists become too close or overidentified they lose their ability to think objectively about the client. Therapists will have a heightened emotional reactivity to the client that will cloud their understanding of the client. When this occurs, the therapists' accurate empathy will be lost to a global, undifferentiated sympathy. Most important, therapists will not be able to discriminate the differences between themselves and the client that inevitably exist and therapists will begin to see the client as being just like themselves. Although this closeness or sameness may be reassuring to clients at first, enduring change will not occur in an enmeshed relationship.

Disengagement

At times, all therapists will also hold themselves too far away from certain clients. This usually occurs when the client arouses the therapist's own personality conflicts. Also, some therapists will consistently err on the side of being too removed from most of their clients. This distance, which renders therapy ineffective, occurs because of the therapist's own enduring personality conflicts. When the therapist is not emotionally available to the client, therapy loses its intensity and becomes intellectualized. Therapists do not "feel with" the client and they lose their intuition, empathy, and creativity. When this occurs, the client does not have the supportive relationship necessary to explore her conflicted emotions. Psychotherapy is more than an intellectual discourse, and enduring personality change will not occur in an emotionally disengaged relationship. Without the impetus provided by genuine personal involvement, a corrective emotional experience will not occur.

Client conflicts will also be recapitulated in the therapeutic relationship when the therapist is too distant or uninvolved. For example, many clients had aloof, self-centered, or authoritarian parents who could not meet their childhood needs for emotional contact and support. A distant therapist will be safe for these clients because their anxieties over their unmet dependency needs—and their conflicts associated with being close to others—will not be aroused in the therapeutic relationship. Unfortunately, however, just as the client's conflicts are not aroused in a disengaged relationship, the opportunity to resolve these conflicts is lost as well. Thus, when therapists defend themselves against their own anxieties that are aroused by closer involvement with clients, many clients will not be able to change.

An Optimum Middle Ground of Involvement

In order to be effective, the therapist must find an optimum middle ground of involvement. For several reasons, maintaining this effective middle ground of involvement throughout the course of therapy is one of the most challenging aspects of psychotherapy. First, therapists are repeatedly confronted with anxiety-arousing issues *in their own lives* by the affect-laden material that clients present. All therapists must become aware of how they tend to respond when clients arouse their own anxieties. For example, some therapists will become passive or withdraw from the client. Some therapists will distance themselves by intellectualizing the relationship, as in interpreting the client's affect before the client fully experiences it. Other therapists become controlling and overly directive, telling clients what they should do in a particular situation. Therapists must examine how they tend to respond when their own anxieties are aroused by the material that clients present and learn to hold these propensities in check.

Second, the balance between overinvolvement and underinvolvement is also difficult because clients often try to move their therapists along this continuum of involvement. Clients do this as an interpersonal strategy to defend against their conflicts. That is, when the therapist has been responding effectively, clients may become threatened by the anxiety-arousing material that begins to emerge for them. Clients will often defend against their own difficult emotions that are being aroused by creating either distance or enmeshment in the therapeutic relationship. For example, clients may try to bore the therapist or push the therapist away by talking about issues they are not really concerned about. Or clients may try to elicit too much involvement from the therapist, such as by exaggerating their distress and escalating their demands for help. Thus, forces both from within the therapist's own dynamics and from the client's defensive eliciting behaviors will pressure the therapist away from an effective middle ground of involvement.

Therapists who are able to maintain their own middle ground of involvement are more dependable and provide a more even therapy. There are no stormy ups and downs or lengthy impasses of emotional disengagement. It is also safer for the client to be vulnerable and trust when the therapist is consistently concerned and available without becoming controlling, unresponsive, or overreactive. Furthermore, if the therapist maintains an optimum interpersonal distance, the client does not have to be concerned about disappointing an overinvolved therapist. Nor, on the other hand, does the client have to elicit the attention or concern of an uninvolved therapist, which often recapitulates the client's generic conflict as well.

The important balance is for therapists to maintain their own objectivity and separateness while at the same time they are available and responsive to the client. *Therapy is usually successful when the therapist can maintain this optimum interpersonal involvement throughout the course of therapy.* Conversely, therapy usually reaches an impasse and ends prematurely when the therapist and client become enmeshed or cannot emotionally connect with each other.

One exercise to help therapists recognize the process they are enacting with their clients is to consider the following questions after every session:

1. What are my feelings/reactions toward this client?
2. How do my feelings/reactions parallel those of significant others in the client's life?
3. What is the client doing to arouse such feelings/reactions in me, and how do these behaviors tie into my conceptualization of the client's generic conflict and interpersonal defenses?
4. Do my feelings/reactions typify my feelings/reactions to other clients and/or significant others in my life?

If therapists write answers to these questions after each session it will ensure that they are attending to the process dimension. Asking themselves such questions will also help therapists discriminate their own countertransference reactions toward the client from the client's eliciting behaviors and interpersonal coping style.

In sum, all therapists will sometimes become locked in one of the extremes of over or underinvolvement. However, beginning therapists are especially prone to become overidentified with their clients and see their clients' problems and lives as being too similar to their own. This is the most common way in which clients' conflicts come to be reenacted in the therapeutic process. It is discouraging for beginning therapists when their supervisors repeatedly point out how they are metaphorically reenacting the client's conflict in how they are interacting. Beginning therapists must be patient with themselves and accept the fact that it is difficult to maintain this effective middle ground of involvement that safeguards against recapitulating the client's conflict.

When therapists do become over or underinvolved, however, they must reestablish an effective middle ground with their clients. When therapists cannot realign the relationship on their own, they must consult with a colleague or supervisor. In fact, *the most productive use of supervision is to help therapists regain control of their own emotional reactions so that they can reestablish an effective degree of involvement*. Maintaining this optimum interpersonal distance is the best way to keep from recapitulating the client's conflict in the therapeutic relationship.

CLOSING

Throughout the course of therapy, therapists must repeatedly ask themselves: What is this client's generic conflict? What expectations has the client learned in past relationships that will be transferred onto the therapist? What type of responses does the client tend to elicit from the therapist and others to defend against his generic conflict? Attending to questions such as these will enable the therapist to anticipate how clients will reenact their conflicts in the therapeutic relationship. Answering these questions will also enable therapists to provide a different and more satisfying response to the client's conflict than the client has received in the past. The next chapter will show how therapists can help clients generalize this corrective emotional experience to other problems beyond the therapy setting.

SUGGESTIONS FOR FURTHER READING

1. Margaret Mahler's developmental theory provides an invaluable conceptual model for helping therapists establish an optimum interpersonal distance with their clients. The reader is strongly encouraged to read chapter six (Rapprochement) of: M. Mahler, F. Pine, and A. Bergman, *The Psychological Birth of the Human Infant: Symbiosis and Individuation* (New York: Basic Books, 1975).

2. Family systems concepts of cohesion and adaptability can also be used to describe an optimum interpersonal distance. Interested readers may examine: D. H. Olson et al. *Families: What Makes Them Work* (Beverly Hills, Calif.: Sage Publications, 1983).

3. The film *Ordinary People*, (directed by R. Redford, 1980) provides an effective illustration of the *corrective emotional experience* presented here. It shows how clients can resolve their conflicts with others only after they have been able to resolve them in their real-life relationship with the therapist.

4. An excellent presentation of how theory guides practice is found in Chapters 2–6 of J. Weiss and H. Sampson, *The Psychoanalytic Process: Theory, Clinical Observation and Empirical Research* (New York: Guilford, 1986). These authors clarify the role of unconscious guilt in psychopathology, and explain how clients attempt to resolve their conflicts by disconfirming certain grim pathogenic beliefs. These beliefs were learned in early parent-child relations and must be resolved in the interpersonal process that transpires between the therapist and client.

10

Working Through and Termination

CONCEPTUAL OVERVIEW

Working through and *termination* are two distinct phases of therapy. Once clients have experienced a more satisfying response to their generic conflict from the therapist, the task is to generalize this experience of change beyond the therapy setting. That is, the central conflict that has just been resolved in the therapeutic relationship must now be worked through in other relationships as well. Although this may be the longest phase of therapy for some clients, it is a period of growth and change. During this phase, clients are assimilating and applying the emotional relearning that has occurred with the therapist. As clients now go on to address and resolve with others the same conflicts that they have been able to resolve with the therapist, therapy evolves to a natural close. The final termination phase then provides one last opportunity to reexperience and master the old generic conflict, to internalize the helping relationship with the therapist, and to successfully emancipate from therapy.

CHAPTER ORGANIZATION

The first section of this chapter describes the working-through process. First, it provides an overview of client change that places the working-through phase within the context of the overall course of therapy. Following this overview of client change, we describe the working-through process. Sample therapist-client dialogues illustrate how the emotional relearning that has occurred with the therapist can be generalized to other conflict areas. The third part of this section highlights the client's transition from concerns about problems and conflicts to future plans that reflect life-enhancing aspirations and goals. This transition from conflict- to growth-oriented concerns is often marked by the emergence of the client's *Dream*.

In the second section, we discuss the critically important phase of termination. The section offers specific guidelines for effecting successful terminations and highlights common pitfalls that occur around termination. Finally, in the third section, we provide two case studies of a moving-against and a moving-away client. These two case summaries provide an overview of the change process with different types of clients, and show how a corrective emotional experience with the therapist can lead to broad-based personality and behavioral change.

WORKING THROUGH

The Course of Client Change: An Overview

Beginning therapists usually lack a conceptual overview of how client change comes about. Because they have not worked with many clients, or may not have experienced their own effective therapy, most beginning therapists do not have a sense of the ordered sequence in which change often occurs. In the previous chapter, the sequence of therapist activities over the course of therapy was reviewed. The first part of this section extends this framework for conceptualizing the course of therapy. This section offers an overview of the change process by outlining when and how clients resolve their conflicts and adopt new, more adaptive responses. Clients usually change in a predictable sequence of steps and this unfolding course of change is reviewed from the beginning of therapy up to the final working-through and termination phases.

Some change occurs for some clients as soon as they decide to enter therapy. The decision to enter therapy involves acknowledging that there really is a problem that the client is no longer going to deny or avoid. This decision is also an acknowledgment that clients recognize they cannot resolve the problem alone and that they accept their need for help. Most clients recognize that their resolution to seek help is a healthy step forward and they feel good about making this decision. As a result, some clients will feel more in control of themselves—which may precipitate some initial change. Although this internal commitment to work on their problems usually produces little relief initially, it is a crucial step that will allow change to occur later in the course of treatment.

Some small changes in feeling and behavior may also occur during clients' initial sessions with the therapist. Clients are reassured when the therapist invites them to express their concerns directly, listens intently and nonjudgmentally to them, and articulates the subjective meaning that their concerns hold for them. Clients' anxiety often diminishes as they find that the therapist can understand their experience and respond compassionately to them. This validation and support does not resolve clients' conflicts but it does engender hope and help to relieve their distress—which may in turn diminish their symptoms.

More substantial changes begin to occur when the therapist succeeds in focusing clients inward on their own thoughts and feelings and away from their preoccupation with the problematic behavior of others. When clients examine their own internal and interpersonal reactions they often recognize how their behavior contributes to an interpersonal conflict—and may be able to change their participation in it. Adopting an internal focus for change is also one important way to reframe how clients think about their problems. Redefining the conflict with the other person as being, in part, an internal problem usually reveals new and more adaptive alternatives that clients can adopt.

Next, as the therapist focuses clients inward on their own experience, their conflicted emotions will emerge. These conflicted emotions are the basis of clients' problems. The pace of change accelerates as clients begin to experience and express the emotions that accompany their problems, and as the therapist responds to each sequential feeling in clients' affective constellation. Clients have the opportunity to resolve their problems when they stop defending against their recurring conflicted emotions and, instead, start experiencing, expressing, and understanding them. Far-reaching changes are set in motion when clients begin to master their affective constellation in this way. For the first time, clients will then be able to change maladaptive, repetitive responses that are integrally linked to their generic conflicts and interpersonal coping styles.

As clients' conflicted emotions emerge, the therapist is also better able to conceptualize clients' generic conflicts and interpersonal coping styles. The therapist then focuses treatment along these conceptual lines and clarifies how clients are reenacting the same dynamic patterns throughout the various issues and concerns they present. Some further change may occur as the therapist helps clients recognize these dynamics and as clients further reframe their definition of their problems. In and of itself, this intellectual awareness may not lead to significant behavioral change but it does facilitate the next and most significant point of change.

The same conflicts that originally led clients to seek therapy, and that they have been discussing with the therapist, will usually be reenacted in the therapeutic relationship. This reenactment in the therapeutic relationship provides both an opportunity for therapy to fail—by recapitulating the client's conflict—and an opportunity for therapy to succeed—by resolving the conflict that has emerged in the therapeutic relationship. A critical incident often occurs when clients feel the therapist is responding in the same problematic ways that significant others have in the past. This usually occurs in one of three ways. First, although the therapist actually may not have responded in this problematic way, the client has a transference reaction and systematically misperceives what the therapist has said or done. Second, the client's interpersonal style may actually elicit the same problematic response from the therapist that she has received in the past. Third, the client's conflict may be brought into the therapeutic relationship when countertransference reactions are stimulated in the therapist that recapitulate the client's conflict.

Although therapists often fail to recognize it at first, this type of reenactment predictably occurs in most therapeutic relationships. Clients cannot resolve their conflicts unless this reenactment is resolved, however, and the therapist and client can work out a different and more satisfying solution to the client's conflict in their real-life relationship. Only when the therapist and client can resolve this conflict in their relationship does the client have a real-life *experience* of change. This interpersonal resolution in the therapeutic relationship is the pivotal step that determines whether change will occur.

Finally, in order to change, clients must reenact these types of corrective emotional experiences with the therapist many times and generalize this emotional relearning to other relationships. This working-through phase of therapy in which client change is integrated and generalized is described next.

Working Through

Change first occurs with the therapist. With just the therapist's encouragement and advice, some clients who function well can successfully adopt new behavior. When the new behavior is integrally linked to the client's generic conflict and interpersonal coping style, however, most clients will need to practice this new response in the therapeutic relationship. Thus, therapists must give clients permission to try out new ways of responding within their relationship and clarify that they do not wish to respond in the same problematic ways that others have in the past. If the therapist gives this permission and encouragement repeatedly, clients will eventually test the therapist and try out anxiety-arousing new responses with him. If the therapist responds positively, rather than metaphorically recapitulating unsatisfying responses that clients have received in the past, clients can resolve their conflicts and change.

This corrective emotional experience is a powerful agent for change but one-trial learning is not sufficient to effect change. The client will need to reenact this and other dynamic themes over and over again in the therapeutic relationship. In addition, the therapist must also help clients generalize this new experience of change to other relationships beyond the therapy setting. Typically, clients try out new ways of responding in the following progression.

First, change occurs in the client's relationship with the therapist. Clients then change with acquaintances they do not know well or with others who are not especially important to them. This is often followed by change with supportive others who are important to the client, such as caring friends, teachers, or mentors. Next, clients often change old response patterns with historical figures with whom the conflicts originally arose, such as parents. Finally, the last arena for change is often with primary others with whom the conflict is currently being lived out, such as spouses or children.

Some clients will spurt at the working-through stage of therapy, rapidly assimilate the new ways of responding, and readily apply it throughout their lives. In contrast, other clients with more pervasive conflicts will work through their conflicts slowly. These clients must repeatedly confront the same conflicts, fears, and habitual patterns of response over and over again. Each time, the therapist must patiently point out how the same dynamic issues are being played out again in this situation and help clients master this particular manifestation of their generic conflict. In this regard, the generic conflict will be repeatedly expressed in four areas of client functioning:

Current interaction with the therapist.

Reviewing crisis events that have recently occurred for the client or that originally precipitated the client seeking treatment.

Current relationships with others where the client's emotional problems are being aroused.

Historical relationships with family members.

For many therapists, working through is the most enjoyable phase of therapy. The therapist often serves as a cheering squad who takes pleasure in clients' newly obtained mastery and encourages them as they successfully adopt new responses in progressively more challenging situations. At this late stage of therapy, the therapist can also become more actively involved in providing information, suggestions, and guidelines to help clients enact new behavior. The nature of the therapeutic relationship also changes during this period. As clients improve through the working-through period, they will gradually come to perceive the therapist in more realistic terms. As this occurs, the therapist can disclose more about himself to the client. That is, once the transference projections and eliciting phenomenon have been addressed and resolved, therapists are able to share more of themselves with their clients.

In working through, however, the therapist must still be prepared to respond to all of the conflicts, resistances, and defenses that have come before. Although some others in the client's life will respond positively to the client's new changes, others will not. As a result, clients will continue to have experiences with others that arouse their old developmental conflicts again. This also provides an opportunity to further work through the client's generic conflict, however. Through each setback or crisis, the therapist and client again gain access to the client's conflicted affective constellation. They can recognize how the client's conflict is being expressed in this particular relationship and can observe how the same resistances, defenses, and interpersonal coping patterns are still being employed. Most important, in each successive encounter with the generic conflict, clients have the opportunity to receive a more satisfying response from the therapist. Repeatedly enacting a more satisfying interpersonal solution with the therapist will enable clients to continue to adopt more effective ways of responding with others beyond the therapy setting.

It is not always easy for therapists to provide this corrective emotional experience, however. Although clients are improving during the working-through period, they will still be struggling intensely with their central conflicts. This means that strong resistances and negative transference reactions toward the therapist will still have to be negotiated. Therapists must be able to tolerate and work patiently with clients' transference reactions, such as accusations that the therapist "doesn't really care about me," "is trying to control me," "isn't strong enough to handle me," "needs too much from me," "is afraid of a strong (or dependent) woman," "will take advantage of me," and so on.

Furthermore, at times most clients will become discouraged by the repetitious working-through process. Seeing that the same old conflict is confronting them again, clients may feel that nothing has changed, that it is futile to keep trying, and that they should consider dropping out of therapy. At these critical points in therapy, the therapist must provide clients with a relationship that offers them the promise of change. Therapists can make no guarantees of change and they cannot assume responsibility for the client's motivation to continue. However, *therapists must actively reach out and extend their care and concern to the client*. The therapist must communicate that there can be another way and that the therapist remains committed to working with him even though the therapist knows how discouraged the client feels at this point. It is the therapist's belief in the potential for change, and *personal commitment to helping this particular client change*, that pulls clients through these expectable crisis points in the working-through phase.

In the therapist-client dialogue below, we will see how clients first change in their relationship with the therapist and how the therapist can then help clients generalize this to other conflict areas in their lives. As we will see later in this chapter, this *critical incident* may occur as a dramatic, transference-laden confrontation. Alternately, as in the example below, the critical incident may be so subtle as to almost go unnoticed.

A therapist has observed that her client, Tracy, has habitually responded to others in a compliant, pleasing manner. Tracy always goes along with others, believing that her wishes and feelings do not matter. Tracy said that she did not believe that others would ever be interested in listening to her or doing what she wanted to do. In therapy, the therapist repeatedly pointed out how Tracy often acted in this compliant way with others. The therapist linked this behavior to Tracy's presenting symptom of crying spells and used this issue as an entré to explore her low self-esteem and feelings of worthlessness.

In addition, the therapist encouraged Tracy to respond differently in their relationship. That is, the therapist showed that she cared about what Tracy had to say and invited Tracy to express her own opinions in therapy—even if that meant disagreeing with the therapist. After two months in therapy, this significant new behavior emerged in the therapeutic relationship:

Tracy:
You're right, I guess I never have felt very good about myself.

Therapist:
From other things you've said, it seems to me that your mother just wasn't there for you as a child. You didn't get the support you needed from her. We need to explore that further.

Tracy:
No, I don't really want to talk about her. I remember my mother fondly, although my father was pretty harsh with us.

Therapist:
You just said no, you don't want to talk about your mother, and that I was wrong about her.

Tracy:
I'm sorry; sure we can talk about her. What do you want to know?

Therapist:
Forget your mother, you just disagreed with me! You just told me you didn't want to do what I wanted to do, and suggested what you thought would be better. That's great!

Tracy:
What?

Therapist:
You just did what we have been talking about for so long. You expressed your own opinion, said what you thought, disagreed with me. I am so happy for you!

Tracy:
Aren't you mad at me?

Therapist:
Oh no, we can disagree and still be close. That was a brave thing you just did.

Tracy:
I guess maybe it is okay for me to say what I think sometimes?

Therapist:
Sure it is. I care about what you think. I want to know what you feel, and I want to do things your way too.

Tracy:
[*tearing*] But you're safe. It's easy to do that with you. You're not like other people.

Therapist:
Yes, I am "safe," and it is easier to do things like that with me than with other people. But you have changed to be able to do that with me, you've grown. You couldn't do that before, you know.

Tracy:
Yeah, that's right.

Therapist:
And if you can value yourself enough to express what you think in here with me, then you can begin to do that out there with other people as well.

Tracy:
Do you really think so?

Therapist:
Yes, I'm sure you can. If you can do it with me, you can do it with them.

Tracy:
Oh, I would love to be able to do this with my boyfriend.

Therapist:
What do you want to be able to say to him?

Tracy:
Well, the next time he . . .

Why is the therapist in this example so excited about such a seemingly small change? Is this single manifestation of a new behavior all that is necessary for Tracy to resolve her problems? No, but this is a highly significant event and it brings her to the working-through phase of therapy. Within the safe orbit of the therapeutic relationship, Tracy could try out a new behavior that taps into her generic conflict and arouses intense anxiety. For Tracy, adopting such a seemingly insignificant, self-assertive behavior arouses lifelong feelings of worthlessness. And, simultaneously, it discards the primary means she has developed to protect herself from these painful feelings (i.e., to go along with others). In order to master her conflict, Tracy will have to reexperience over and over this same sequence. This sequence involves: (1) having her old conflict aroused (having to go along), (2) trying out a new and more adaptive response with the therapist (asserting her own preference), (3) receiving a different and more satisfying response from the therapist (accepting Tracy's initiative), and (4) generalizing the new behavior to others beyond the therapy setting. This repetitious reworking of the new behavior and the old conflict is called working through.

The next week when Tracy returned for her session, she made no mention of this incident with the therapist and said nothing about what went on with her boyfriend. Recognizing this as resistance, the therapist waited for the opportunity to acknowledge what had occurred between them the week before and to reassure Tracy that she was supportive of her new assertive response.

Therapist:
We haven't talked yet today about the important new way that you responded to me last week. Did you have any thoughts about that during the week?

Tracy:
No, not really.

Therapist:
Fine, but I just wanted to say again how happy I was for you. It felt very good to me to see you express your own opinion and be able to disagree with me.

Evidently, this reassurance must have given Tracy the permission she needed. The following week, Tracy was able to adopt the same type of assertive behavior with her boyfriend for the first time. This successful experience, in turn, encouraged her to confront the same issue in another more threatening relationship—with her father.

Tracy:
[*beaming*] Guess what! I did it! I've been dying to tell you all week!

Therapist:
Ha! What did you do?

Tracy:
I did what we talked about with my boyfriend. He was talking about some-

thing, and I disagreed with him and told him what I thought. It felt great! I don't think he minded either.

Therapist:
Good for you! You're on your way.

Tracy:
I can't believe how easy it was. I wish it could be that easy with my father. He's always putting me down when I say something.

Therapist:
Maybe you're ready to start changing your relationship with your father as well. How do you respond to him when he puts you down?

Tracy:
I get real quiet when he does that. I feel like crying, but I don't. I wish I could just tell him that I don't like it and I want him to stop.

Therapist:
Yeah, confronting him at the time he does that and setting limits with him would certainly change your relationship. It would be saying to him, and to yourself, that you value who you are and what you have to say, and you're not going to let him hurt you like that anymore.

Tracy:
But I could never do that. I'd like to, but I just couldn't.

Therapist:
You haven't been able to do that in the past, but you have been changing in here with me, and now with your boyfriend, too. So maybe you can do something different with him as well. What holds you back from setting limits with him; what are you most afraid of?

Tracy:
He wouldn't take me seriously; he'd just laugh at me.

Therapist:
How would that make you feel?

Tracy:
Worthless. [*begins crying*]

Therapist:
So that's where that awful feeling comes from.

Tracy:
Yeah. [*long pause*] It makes me mad too.

Therapist:
Of course it does. He's hurt you very much. You have every right to be angry at him for treating you like that!

Tracy:
It's not fair. I don't want to let him do that anymore. It's not good for me.

Therapist:
That's right, it's not good for you and you don't deserve it. Now that you can see that clearly, you don't have to go along with it the way you used to.

Tracy:
What can I do?

Therapist:
What would you like to do the next time he does that?

Tracy:
Well, maybe I can tell him to stop it. Tell him that I just don't want to be treated like that anymore . . .

In ever-widening circles such as these, clients confront and work through the same dynamic conflicts in the different spheres of their lives. Unless the therapist conceptualizes the client's dynamics and hypothesizes how the client might reenact this conflict in their relationship, however, it is easy for the therapist to miss these subtle transactions. For example, at the beginning of this sequence, Tracy said she did not want to follow the therapist's suggestion of discussing her relationship with her mother. If the therapist had not anticipated that Tracy would tend to comply with her in therapy—and if the therapist had not been alert to supporting any budding sign of self-direction or assertiveness from Tracy—this change-producing sequence would have been missed. In addition, if the therapist had responded by focusing on the content (e.g., "But it is important for us to look at your relationship with your mother because . . .") rather than by focusing on the process (i.e., Tracy asserting herself and disagreeing with the therapist), this opportunity for change would also have been lost. Tracy would have complied with the therapist and dutifully talked about her relationship with her mother. In the context of this interpersonal process that recapitulates her central conflict, Tracy would not be able to become more assertive or to uncover the long-standing emotional conflicts that led to her compliant interpersonal style.

Oftentimes, the therapist will eventually become discouraged about working with clients such as Tracy who are not able to try out or successfully incorporate new, more adaptive responses. The therapist may become either critical toward or disengaged from the client for not changing without realizing that the client's generic conflict has been recapitulated in their relationship. Thus, the client is unable to change even though the therapist and client continue to talk about adopting more assertive behaviors with others, the therapist sincerely supports and encourages this, and the client learns useful skills that facilitate performing the new behavior. Generating working hypotheses will help therapists respond more effectively to the process and relationship dimensions that determine whether change will occur.

The Dream

Clients make adaptive behavioral changes and feel subjectively better as they work through their conflicts. As clients improve, the therapist and client become less concerned with conflict resolution and more involved with issues regarding health and personal growth. This exciting transition from psychopathology/neurosis/conflict to health/growth/creativity is signaled by the emergence of *the Dream*.

In his book, *The Seasons of a Man's Life*, Levinson (1978) describes the profound influence of the Dream in shaping the structure of adult life and the course of personality development. As Levinson points out, the Dream does not refer to casual daydreams or night dreams but, in the largest sense, to the kind of life that one wants to lead. At first, the Dream may be poorly articulated and tenuously connected to reality but it holds imagined possibilities of self-in-adult-world that generate excitement and vitality. It is the central issue in Martin Luther King's historic "I Have a Dream" speech or in Delmore Schwartz's story, "In Dreams Begin Responsibilities."

The Dream has roots in the grandiose and unrealistic hero fantasies of adolescence, but it is more than this. In early adulthood, the Dream still has the quality of a vision—of who and how one would like to be in the world. In this way, the Dream is both inspiring and sustaining for the individual even though it may be mundane to others. For example, individuals have Dreams to be a certain kind of husband and father; an excellent craftsman; a respected community leader; an ethical attorney; a medical doctor who uses science to relieve suffering; a good teacher who helps children grow; a tough and successful, but honest, businessperson, or someone who can express himself artistically or spiritually. *In order to have purpose and a sense of aliveness, occupational and marital choices must incorporate some aspects of the Dream. When the Dream has been abandoned or is unconnected to the life structure, the life will not be infused with vitality and meaning even though the person may be successful.*

Up until the working-through phase of therapy, therapists are usually responding to the despair of broken dreams, the disillusionment of unfulfilling dreams, and the cynicism of abandoned dreams. In many cases, the life-infusing Dream that Levinson has articulated has not yet been addressed in therapy. In the working-through phase, however, clients are resolving their conflicts and emerging as healthier individuals. At this point, therapists must help clients to articulate and renew their Dreams and to find ways of incorporating aspects of their Dreams in their everyday lives. To achieve this, therapists must first be able to differentiate the Dream from the broken dreams that often underlie clients' presenting symptoms. As we will see below, the broken dreams that clients present to therapists often reflect failed attempts to rise above their conflicts and become special.

In the process of working through, clients are progressively relinquishing their interpersonal coping styles of moving toward, away, or against others. Clients gradually recognize their compensatory strivings to be special and rise above their conflicts by pleasing others, achieving success and power, or becoming safely aloof and cynically superior. As clients give up their characterological coping strategies they stop blocking the expression of their generic conflict. This allows their conflicts to be expressed, and potentially resolved, in the therapeutic relationship. However, therapists must anticipate that it will be a devastating failure and a total loss of self-esteem for clients to reliquish these attempts to rise above their conflicts. Thus, one important component of helping clients resolve their conflicts is to replace these defensive, grandiose strivings with the client's own attainable, yet sustaining, Dream.

Arthur Miller's Pulitzer prize winning play, *Death of a Salesman*, poignantly illustrates how the neurotic striving to rise above the conflict inevitably fails, how it can lock clients in their generic conflict for a lifetime, and how it stifles the Dream. The protagonist, Willy Loman, has adopted a moving-toward interpersonal style to cope with his profound feelings of inadequacy and shame. With a smile and a shoe shine, Willy pathetically strives not just be liked but to be well-liked. In a brilliant exposition of multigenerational family roles and relationships, Miller shows how Willy's grandiose strivings to rise above his conflicts by being well-liked are also acted out through his oldest son, Biff. Willy exaggerates Biff's accomplishments as magnificent, excuses or ignores his shortcomings, and never responds to the reality of his son's actual feelings, needs, or wishes.

Near the end of the play, both father's and son's defensive strivings to rise above fail. Willy is fired from his job—a crushing humiliation that shatters his myth of being well-liked and his lifelong coping strategy of winning approval. That same day, Biff fails to secure an important business opportunity that his father has encouraged. With this setback, Biff realizes that he has been living out his father's myth that he would become a fabulously successful entrepreneur. In the closing scene, however, the father and son each respond very differently to their respective crises.

Biff is able to relinquish the unrealistic script of superachievement and success that his father has demanded of him. In the last scene, Biff begs his father to release him from this grandiose role, "speak the truth" in the family for the first time, and acknowledge that he is just another regular guy—nothing more, nothing less—and to let that be good enough. However, Willy cannot relinquish his own rising-above defense and, therefore, cannot grant Biff's request to "let me off the hook." Alternately, Willy rejects and condemns Biff and continues to idealize him as magnificent.

Biff finally recognizes the conflict and interpersonal process that he and his father have been enacting all of their lives. By directly confronting his father, Biff is able to change his part of their conflict. Although this confrontation does not lead to an interpersonal resolution with Willy, it does lead to an internal resolution for Biff. Soon after the confrontation Biff decides to leave home. He states that he now knows who he is and what he wants to do with his life. He is going to pursue his own Dream and do what he has always wanted to do: leave the city, move out west, and work outdoors where he can feel the sun on his back and smell the grass. Whereas Biff could relinquish the neurotic strivings to be special and allow his own attainable Dream to emerge, Willy could not.

In one last attempt to change their relationship and have a genuine closeness, Biff reaches out and puts his arms around his father. Horrified, Willy recoils in fear and disgust. Although his lifelong obsession has been to win the approval and respect of others, he must rigidly reject exactly what he has always wanted from his son. To accept the love that Biff was offering, his own unacceptable, generic conflict would emerge. That is, Willy's own unmet needs to be respected and wanted, his profound sense of being unlovable, and his intense feelings of inadequacy and shame would overwhelm him. Thus, Willy is now trapped in his conflict: He is no longer able to maintain his own (or Biff's) defensive strivings to rise above and he is unable to let his true feelings and concerns emerge. Desperately bound in that unresolvable conflict, Willy's only solution is to end his own life.

As clients' neurotic strivings to be special and rise above their conflicts fail, their generic conflicts are revealed. If the therapist can provide a different and more satisfying response to the conflict than clients have received in the past, however, clients can resolve their conflicts and change maladaptive behavior. As this occurs and clients begin to improve during the working-through phase, the Dream will often emerge.

In order to help clients change, therapists must support and encourage the Dream. They can do this in many ways. First, therapists must listen for what it is that clients really want to do and inquire about what holds a feeling of rightness for them. Therapists can also help clients discover and articulate their Dreams. In this regard, therapists must provide a safe, "practicing" sphere in which clients can discuss and explore various possibilities of their Dream without prematurely having to become committed to any action. Therapists can also help clients tailor their Dreams to reality and find ways that clients can express components of their Dreams in their everday lives. Still another way to bring aspects of their Dream into their everyday lives is to help clients identify training or education routes that will facilitate realization of their Dreams. Similarly, therapists must also give clients permission to develop close relationships with others who can inform them and act as mentors in their chosen fields and pursuits.

Finally, clients will confront the same generic conflicts in exploring their Dreams that they have experienced in other aspects of their lives. Thus, therapists will also have to help clients work through their old conflicts that are aroused by pursuing the Dream. In particular, therapists will have to help clients differentiate between the Dream and clients' interpersonal coping style and defensive strivings to rise above (e.g., to be loved by everyone, to be wealthy and powerful, or to be safely aloof and superior). As clients successively work through their conflicts and start to follow through on realistic plans for manifesting aspects of their Dreams, therapy evolves to a natural conclusion.

TERMINATION

Termination is an important and distinct phase of therapy that must be negotiated thoughtfully. Ending the therapeutic relationship will almost always be of great significance to clients. The way in which this separation experience is resolved is so important that it influences how well clients will be able to resolve future conflicts in their lives. More specifically, the way in which the termination is dealt with helps determine whether clients leave therapy with a greater sense of their own personal resources and ability to manage their own lives. Termination is a potent and far-reaching experience for clients. It holds the potential either to undo the growth and resolution that has come before or to confirm and extend the changes that have come about in therapy. Thus, therapists must be prepared to utilize the potential for change that is still available as therapists and clients prepare to end their relationship.

Beginning therapists often ask: "How do you know when it's time to end therapy"? It is time to end when clients no longer have symptoms, can respond more flexibly and adaptively in current situations that arouse their old generic conflicts, and have begun to take steps toward promising new directions in their lives. Therapists are also informed that clients are ready to terminate when they have converging reports of client change from three different sources. First, therapists know that clients are ready to terminate when clients report that they consistently feel better, can respond in more adaptive ways to old conflict situations, and find themselves capable of new reponses that were not available to them before. Second, the therapist knows that termination is approaching when clients can consistently respond to the therapist in new and different ways that do not enact their old interpersonal coping styles, defenses, resistances, transference reactions, or eliciting behaviors. Third, termination is approaching when significant others in clients' lives give clients feedback that they are different, or have changed, or make comments such as "you never used to do that before." With this convergence of perceptions that important changes have occurred, it is time for therapy to end. We must now discuss issues essential to successful termination.

The Ending Must Not Be Avoided

It is usually difficult for both the therapist and the client to end their relationship. In many cases, bringing up the topic of termination will arouse emotional responses that are far more intense and difficult than either the therapist or the client have anticipated. As a result, therapists and clients regularly collude to deny the reality of the impending ending and to avoid the separation anxieties that it arouses for both of them. When therapists and clients stumble in this way and do not confront the ending squarely, their interpersonal process will usually recapitulate clients' generic conflicts and prevent clients from fully resolving their conflicts.

The single most important guideline for negotiating a successful termination is to unambiguously acknowledge the reality of the ending. The therapist and client must then discuss all of the client's emotional reactions about the ending, especially the client's reactions toward the therapist. Although the therapist and client may both want to avoid this topic, the therapist cannot let this occur. Once the therapist and client mutually decide that the client is ready to terminate, they must *set a specific date* for the final session. Because the therapist and client need time to work through their ending, the final session must be scheduled several weeks hence.

In order to have a successful ending, the therapist must insist upon establishing a final date and then explore the client's reactions to ending their relationship. Clients may angrily disapprove when therapists insist upon setting a termination date and some therapists will feel that they are being unnecessarily harsh, mean, or rigid. It is difficult to set a specific termination date and discuss the ending because this will arouse both the therapist's and the client's conflicts over endings. In addition, setting a clear termination date will often bring up the client's generic conflict again. In order to definitively resolve their central conflicts, however, clients must again work through in the termination phase the same issues that have been dealt with before. For these reasons, therapists must count down the final sessions and repeatedly invite clients to discuss their reactions to the termination:

> After today, we will have only three sessions left. How is it for you to hear me say that?

> We have only two sessions left now. It's important that we talk about our ending. What comes up for you when I acknowledge the fact that we will soon stop working together?

> Next week will be our last session. What do you find yourself thinking about our relationship and the work we have done together?

> This is our last session. What are you feeling toward me right now?

This type of countdown precludes any ambiguity that clients may have about the ending (e.g., client at end of last session: "Will I be seeing you next week"). This approach also keeps the therapist from acting out and avoiding the separation as well (e.g., therapist at end of last session: "Oh, I see our time is up. Well, I guess that's it"). When therapists do not address the termination directly, they are usually acting out their own separation anxieties. This commonly occurs, however, and when it does, therapists need to seek consultation from a supervisor or colleague.

Therapists must address the termination forthrightly and give clients the opportunity to work through their reactions to it. Why is this so important? In most clients' pasts, they have painfully experienced endings with significant others as "just happening to them." In many cases, either they were not prepared in advance for the separation, they did not understand when or why this particular ending was occurring, or they were not able to participate in the leave-taking by discussing it with the departing person. These types of responses have left many clients feeling powerless and out of control in regard to some of the most important experiences in their lives. In contrast, the approach suggested here gives clients a mastery experience by allowing them to be active, informed participants in the ending. Therapists offer many clients an opportunity to resolve long-standing conflicts when they help clients differentiate this type of mutually shared ending from other incomplete or unsatisfying endings with which they have had to cope in the past.

Termination Arouses the Client's Conflicts Again

Once the therapist and client mutually agree to end and set a termination date, the client's generic conflict may be aroused again. Some clients will begin to feel that they have not changed in therapy after all and their initial presenting symptoms will return. Therapists must be alert for how the termination may tap into the client's generic conflict and how this may be reenacted in their relationship. Then, therapists must ensure that their interpersonal process enacts a resolution of the client's conflict rather than a recapitulation of it. The best way for therapists to accomplish this is by drawing out and responding to all of the client's emotional reactions to the ending.

During the termination period, clients may have a diverse range of sad, hopeful, angry, excited, disappointed, and grateful feelings toward the therapist. As therapists track the client's reactions to the ending, they will often see how the client's central conflict is simultaneously being aroused in two contexts. First, the client's primary feelings toward the therapist about the ending (e.g., anxiety, anger, guilt, helplessness) may match the feelings that existed in relation to the earlier, formative relationship in which the generic conflict originally arose. Second, the client's reaction toward separating from the therapist may also match the feelings that were aroused in the crisis situation that originally brought the client to treatment.

If the therapist can respond to the client's feeling and clarify its connection to these two sources, the therapist is helping the client further resolve his central conflict. In contrast, if the therapist avoids or cannot respond to all of the client's reactions to termination, this will usually recapitulate the client's conflict in some way. When this occurs, it prevents clients from resolving their conflicts: They cannot access their own resources and capacity for autonomous functioning, cannot outgrow their dependency on the therapist, and cannot disengage from therapy as they need to do.

For all of these reasons, the therapist must address and help clients work through their feelings about ending the relationship. This is difficult to do, however, when in part both the therapist and the client wish to avoid the ending. The therapist and client have become close through their work together and the relationship holds significant meaning for both of them. In order to defend against the separation anxieties that are aroused by the termination, clients (and therapists too) may try to deny the reality of the ending. Or, some clients may try to devalue the significance of their relationship with the therapist or to diminish the importance of the work that has been accomplished. Still other clients will become symptomatic again and anxiously communicate that they are still too troubled to terminate and make it on their own.

Resolving such separation anxieties is the prototype for mastering all conflicts. Therapists must not overreact to these defenses but, instead, recognize and respond to the underlying concerns that are aroused by the impending separation. Too often, the client's defensive maneuvers elicit countertransference reactions in therapists that prevent them from responding to the client's real concerns. That is, therapists may feel guilty, angry, or inadequate because of the client's attempts to undo the importance of their relationship or the work they have accomplished. Whenever therapists are immobilized by such countertransference reactions they must seek consultation to help manage their emotions more effectively. Only then will therapists be able to effectively return to the task of responding to the client's concerns over ending.

Ending the Relationship

Although some clients will reexperience their central conflicts at the time of termination, others will not. Both clients and therapists still need to talk about the ending, however. For example, therapists can talk with the client about the different ways in which they have seen the client change over the course of therapy. Therapists can also acknowledge the limitations of their relationship and the unfinished issues that the client will need to continue to work with on his own. Recollections of close moments, awkward misunderstandings, threatening confrontations, and humorous incidents can all be recounted as well. This is also a time when therapists can share their own feelings about the client: what they have learned about themselves and life from the client, how the client has changed, enriched or influenced them, and ways in which therapists have cared about and will miss the client.

Finally, termination brings the therapist and client back to the separateness-relatedness dialectic again. On the one hand, therapists must give clients permission to leave. That is, clients must know that the therapist enjoys their success, is pleased by their independence, and wants them to become committed to other, new relationships. Conversely, just as all clients need permission to emancipate, they also need to be reassured that they can have future contact with the therapist if necessary. Clients will be reassured to know that the therapist is available to help them with future crises should the need arise. Knowing that the therapist is available if needed, but also supporting the client in leaving, allows the client to internalize the therapist and the help she has provided. This type of termination supports the client's own individuation and mastery strivings and helps clients to further claim their own personal power and identity.

TWO CASE SUMMARIES

In Chapter 7, a model for conceptualizing client dynamics was presented and illustrated with the case study of Peter—a moving-toward others client. Now, further guidelines for conceptualizing clients have been provided and the entire course of therapy has been detailed. With this conceptual framework and treatment course complete, two case studies illustrate the other interpersonal styles. Below, salient features in the treatment of a moving-against and a moving-away client are summarized.

Chuck—Moving Against Others

Chuck had improved dramatically since he entered therapy a year ago. Chuck had been riding high, on his way to becoming a real estate king when his business failed. Buoyed by his initial success in a booming real estate market, Chuck was woefully overextended when interest rates rose unexpectedly. His business went bankrupt, his new home and sports car had been repossessed, and friends deserted him as creditors and the IRS aggressively pursued him. Chuck entered therapy when his dreams of wealth and power were dashed, leaving him desperate, frightened, and suicidally depressed.

With the therapist's help, however, his suicidal preoccupation and other concerns had greatly improved. Chuck recognized how helpful the therapist had been to him and had recently told someone that he probably would not be alive today if not for the therapist's expertise and genuine concern. On this particular day, however, Chuck was ready to quit therapy. He was frustrated by having to come to therapy for such a long time and he did not want to need the therapist anymore. In particular, he was fed up with the therapist's high fees. Chuck began the session by bitterly taunting the therapist:

> Who do you think you are to charge so much?! Do you really think you're worth all that?!

The therapist acknowledged the feeling in Chuck's provocation:

Therapist:
You're angry about my fees. Let's talk about them.

Chuck: [continuing his assault]

> What are you doing, trying to prove that you can gouge as much money as the psychiatrist next door?! Did your mother want you to be a "real" doctor and make a lot of money or what?!

Fortunately, Chuck's therapist was able to stay in relationship with Chuck during this critical incident. The therapist did not retreat or counterattack, which is what Chuck's provocations usually elicited from others. Instead, the therapist mediated his own reflexive response to justify and explain and tried to maintain an effective middle ground of involvement:

> Yes, of course you're angry with me. I do charge you a lot of money, and it's a hardship for you. And there are still many problems in your life that therapy hasn't been able to change yet.

The therapist's accepting response only infuriated Chuck further:

Chuck:

> I hate your "understanding," I hate coming here, I don't want to do this anymore! What do you do, be nice to people when they're falling apart so they become dependent on you? Then they can't leave you and you can keep taking all of their money. There's something wrong with you; you're sick!

Therapist:

> It seems like I am trying to make you dependent on me so that I can take advantage of you financially?

Chuck: [livid]

> Yes, you idiot, I want to leave and get out of here, but I can't. I know I'll just get depressed again if I leave, and probably go kill myself. I need you and you know it, and you use that to take the little money I have left. I'm trapped by you. You've got me and I hate it, I hate *you!*

The intensity of Chuck's reactions told the therapist that a central conflict was being reenacted in this transference reaction. Based on other hypotheses he had already formulated the therapist reasoned that, for Chuck, having a need of someone automatically meant being used by them. Trying to articulate what Chuck was experiencing in their relationship right then, the therapist responded:

> It's as if you don't experience the decision to remain in therapy as your own choice, Chuck. You feel trapped by your own need to be helped or understood. You have learned that to let yourself need somebody puts them in control of you and subject to their own selfish needs. Your only choice then is to resist by leaving the help you still want or stay in treatment with me but be exploited. You may have experienced this with others, Chuck, but I want you and I to have a different kind of relationship. I want to respond to your need for help, not use your trust and vulnerability for my own gain.

Over the course of the session, Chuck gradually calmed down and was somewhat able to accept what the therapist was saying. Chuck's transference reaction—that the therapist had manipulated his dependency in order to meet the therapist's own financial need—encapsulated

Chuck's generic conflict. Chuck had grown up in an orphanage and had been emotionally deprived throughout his early childhood. When he was placed with foster parents, they took advantage of his intense, unmet dependency needs. They manipulated Chuck to respond to their needs under the guise of their love for him.

By the time he was seven years old, Chuck had become an exploited laborer on his foster parent's farm. In order to earn their approval and affection, he worked sunup to sundown most days of the week. By the time he was eighteen and ready to leave home, Chuck had long since realized that his foster parents were taking advantage of him and were not to be trusted. At some point during his early adolescence, Chuck's anxious efforts to please his foster parents had evolved into an angry defiance toward them and others. He had vowed to himself that he was never going to be dependent on or one-down to anybody again. Chuck decided that he was going to be rich and powerful—strong enough that no one would ever be able to take advantage of him again.

The dramatic confrontation described above was a critical incident in therapy that proved to be a corrective emotional experience for Chuck. Chuck's old fear of being used was aroused in relation to the therapist, just as it was aroused whenever Chuck began to trust or get close to anyone. This angry encounter was a corrective experience for Chuck because his old conflict was intensely aroused but his defensive eliciting behavior did not push the therapist away. The therapist was able to tolerate Chuck's provocative attacks and continue to remain engaged with him and responsive to his concerns.

As the therapist remained available to him—and provided a different response to his conflict than Chuck had received in the past—the next feeling in his affective constellation emerged. That is, once Chuck's reactive feeling of anger was responded to, his primary feelings of hurt and deprivation emerged as the predominant issue in therapy. The therapist responded to these primary feelings effectively and they soon began to diminish. Chuck's accompanying shame about not being "strong," however, and his recurring fear of being used by the therapist continued to be acted-out in the therapeutic relationship. Thus, Chuck reexperienced over and over again with the therapist his same conflicts and fears. Each time these concerns were manifested in a conflict between them, however, Chuck received an understanding response from the therapist that was different from what he had experienced in the past.

In addition, the therapist validated Chuck's perception that he had indeed been taken advantage of as a child, but stressed that others were not always trying to do this to him now in his current relationships. The therapist also observed that as a child, Chuck had made the best and only adaption that he could have made to his unsolvable childhood predicament. Emphasizing the health component, the therapist pointed out that there was courage and strength in Chuck's defensive attempt to rise above his conflict by adopting an aggressive and defiant interpersonal style. Although this defensive attempt to rise above his conflict was no longer necessary or effective, it had served to protect him from his old feelings of vulnerability that he was determined never to expose again. Eventually, Chuck understood what the therapist meant when he said that it took just as much strength to confront his old conflicts and "weak" feelings now as an adult as it originally did to defend against them as a child by trying to achieve success and power.

With the therapist's consistent support, Chuck was gradually able to reexperience his old feelings of desperate need and simultaneous outrage at being used by his foster parents. As he gradually let go of his strong combative and competitive stance with the therapist, and let himself undergo those painful feelings of his childhood that had always seemed "disgusting and weak," Chuck began to change. First, his combative, argumentative style gave way to a friendlier comradery with the therapist. Chuck began to disclose more easily and felt less competitive with the therapist. In particular, Chuck's heightened sensitivity to needing the therapist and being taken advantage of by him diminished.

In turn, these changes with the therapist began to carry over to other relationships as well. Chuck began to establish male friendships for the first time, which his competitiveness had always precluded in the past. Previously, Chuck's relationships with women had been short-lived, superficial sexual contacts that, at times, were exploitative. As Chuck stopped defending against and came to terms with how he had been used in his childhood, he no longer continued to use women as well. This symptom abated, but Chuck was still unable to establish an intimate, egalitarian love relationship at this time in his life.

Other evidence of change came from business associates who remarked that Chuck seemed less driven and less pressured than he used to be. Chuck's compensatory attempts to rise above his conflicts through achieving wealth and power were modulated and gave way to merely an ambitious, achieving work ethic. When an established banker in town offered Chuck a good job as a loan officer/appraiser in his real estate division, Chuck felt ready to terminate. All of his problems were certainly not solved but Chuck now felt capable of successfully moving on in life on his own. Chuck did not recapitulate his conflicts as therapy ended but it was important to him that the therapist remain available should future crises arise. Assured of the therapist's continuing availability, Chuck terminated and did not recontact the therapist.

Pamela—Moving Away From Others

Four months after her adolescent daughter had been raped, Pamela was still in crisis. Nightmares stole her sleep, tension headaches persecuted her days. Helpless to comfort her daughter, enraged at the casual indifference of the police and courts, Pamela was afraid she was going out of control. At work, her supervisor evaluated her as irritable, sullen, and withdrawn and suggested that she seek counseling. Although she had always been reluctant to ask for help with anything, Pamela contacted a therapist when she realized that her job was in jeopardy.

The therapist was empathic to all of the different feelings and concerns that her daughter's tragedy had aroused for her. To her surprise, Pamela felt understood by the therapist and soon began looking forward to their meetings. Over a slow period of months, Pamela gradually came to trust the therapist and increasingly invested herself in their relationship. After several months in treatment, Pamela reported a dream from the previous night—a recurrent dream that she had dreamt throughout her life. In the dream, Pamela was alone in a vast desert night. No other people existed in this great, silent space. The desert night was black, no light shone from stars or moon. As she walked across the endless sand, a cool, dry wind began to move lightly across her face. Pamela laid down on the sand, closed her eyes, and silently slipped away into the darkness.

Because variations of this dream had recurred throughout her life, the therapist knew that the dream expressed a lifelong generic conflict. Hoping that the dream could also provide an avenue to reach her central feeling of aloneness, the therapist tried to bridge her moving-away orientation:

Therapist:
Can you close your eyes and see the dream again?

Pamela:
Yes. [*settles back and closes her eyes*]

Therapist:
Describe what you see to me.

Pamela:
I'm walking; it's quiet and dark. I'm alone. I can feel the breeze. Now I'm lying down on the sand and I close my eyes, like going to sleep.

Therapist:
I don't want you to be there alone. Will you let me join you?

Pamela:
[*pause, then slowly*] Yes, you can.

Therapist:
Keep your eyes closed, and hold that same, familiar image. But you're not

alone this time. I am walking toward you and I reach my right hand out toward yours. Will you take it?

Pamela:
Mm hmm.

Therapist:
I'm now in the dream with you. We're holding hands, and walking together through the desert night. Can you see that?

Pamela:
Yes, we're walking toward the lights of a distant city. [*opens her eyes, and looks kindly at the therapist*] I'm not alone. It's good to have you with me.

This *joining* experience was a turning point in therapy. Pamela had grown up in a silent void—much like the setting in her dream. She had never known her father and her mother was usually away. By ten years of age, Pamela was regularly spending entire weekends alone, fixing her own meals, and putting herself to bed while her mother was out. The dream reflected both the aloneness and emptiness of her childhood and her lifestyle adaptation of moving away from others. However, the crisis with her daugher overwhelmed her lifelong coping strategy to withdraw and be self-sufficient and aloof. In letting the therapist join her in her dark, empty space, Pamela was accepting the human contact that she longed for but had long since learned to defend against. This single experience did not resolve her conflict but as other incidents of shared mutuality continued to occur in their relationship, Pamela began to change in three ways.

First, Pamela's conflicted affective constellation emerged. The emptiness and longing of her childhood abandonment became accessible and was shared with the therapist. To ensure that the lack of response that Pamela had experienced as a child was not recapitulated, the therapist was careful to let Pamela know that her feelings were being listened to this time. The therapist was skilled in communicating to Pamela that she was not in a dark, silent void anymore, but in a caring and concerned relationship. Pamela became more comfortable sharing her deprivation and longing with the therapist. However, the intense anger at her mother for abandoning her, and the frightening separation anxieties aroused by her rage at her mother to whom she was so insecurely attached, were worked through much more slowly. As the therapist continued to provide a corrective emotional experience in which all of these difficult feelings were supported and understood, Pamela began to change in her relationship with the therapist.

Although Pamela had become attached to the therapist because of her crisis state, she still hated that she needed help from anyone and still kept part of herself held away from the therapist. Only at this later point in treatment was Pamela able to further let go of her coping style, give herself up to her need of the therapist, and allow the therapist to help her. As a result, Pamela began to act less reserved toward the therapist and became more expressive than she had ever been with anyone else. She talked freely about herself with the therapist and found herself being curious and interested in the therapist's own life. Her nightmares and headaches had been alleviated several months ago, but now a sense of humor, interpersonal warmth, and graciousness were flowering as well. As Pamela talked about feeling "fuller" inside, the therapist observed that changes were also occurring in her other relationships as well.

At work, her supervisor was pleased to observe that Pamela was more involved and available than she had been, which made it easier for others in the office to work with her. Whenever interpersonal conflicts surfaced at work, Pamela's initial reaction was still to withdraw and "go away." Now, however, she was able to freely discuss the problems and her reactions to them with the therapist. Together, they would find new ways for her to remain involved in the situation rather than withdraw or remain aloof as she had always done in the past. Pamela also became more accessible to her two adolescent children. For the first time, she talked more about her own feelings, interests, and personal history with them. The nearly grown children welcomed this contact and, in turn, they began to disclose more to her as well. In general, Pamela felt closer to her children than she had ever been before and even felt somewhat more capable of helping her daughter cope with the painful aftereffects of her assault.

Finally, Pamela also began to change how she responded to her long-term boyfriend. Pamela asked for more personal sharing and for more commitment from him. She asked him to talk about his feelings more, and to spend more time with her. She initiated an agreement that they not date other people. It was exciting but anxiety-arousing to take each of these steps forward. Her old coping style of moving away was activated each time she took a step toward others, as she still reflexively defended against the hurt that relationships had originally held for her. As the therapist repeatedly helped her work through her concerns in each of these arenas, Pamela tentatively suggested that it may be approaching time to end.

Although things had been going well for the past few months, Pamela became depressed as soon as they talked about ending. She forgot the next appointment and arrived late to another session. As before, the therapist continued to focus Pamela inward and her old feelings of emptiness and abandonment emerged again. The therapist suggested that they put off setting a termination date for awhile and work further with these conflicted emotions. With more vividness and detail than before, Pamela recalled her childhood abandonment depression. Painful memories returned such as being eight years old, sitting alone on the living room couch, and listening to the clock tick the empty afternoon away. Pamela sobbed as she recalled her desperate childhood wish for someone to come home to. Touching the original pain so directly relieved the depression that the suggestion of terminating had precipitated. In six weeks, Pamela again felt ready to terminate. This time, with the therapist's reassurance that she could recontact her if necessary, Pamela successfully terminated.

CLOSING

This book has paralleled the course of therapy from beginning to end. Just as clients still have some unresolved conflicts when treatment ends, many questions and concerns about therapy remain unanswered for therapists-in-training. Complex psychological issues and interpersonal processes have been introduced here but further reading and supervision is needed to help with the myriad exceptions, nuances, and complications that occur in every therapeutic relationship. Despite these limitations, essential guidelines for working with process and relationship in psychotherapy have been provided. The conceptual and intervention framework presented here should enable beginning therapists to function more effectively and autonomously as professionals and to better assimilate further training experiences. In closing, therapists have been encouraged to utilize themselves and the relationships they provide their clients as the most effective way to help clients change.

SUGGESTIONS FOR FURTHER READING

1. *The Dream* is an important psychological dimension in people's lives that has received too little attention. The reader is encouraged to read Daniel Levinson's groundbreaking work in this area, *The Seasons of a Man's Life* (New York: Ballantine, 1978). See especially pp. 91–109.

2. A dramatic illustration of Horney's concepts of rising above and interpersonal coping styles can be found in Arthur Miller's play, *Death of a Salesman* (New York: Penguin, 1949).

3. Useful information about identifying clients' generic conflicts and about negotiating successful terminations can be found in J. Mann, *Time-Limited Psychotherapy* (Cambridge: Harvard University Press, 1973).

4. Readers who have found the ideas presented here to be helpful are likely to enjoy Irving Yalom's modern classic, *Existential Psychotherapy* (New York: Basic Books, 1980).

BIBLIOGRAPHY

Alexander, F. and French, T. *Psychoanalytic Therapy: Principles and Applications*. New York: Ronald Press, 1946.

Anderson, C. M. and Steward, S. *Mastering Resistance: A Practical Guide to Family Therapy*. New York: Guilford Press, 1983.

Bandura, A. "Self Efficacy: Toward a Unifying Theory of Behavioral Change." *Psychological Review* 84, no. 2 (1977), pp. 191–215.

Baumrind, D. "Child Care Practices Anteceding Three Patterns of Preschool Behavior." *Genetic Psychology Monographs* 75 (1967), pp. 43–88.

Baumrind, D. "Current Patterns of Parental Authority." *Developmental Psychology Monograph* 4, no. 1, part 2 (1971).

Boszormeni-Nagy, I. and Spark, G. *Invisible Loyalties: Reciprocity in Inter-Generational Family Therapy*. New York: Harper & Row, 1973.

Bowen, M. "The Use of Family Theory in Clinical Practice." *Comprehensive Psychiatry* 7, (1966), pp. 345–376.

Bugental, J. *The Search for Authenticity: An Existential-Analytic Approach to Psychotherapy*. New York: Holt, Rinehart & Winston, 1965.

Erikson, E. *Childhood and Society*, 2nd ed. New York: W. W. Norton, 1964.

Farley, J. "Family Separation-Individuation Tolerance: A Developmental Conceptualization of the Nuclear Family." *Journal of Marital and Family Therapy*, January 1979, pp. 61–67.

Fisch, R., Weakland, J. H., and Segal, L. *The Tactics of Change: Doing Therapy Briefly*. San Francisco: Jossey-Bass, 1982.

Fromm, E. *Escape from Freedom*. New York: Rinehart, 1941.

Fromm-Reichmann, F. *Principles of Intensive Psychotherapy*. Chicago: University of Chicago Press, 1950.

Gilligan, C. *In a Different Voice: Psychological Theory and Women's Development*. Cambridge: Harvard University Press, 1982.

Greenson, R. *The Technique and Practice of Psychoanalysis*, vol. 1, chap. 1. New York: International Universities Press, 1967.

Guest, J. *Ordinary People*. Film directed by R. Redford, 1980.

Guggenbuhl-Crain, A. *Power in the Helping Professions*. New York: Springer Publications, 1971.

Haley, J. "Toward a Theory of Pathological Systems". In G. H. Zuk and I. Boszormenyi-Nagy (eds.), *Family Therapy and Disturbed Families*. Palo Alto: Science and Behavior Books, 1967, pp. 11–27.

Haley, J. *Leaving Home: The Therapy of Disturbed Young People*. New York: McGraw-Hill, 1980.

Horney, K. *Self Analysis*. New York, W.W. Norton, 1942.

Horney, K. *Our Inner Conflicts*. New York: W.W. Norton, 1945.

Horney, K. *Neurosis and Human Growth*. New York: W.W. Norton, 1950.

Kafka, F. *Letter to his Father*. New York: Shocken, 1966.

Kelly, G. *The Psychology of Personal Constructs*. New York: W.W. Norton, 1955.

Laing, R. D. and Esterson, A. *Sanity, Madness and the Family*. Middlesex, England: Penguin, 1970.

Leary, T. *Interpersonal Diagnosis of Personality*. New York: The Ronald Press, 1957.

Levinson, D. *The Seasons of a Man's Life*. New York: Ballantine Books, 1978.

Mahler, M., Pine, F., and Bergman, A. *The Psychological Birth of the Human Infant*. New York: Basic Books, 1975.

Mann, J. *Time-Limited Psychotherapy*. Cambridge: Harvard University Press, 1973.

Masterson, J. *Treatment of the Borderline Adolescent: A Developmental Approach*. New York: John Wiley & Sons, 1972.

Masterson, J. *Psychotherapy of the Borderline Adult: A Developmental Approach*. New York: Bruner/Mazel, 1976.

Miller, Alice. *Prisoners of Childhood*. New York: Basic Books, 1981.

Miller, Arthur. *Death of a Salesman*. New York: Penguin, 1949.

Minuchin, S. *Families and Family Therapy*. Cambridge: Harvard University Press, 1974.

Mueller, W. and Kell, B. *Impact and Change: A Study of Counseling Relationships*. Englewood Cliffs, N.J.: Prentice-Hall, 1966.

Olson, D. H., McCubbin, H. I., Barnes, H., Larsen, A., Muxen, M., and Wilson, M. *Families: What Makes Them Work*. Beverly Hills, Calif.: Sage Publications, 1983.

Passons, W. *Gestalt Approaches in Counseling*. New York: Holt, Rinehart & Winston, 1975.

Rogers, C. *Client-Centered Therapy*. Boston: Houghton Mifflin, 1951.

Rogers, C. "A Theory of Therapy, Personality and Interpersonal Relationships as Developed in the Client-Centered Framework." In S. Koch (ed.), *Psychology: A Study of Science, vol. 3, Formulations of the Person and the Social Context*. New York: McGraw-Hill, 1959.

Satir, V. *Conjoint Family Therapy*. Palo Alto: Science and Behavior Books, 1967.

Seligman, M. *Helplessness*. New York: Freeman, 1975.

Shapiro, D. *Neurotic Styles*. New York: Basic Books, 1965.

Steinbeck, J. *East of Eden*. New York: Viking, 1952.

Stierlin, H. *Separating Parents and Adolescents*. New York, Quadrangle, 1972.

Sullivan, H. S. *The Interpersonal Theory of Psychiatry*. New York: W.W. Norton, 1968.

Sullivan, H. S. *The Psychiatric Interview*. New York: W.W. Norton, 1970.

Teyber, E. "Structural Family Relations: A Review." *Family Therapy* 1 (1981), pp. 39–48.

Teyber, E. "Effects of the Parental Coalition on Adolescent Emancipation from the Family." *Journal of Marital and Family Therapy* 9, no. 1 (1983), pp. 89–99.

Teyber, E. *Helping your Children with Divorce.* New York: Pocket Books, 1985.

Wachtel, P. *Psychoanalysis and Behavior Therapy: Toward an Integration.* New York: Basic Books, 1982.

Weiss, J. and Sampson, H. *The Psychoanalytic Process: Theory, Clinical Observation and Empirical Research.* New York: Guilford, 1986.

Wenar, C. *Psychopathology from Infancy through Adolescence.* New York: Random House, 1982.

Wheelis, A. *How People Change.* New York: Harper & Row, 1974.

White, R. "Motivation Reconsidered: The Concept of Competence." *Psychology Review* 66 (1959), pp. 297–333.

Woodward, B. *Wired.* New York: Simon and Schuster, 1984.

Yalom, I. *Existential Psychotherapy.* New York: Basic Books, 1980.

Name Index

Subject Index

iii

ABOUT THE AUTHOR

Edward Teyber, Ph.D., a clinical psychologist, is Professor of Psychology and Director of the Community Counseling Center at California State University, San Bernardino. He is also the author of *Helping Your Children with Divorce*. He has published numerous research articles on the effects of marital and family relations on child adjustment, and he regularly contributes articles on parenting and postdivorce family relations to newspapers and magazines. Dr. Teyber is also in private practice.

A NOTE ON THE TYPE

The text of this book was set in 10/12 Palatino using a film version of the face designed by Hermann Zapf that was first released in 1950 by Germany's Stempel Foundry. The face is named after Giovanni Battista Palatino, a famous penman of the 16th century. In its calligraphic quality, Palatino is reminiscent of the Italian Renaissance type designs, yet with its wide, open letters and unique proportions it still retains a modern feel. Palatino is considered one of the most important faces from one of Europe's most influential type designers.

Composed by The Saybrook Press, Old Saybrook, Connecticut.

Printed and bound by Arcata Graphics/Fairfield, Fairfield, Pennsylvania.